INTERNET M.

BIBL.

FOR ACCOUNTANTS

THE COMPLETE GUIDE TO USING SOCIAL MEDIA AND ONLINE ADVERTISING INCLUDING FACEBOOK, TWITTER, GOOGLE AND LINKEDIN FOR CPAS AND ACCOUNTING FIRMS

BY

NICK PENDRELL

www.informerbooks.com

Published by Informer Books

Farnborough House

Alveston, Stratford-upon-Avon

Warwickshire

CV37 7QZ

United Kingdom

British Library Cataloguing in Publication Data

A catalogue record for this book is available from the British Library

ISBN-10: 0-9561448-2-9

ISBN-13: 978-0-9561448-2-9

www.informerbooks.com

The book is dedicated to the Internet.

Since the moment I first met you back in 1996, it was love at first sight. As we move towards our third decade together, my love for you continues to grow more and more each day.

Thanks for being there for me each day – my muse, my mentor and my constant companion.

*　　　*　　　*

DISCLAIMER

*　　　*　　　*

I am very much indebted to Tracy B. Stewart CPA of College Station, TX for reading through the first draft of the manuscript and correcting errors. This book would be not nearly as polished without her kind assistance.

Contents

INTRODUCTION

WHY DO YOU NEED A BOOK ON INTERNET MARKETING?

IF YOUR PRACTICE is currently doing just fine – you have enough existing clients and a regular pipeline coming through from referrals that you have no need of any more and you're not currently advertising, then you don't need one. Just because everyone else is jumping on the social media and internet marketing bandwagons doesn't mean that you need to as well just to follow the crowd.

Creating and running an internet marketing and social media campaign is going to cost you a fair bit of time and effort, plus some money as well. So if you don't need to make that investment – don't make it.

But if you are currently spending good money each month on advertising and want to see a better return – you need to read a book on internet marketing. If you need to reach more prospects and turn those prospects into paying clients who stay with you longer – you need to read a book on internet marketing.

Already 50% of small and medium-sized businesses have a presence on social media such as Facebook and Twitter and a large proportion of the remaining 50% who don't are planning on having one in the next 12 months. According to research group BIA/Kelsey, 25.4% of all local business marketing budgets in the US will be spent upon digital advertising and social media by 2015, worth $37.9 billion. As accounting is not the most marketing orientated from all the different categories of small and medium-sized businesses, maybe your local competitors are not actively using the Internet to market their businesses. Yet. But, if and when they do (and if the BIA/Kelsey figures are correct, it's more a question of 'when') their campaigns will give them a tremendous advantage over those who are either not running any marketing activities or who are still spending their promotional budgets on 'old media' such as newspaper advertising, the Yellow Pages, local radio advertising, etc., where businesses get a much lower return on investment than they will see on even the most disastrous internet marketing campaign.

The Internet has changed the world of marketing forever. The large multinationals were the first types of business to harness its power. However, over the past few years, it is small and medium-sized businesses that have been most active in terms of taking more and more of their promotional activities online.

WHY DO YOU NEED THIS BOOK ON INTERNET MARKETING?

When it comes to internet marketing, there is no 'one size fits all' solution. This book is not some generic internet marketing book that has simply had the word 'accountant' copied and pasted on every page to make it seem relevant. It has been written from the ground up with just accountants in mind, focusing on their unique requirements – their problems and their opportunities.

By way of example, let's compare and contrast two small businesses:

John Smith, ACCA is a newly-qualified Chartered Accountant living in the small town of Grantham, Lincolnshire, UK.

Coats4Goats is a one-man-band company selling luxury fashion coats for pet goats, which is based in San Francisco, USA.

These two businesses' internet marketing requirements are almost exact opposites.

In particular:

Location vs. Market Size

John Smith's market is nearly everyone who owns a local business in a small geographical area – the town of Grantham and perhaps a twenty mile radius. Any effort or money he invests in attracting the attention of anyone outside his geographical area is probably wasted.

Coats4Goats' market is a tiny proportion of clients in a vast geographical area (they ship all over the world). Any effort or money they invest in attracting the attention of anyone who is not passionate about their pet goats is probably wasted.

Needs vs. Wants

John Smith's clients **need** his services, even if they may not **want** them. His potential clients know what accountants are, why they need them and so will need to go to the effort of hunting for one if they don't know of any.

Coats4Goats' clients don't **need** their services, but they might **want** them. Their potential clients probably don't even realize that someone in the world is making designer coats for their pet goats and so will not be actively searching for them. Therefore, Coats4Goats needs to look for websites that pet goat owners will visit and tell them why they should use the company's services.

Required Results

John Smith's desired result from his internet marketing is a phone call or an email from a potential client asking for a meeting or for more information on the services which he provides.

Coats4Goats desired result from their internet marketing is for a potential customer to come to their website and order a coat for their goat online.

Relationships vs. Quick Sales

John Smith realizes that not every business in his local area is in the market for his services today – most of them will already have accountants. His internet marketing activities need to be focused on the long term so that, one day, when a company is ready to change its accounting firm, he is the first person they think of.

Coats4Goats' main customers will be impulse buyers. Their products are relatively inexpensive and not at all essential. They need to capture a client's interest quickly and get them to buy. If a potential client is not ready to buy their products today, they are not much more likely to be interested in buying them three years from now.

Most books you will see on the subject of internet marketing for small businesses either can't tell the difference between these two types of clients, or else they assume that they all have the same needs as Coats4Goats rather than John Smith. So these books will go on at great length about costly or time-consuming internet marketing methods which would just be a waste of time and money for John Smith.

Blogging, Vlogging, YouTube channels, Podcasts, etc. – these activities are all tricky to understand for beginners, time-consuming to master or expensive to hire someone else to do. For Coats4Goats, the investment will probably be worth it because they need to attract attention from a tiny percentage of the total internet audience (i.e. pet goat owners) who are unaware that their products exist at all. For John Smith though, even if he was to spend a lot of effort on such activities, 99.9% of his hard work would be wasted because those people who did see his marketing activities would be from outside his local area and so would be unable to use his services anyway.

This book is not a general internet marketing guide for all small businesses. It is specifically written for accountants so that you can spend the minimum amount of time, effort and money attracting targeted new clients in your local area and keeping existing ones happy. It avoids any talk of marketing methods which are going to be irrelevant to your needs or will require too much investment for too little reward.

INTERNET MARKETING HAS BEEN EVOLVING RAPIDLY

If you have a book on internet marketing which was written before 2008, then throw it away – it's out of date and next to useless now.

Chances are that you have a website already. For a business of any size, not having a website a decade ago was tantamount to saying that you were clueless, a Luddite or that you'd just crawled out from under a rock.

"It's the 21st Century – you've **got** to have a website," was the common wisdom – especially from web designers who grew rich from building websites for butchers, bakers and candlestick makers, whether it brought their clients any benefit or not.

So a vast amount of local businesses paid up to get themselves a website – with as many bells and whistles as the web designer could convince them that they needed.

And then what happened once their all-singing, all-dancing websites were live? In many cases, hardly anyone stopped by to visit it. So maybe then they started to put their web addresses in all their advertising trying to get people to stop by.

For Coats4Goats, this would make sense. After all, Coats4Goats' website is their shop front – so all of their marketing activity needs to be aimed at getting people to visit their site. But John Smith isn't going to make any more money simply by having potential clients visit his website. He only makes money after meeting with a client. So all John Smith's website is to him is a marketing tool. But now people are telling him that he has to spend more money or time and effort on marketing his marketing tools?

Something is definitely wrong with this picture.

In the past, too few local business owners have asked themselves the question, "But what do I actually need a website for?"

A major problem with most websites is that they are a 'passive' means of advertising as opposed to an 'active' means of advertising such as TV and radio. These 'active' means of advertising reach potential clients' eyeballs and ears respectively whether they want to see or hear it or not. 'Passive' advertising like websites only work when people have **chosen** to track down this information in the first place.

If your website is simply somewhere online where people can find the basic information about your company – your contact details, your opening hours, your areas of expertise, etc., then your website will still be of use. But these days, there are plenty of ways of producing or maintaining a highly professional looking web presence either for free or at negligible cost.

While having a simple website is still a major element of any internet marketing campaign, more useful tools for reaching out and **actively** seeking new prospects are networks such as Facebook, Twitter and LinkedIn – collectively known as 'social media'. Social media is not only a free promotional tool, but it is also a great leveler – in ten minutes, your Facebook, Twitter and LinkedIn pages can look as good as those of the huge multinational corporations. They also give you a place to put all the vital information about your business that potential clients might need to know. If used correctly, they can 'actively' advertise your practice as would be the case were you to use such methods as TV or radio advertising.

Social Media is Local Media

The stunning rise of social media such as Facebook, Twitter and LinkedIn over the past couple of years has dramatically changed the landscape for internet marketing. Ironically though, it seems as if those businesses who have the most to gain from using social media are the last ones to actively use these methods.

I have to smile when I see big brands for everyday objects such as fabric softeners or detergents desperately urging people to 'Like' them on Facebook. Do people actually 'Like' their detergent in a literal sense? Does anyone want to interact socially with a brand of fabric softener (or, more accurately, the intern whose job it is to post some random twaddle a couple of times each day because 'everyone's on Facebook these days'?) No, perhaps some people can be bribed into 'Liking' these brand names from faceless multinationals in return for receiving a benefit such as discounts or entry into sweepstakes, but no one's going to be inviting their favorite brand of mouthwash to their birthday party any time soon.

If you have a small, local business, however, then **you** are your 'brand' – a living, breathing human being who all your clients are probably going to know personally. Your current clients really do 'Like' you in a literal way, and your future clients will need to do so as well because, if they actively 'Dislike' you, then they are going to take their business to one of your competitors who they 'Like' more.

Social networks were originally designed solely for the purpose of 'Friends' (or at least 'Acquaintances') to interact with one another – not for big brands to bore the pants off people. Maybe you already have a Facebook account. If so, you're already social and you probably have many of your existing clients as 'Friends' there. Using social media for marketing purposes is not so different from using it just to keep in touch with your close friends. The basics are the same - just the focus of your activities there will be different.

Social Media is Cheap (or Even Free) Media

How much are you spending on advertising and marketing for your business at the moment? Chances are that it is a not insignificant amount when even the tiniest ad in the cheapest local newspapers will cost a minimum of $100/£60. And that's for one tiny ad, for one week, surrounded by the clutter of all the other advertising in the newspaper. The high prices of local newspaper advertising continue despite the fact that less and less people are reading local newspapers as more and more people turn to the Internet to get their news. Advertising revenues for local newspapers across the world are nose-diving as more and more people realize that they are spending too much money there for too little return.

In comparison, how much money did it cost you to set up your Facebook account? Absolutely nothing, of course, and that's how much it is going to cost you to employ most of the marketing techniques in this book. In the majority of cases, your only investment will be a little time and imagination.

SOCIAL MEDIA IS FOR CREATING LONG-TERM RELATIONSHIPS

Internet marketing expert, Seth Godin, had an enormous amount of impact on the field with his 1999 book, 'Permission Marketing', the subtitle of which is 'Turning Strangers into Friends and Friends into Customers'. The main audience for this book was major brands who Seth Godin predicted would need to change the way they marketed their products to consumers. 'Interruption marketing' such as TV and radio, where the consumer has no choice but to be bludgeoned by advertising methods are becoming less important as changes in technology enable people to filter out these messages. Instead, he argued that marketers would need to start a **relationship** with customers so that they actually **chose** to receive promotional messages from them.

For accountants, this is not such a paradigm shift – after all it's this softly, softly approach that sales people have been using since the early days of marketing in order to sell their services. Now accountants finally have a promotional vehicle which works in exactly the same way as their sales process. Facebook is all about making friends and getting closer to them. As a result, it is a perfect tool for taking these new friends just one more step towards becoming paying clients.

WHO IS THIS BOOK FOR?

The title of the book is a major giveaway here – it's for practicing accountants who would like to find new clients, retain their existing clients and increase the amount of business that they get from existing clients through the use of simple and effective internet marketing activities. These methods are all highly cost-efficient, so should see readers' total marketing expenditure coming down as they use it to replace much of their current promotional activities.

Currently, around 75% of all working adults in the English-speaking world have a Facebook account. I am assuming here that you are one of these, or at least you are relatively computer literate. I am not going to waste your time and insult your intelligence by explaining what a 'mouse' is and how to connect to this wonderful new invention called 'the Internet'. If you do need this explaining to you, then may I suggest that you read a more basic book first and then come back to this one after you've finished it!

At the same time though, I am going to assume that you are something of a novice when it comes to internet marketing. I am not going to try and show you how clever I am by trying to use every single buzzword and piece of jargon that I've heard. I will hold your hand through the whole process, taking you through each one in easy-to-follow steps. Most of the steps here are simple – no more complicated than setting up a personal Facebook page. Setting up a good website is not quite such a simple matter, however. You might find that you need a friend who knows a little about websites or to hire a professional to help you set one up to start with. Once it is up and running though, you should be able to handle everything yourself from there on.

All of the sites which I talk about in this book are from large companies whose sites have detailed 'Help' sections and often support forums where you can ask questions and receive answers from other users. So, if you get stuck anywhere, just ask. It's also worth typing your question directly into Google's search engine. Nine times out of ten, you'll find that someone has asked the question before somewhere on the Internet and someone else has already answered it.

I am assuming that you are already working 40 hours a week or more on the day-to-day running of your practice a so you don't have masses of spare time available to invest in your marketing. Instead, you just want simple and straightforward solutions that will get you the best results for the minimum amount of time and effort.

WHAT IS CONTAINED IN THIS BOOK?

Although this book comes bound in one volume, it's more like a complete library of over a dozen different titles, each of them giving you a comprehensive guide to one particular aspect of internet marketing and social media. Think of it as 'Facebook for Accountants Made Simple', 'Twitter for Accountants Made Simple', 'AdWords for Accountants Made Simple', etc.

This book represents the sum of my knowledge gained over 15 years of being involved in internet marketing, plus reading well over 100 books on the subject. In order to keep the size down to a realistic number of pages, I have cut out all of the padding and everything that it not completely relevant to the needs of accountants. If the advice in any of the chapters is not sufficiently detailed for you, there is always the opportunity to buy a book dedicated to that particular subject to learn more about it. In most cases, however, you should find that, unless your practice is so large that it has its own dedicated marketing department, you only need to know the basics. You can save the highly advanced techniques for the Big 4 Accounting Firms who can afford to hire specialists in each different area.

HOW TO USE THIS BOOK

Having bought this book, you're probably ready to rush off and start your internet marketing campaign immediately. That's great and, if you want to start putting your campaign together as you read the book one page at a time, there's nothing that I can do to stop you.

However, my recommendation is that, instead of this approach, it will be better for you to have a quick read of the book from cover to cover first – just a quick scan through will do. Don't worry about which click does what at this stage. Once you have gone through the book once, go back and follow each chapter, section by section, putting the theory into practice. Maybe you want to use the table of contents at the start of this book as your 'To Do' list. Take a highlighter and cross off each section as you finish it to keep track of your progress.

The reason why I suggest reading through the entire book first is because it provides a 'holistic' process to internet marketing – which is a pretentious way of saying that all of the pieces fit together like a jigsaw. Having an idea as to what the 'big picture' that you're aiming for is going to look like will help you to understand how the individual elements fit together.

There are no pictures in this book. If there were, then it would be at least twice the size (and twice the price). Additionally, the major sites featured in this book make minor changes to their layouts so often that the pictures in the book would soon look different to those that you would be seeing on your computer. Therefore, the best way to work through each exercise is by having the book open next to your computer so that you can keep referring back to it as you proceed step-by-step.

Hopefully it shouldn't take you long to have a quick scan through each of the chapters before you read each of them in detail. I hate writing padding as much as you hate reading it and so you will only find solid and practical advice in this book without the filler that a lot of writers add in to make just a little useful information seem more impressive.

PREPARATIONS FOR STARTING YOUR CAMPAIGN

As PART OF your promotional strategy, you're going to be setting up accounts and profiles on a number of different social media sites. These profiles are all going to need the same type of materials in almost every case – logos, photos, a good description of your business, email addresses of your existing contacts, etc. Rather than having to keep stopping and restarting the process, which is going to ruin your train of thought, it will save a lot of time if you prepare all of the materials that you are going to need before you start work on the sites. Once you have everything prepared and filed away in a special 'Marketing' folder, you'll be able to speed through setting up each of the required profiles in a flurry of copying, pasting and uploading.

So here's what you need to prepare:

GET YOUR HOUSE IN ORDER FIRST

Social media is **viral** media, where messages spread through the Internet like a virus spreads through the population. Social media marketing is all about getting your satisfied clients to act as ambassadors or a sales force for your company. Used effectively, it can have phenomenal results (as can be seen from the meteoric growth of Facebook, which grew from one person to over 800 million in a period of seven years).

If you are offering an excellent service to your clients, they should be happy to start recommending you to their friends and contacts. This is incredibly powerful marketing because people have grown cynical of advertising hype. But they still trust their friends' advice.

Let's say you needed a plumber in a hurry. Whose recommendation would you trust more – a good friend of yours who says that the plumber they hired last year did an excellent job or an ad in the Yellow Pages where a plumber claimed to be reliable and inexpensive?

Reviews on the Internet have changed the way that many people choose which businesses to work with. Two decades ago, when booking a vacation, buyers had no choice but to go into a travel agency and trust that the hotel they were going to stay in offered a good service. Today, millions of people check sites such as tripadvisor.com in advance to ensure that they aren't going to be getting any nasty surprises.

The ability to check on virtually any business on the Internet is leading to a paradigm shift in the relationship between client and service provider. The saying that 'the customer is king' has been around for generations, but today this really is the case. It means that scam artists like timeshare salesmen from the mid-nineties simply aren't able to hoodwink potential clients in the same way anymore. This new 'word of mouse' as it is sometimes referred to today, rewards businesses which do offer a good service through their past customers acting as an unpaid team of evangelical salespeople.

Maybe you have seen signs in some restaurants saying, 'If you had a good meal, tell your friends; if you had a bad meal, tell us'. It is important in the 'Internet Age' that every business adopts a similar pro-consumer attitude, because it is now easy for dissatisfied customers to air their grievances in public. As a look through the national newspapers will confirm, bad news sells more papers than good news.

The bottom line is that everything that you will read in this book could actually prove to be **detrimental** to your practice if you are not offering a good service to your clients. Your viral marketing campaign could end up being the virtual equivalent of Ebola in this case, killing it off rapidly as disgruntled former clients use the Internet to tell your potential new customers how they were unhappy with your service.

While you should never allow customers to blackmail you with the threat of bad reviews, if they do have genuine grievances, it is a wise investment to do whatever you can to resolve the issues to their satisfaction. Any expenses incurred in the process will usually end up being minor compared to the loss of business that you can expect if everyone checking you online reads their complaint. I cover the subject of unhappy clients and what to do about them in more detail in chapter 12.

So, before you embark on a social media campaign, ask yourself if your past and current clients are genuinely happy with you and your service. If not, then it will be better to put your marketing plans on hold for a while and first concentrate on improving the service you offer your existing clients.

READY YOUR DATABASE

Unless you are reading this book because you are just starting a new practice, you will have existing clients. Even if you already have a strong personal relationship with these clients, there are good reasons as to why you should add them to your online marketing activities:

(a) There is always the possibility of selling more of your services to existing clients. Research has shown that it costs a minimum of five times as much to find a new client as it does to sell more to existing clients.

(b) Email and other online marketing activities allow you to keep in better contact with your existing clients. It takes a lot less time to email 100 clients to inform them about your new activities in a newsletter than it would do to call each of them individually or to speak with them next time they stop at your office.

(c) Your existing clients can kick-start your marketing activities by joining your social networks where they can start the viral process of promoting your practice to a wider audience. As a highly hypothetical example, if you started off with just ten clients today who each referred two friends to you each quarter, and those friends also started referring two new clients to you each quarter and so on, after 12 months you would have 140 new clients. It's the marketing equivalent of compound interest.

So don't underestimate the potential of your existing clients in your rush to sign up some new ones. Your existing clients provide an excellent nucleus to kick off your social media campaign with a bang.

Hopefully you already have a computer database containing all of your clients' contact information. Most email systems come with an inbuilt address book, whether this is one that resides on your computer, such as Outlook Express or Outlook, or the leading online services such as Gmail, Hotmail, etc. It's well worth getting all of this information up-to-date and adding any other contacts which you may not have included in the past (e.g. from business cards, etc.) before you progress to the next stage. All of the important social media sites have the ability to automatically look through your contacts and invite all of them to join your networks. So, if your database is up-to-date, it is going to be a simple task to launch your online activities.

If you have not been making an effort to capture contact details in the past, then the time to start is **now**. Every person who emails you should automatically be added to your database. In addition, get into the habit of asking **everyone** you meet for a business card so that you can take down their email address, even if you normally only communicate by phone. If you meet a useful contact who doesn't have a business card on them, add their contact information straight into your smartphone if you have one, or jot it down on a piece of paper otherwise.

Don't be too selective about whose contact information you do and don't record. When it comes to social media, **every** contact you make is a useful one. Even if someone who you just met is unlikely to ever have need of your services, they are likely to know someone who will.

Also don't be too shy about asking everyone you meet to join your social networks or for permission to them a newsletter at some time in the future. If they really aren't interested, they will just ignore your requests or politely decline.

So, before you race ahead with the rest of this book, take a little time out to make sure that your contact lists are as complete as possible. Also, set aside a little time each month to ensure that any new contacts you've made are added into your database and all of your different social networks.

IMAGES AT THE READY

As the expression says, 'A picture is worth a thousand words'. This is particularly relevant when it comes to social media where people are used to seeing a lot of images, but only bite-sized pieces of information. As you work your way through the stages of putting your internet marketing strategy into action, you will find that you use the same few images again and again on different sites. So it will save time to get them ready before you get started.

The images that you are going to need often are the following:

A copy of your logo

If you already have a website which features a logo that a designer created, you can copy it and save it to your computer. If you don't have a website yet but have used a designer to make letterheads, business cards or signs, etc., they should be able to provide you with a copy in JPEG, GIF or PNG format.

If you haven't already got a logo for your business, now is the time to get one. There are several different sites on the Web where you can make a logo for free, such as **www.logomaker.com**. The free version should be sufficient for using on the Internet. If you want a logo in high quality for printing though, you need to pay a little extra. Try and come up with a logo that is close to being square-shaped rather than a thin strip, as it will be possible to place this in larger sizes on most websites.

Pictures of yourself

Ideally you should have two different photos – a casual one that represents yourself as a private individual for sites such as Facebook, and a professional one to represent your practice on more professional sites such as LinkedIn. There's no need to go to a professional photographer to get these photos taken as they will probably look too formal on the more laidback medium of the Web, Instead, just get a friend or family member to take a few shots on a digital camera and select the best ones.

Get into the habit of using the same professional photo on every site. In this way, the photo will become as much a part of your personal 'brand' as your logo and will become instantly recognizable to your clients.

Pictures of your office

Many of the location-based sites provide an option for you to upload pictures of your premises. If you have a decent looking office, it is worth uploading these pictures to show that you are a *bona fide* business with a physical location. It will also help potential clients to find your office.

Conversely, if you work from home or your offices don't look particularly impressive, skip this exercise or else it could do you more harm than good.

CHOOSING KEYWORDS

As well as using a handful of images over and over again as you set up your internet marketing and social media campaigns, you're also going to be reusing the same 'keywords' too.

'Keywords' are the words (or, more usually, phrases consisting of two or more words) that people would use to find your practice if they were searching for your practice online.

How would **you** find an accounting firm in your area if you were searching for it on Google? Probably the most obvious way to find it would be by searching for 'accountant' and 'yourtown' and so these should probably be your main keywords.

Without using keywords, much of your marketing efforts are going to be in vain. If you don't have any of your major keywords in your profiles or descriptions, you will be practically invisible in most cases. Search technology is becoming increasingly clever all the time, but unless you put the fact that 'John Smith is an accountant in [yourtown]' into your profiles, the various search engines aren't going to be able to figure it out.

A quick note at this stage - search engines completely ignore capitalization in search results. So a search for 'CPA in Yourtown' produces exactly the same results as 'cpa in yourtown'. Therefore, whenever I mention keywords in the book, I always list them in lower case.

In chapter 13 on Google AdWords, I show you a tool from Google which you can use to find out accurate information on the best keywords for you to use based upon what users in your area are really searching for. So as not to bog you down at this stage, let me give you a summary here of what I have discovered to be the four most popular keywords for accountants so that you can start off by using these to save time:

- accountant
- cpa
- accounting firm
- tax preparation

Put these four keywords together and maybe your profile could look something like:

Need an accountant in [yourtown] to help with your tax preparation? Contact John Smith, CPA, today for a free consultation.

Note that, for British readers, 'CPA' is not such popular search terms in the UK and so there is not much need to add these terms to your profiles. Instead the keyword 'Chartered Accountant' is more often searched for.

Once you have chance to use the Google AdWords tool to come up with a list of the actual keywords which are most commonly searched for in your area, you can go back and change the keywords in your profiles if you find they are slightly different. This is another of the great benefits of internet marketing – nothing you do is ever permanent. You can always make changes in a couple of clicks any time you want to make them.

WRITE YOUR COPY

So now you know the best keywords for attracting potential clients to your advertising and profiles on the Internet. However, simply attracting eyeballs to look at your messages alone is going to be worthless if there is nothing there to capture their attention when they read it.

The Internet might be the cutting edge of communication technology at the start of the 21st Century, but the basics really haven't changed that much since Gutenberg invented movable type over 500 years ago. Despite all of the pictures, videos and flashy animations, people spend most of their time on the Internet simply reading – and acting upon what they have read if it captures their interest sufficiently.

This means that you are going to have to write some copy. And it is going to have to be some effective copy too if you want your visitors to take the action that you want them to take.

Effective copywriting is part art and part science. There have been hundreds of books published on the subject and, such is human psychology, even books written on the subject 40 years ago are still (mostly) relevant today. I'm guessing though that you don't have the time (or the inclination) to read a book or two on the subject of copywriting right now though, so let me give you a quick primer based upon five simple acronyms:

KISS – Keep It Simple, Stupid!

People read from screens differently than they do on paper. Despite advancements with screen resolutions, it's still not as comfortable reading on a monitor (or worse, on the tiny screen of a smartphone) as it is on paper. As a result, people tend to rush through their reading on screen, scanning content rather than lingering on every word. A lot of people simply can't be bothered to read through long pages of content and will simply click away if they find it looks too much like hard work.

For this reason, 'less is more' when it comes to writing online. The quicker you can get your point across, the better. As a result, once you have made your first attempt at writing some content, go through it again. Does every word of every sentence of every paragraph absolutely have to be there to get your point across? If you take some of it out, will it be any less effective in getting people to respond the way you want them to respond? If not, cut it out. Make sure that every single word of content is there for a reason.

Another point to remember is that, 'White space is your friend'. It's hard on the eye and difficult to scan dense paragraphs of text. The solution is to cut up your content into a succession of short and punchy paragraphs. Three or four simple sentences per paragraph are usually the maximum that you need to get your point across.

Wherever possible, use bullet points to list individual ideas rather than trying to explain each of them in long rambling literary paragraphs. Lists with bullet points are a lot easier for readers to scan.

AIDA – Attention, Interest, Desire, Action

Aida is not only a famous opera – it also describes the process of taking someone from casually coming across your information through to persuading them to do whatever it is that you want them to do:

Attention – With so much choice of alternative destinations on the Internet just a click away, you need to hook readers immediately, usually with a punchy headline.

Copy editors of tabloid newspapers are masters of this black art by coming up with headlines which arouse the readers' curiosity - intriguing them so that they start reading the article to find out what it's all about, e.g., "Freddie Starr Ate My Hamster" or, "Headless Body in Topless Bar". Although this might not be relevant for accountants in most circumstances, you will still have a lot more success if you come up with a punchy heading.

Compare the following two headlines:

Effective Tax Planning for Small Business Owners

You Can Reduce Your Next Tax Bill by up to 70%

Both of these articles could cover exactly the same subject, but which of them do you think is going to be most effective in getting people to read further?

Interest – The punchy headline will get readers to start reading (or scanning), but they will soon click away if it takes too long for you to get to the point. Because of this, you need to quickly show them that the article (or profile) is relevant to their interests. Once again, look at how newspaper articles are written. They don't slowly build up to a climax like in a movie or book. Instead they give you a summary as to what the whole article is about first before then going into detail on the subject.

This is how your copy needs to be written as well. Now that you have excited your readers with the headline, don't start to bore them with dull background information. Give them even more reasons as to why they are going to want to read right through to the end of the article.

Desire – The majority of your article or advertisement should be devoted to creating desire in the reader to have whatever it is that you are selling. In your case, it could be a reduction in taxes, saving them time, etc. As quickly and concisely as possible, explain to the readers exactly what you can do for them and why you are the best person or company for the job. By the end of your text, your prospects should be ready to do whatever it is that you want them to do.

Action – Too many people writing advertisements finish at the Desire stage, thinking that the prospects will automatically now do whatever you expect them to do now that you have them sufficiently excited. This can be a fatal mistake to make though. Your marketing copy also has to be its own salesman, and every salesman knows that he has to 'close the deal' or else all their hard work will have been for nothing.

Ask yourself the question, 'What do I ideally want the reader to do now?' Then simply ask them to do it.

Do you want the prospect to pick up the phone to set up a free consultation with you now? Then write:

Call me now on 555-555-5555 to set up your free, no obligation consultation

Or, if you want the readers to fill in a form on your website, give them the link to the relevant page right where the article or advertisement finishes, urging them to 'Click here now'. Don't make them hunt around your site to find the relevant contact form. You might know your way around your website like the back of your hand, but your prospect doesn't. It would be a tragedy if, after all your hard work in selling them on your service, the prospects couldn't find the right link and so simply gave up in frustration.

WII-FM – What's In It For Me?

Are you listening to WII-FM? Or are you going 'we-we' all the time?

Human beings are naturally rather selfish creatures. Sad as it might be, they don't care about your cashflow situation, your need to find new clients, or the fact that you promised your spouse a vacation in the Bahamas this winter and you have no idea how you're going to pay for it. They care only about their problems, their cashflow and how to buy **their** spouse a winter holiday in the Bahamas.

Bear this vital difference in mind whenever you are writing copy. Always put yourself in the mindframe of the reader rather than staying in your mindframe as the writer. All sales basically boil down to one of two things, either, 'Find a need and fill it' or, 'Find a problem and solve it'.

The magic word when writing copy is 'You'. This is what the reader of your text wants to hear about – themselves. Not you, the writer – themselves.

This is why it's a problem if you are going 'we-we' all the time.

I just made a random search for a random accounting firm in a random town and this is what I found on their home page:

[Redacted] offers tax, business consulting, accounting, assurance and exit and succession planning services. Our commitment is to help each client achieve their goals and ultimately peace of mind.

[Redacted] founded [Redacted] in 1985. He has extensive experience in partnership taxation, estate and gift tax planning, extensive financial planning and private foundation consulting and administration.

This is not a **terrible** website, but it's still all about the writer – not one single mention of 'you' – the potential client - and what 'your' problem might be. As a rule of thumb, look for a ratio of around two 'yous' and yours' for every one 'we', 'I', 'us', 'our', etc.

Don't be afraid of being too obvious in this – consider asking the readers direct questions:

Are you looking for a larger tax rebate next year? Are you finding that there aren't enough hours of the day to handle your own payroll? Etc.

For proof that I practice what I preach, take a look at the back cover of this book. Count how many times I used the word 'you' in just a few short sentences. Notice how I started off by asking the one question that I thought anyone browsing for this book would be asking themselves when they were reading the copy. Notice how I generated interest (and exclusivity) by turning convention on its head and telling potential buyers who this book was **not** for. Notice how I created desire with the promise of saving both time and money. All that's missing is the 'Action' part (which the on-line book store where you probably found the book should have provided with their 'Add to Basket' or 'Buy now with 1-Click' buttons).

WMT – Which Means That

I remember a sketch from an old comedy show which had the Sales Manager for an electronics company demonstrating a new hi-fi system to his sales force. He proudly showed them the Dolby HX button, the graphic equalizer, the SCART sockets, etc., before asking for any questions. One of the sales guys shouts out, "But what do they all do?" The Sales Manager then struggles to answer the question. He obviously has no clue what they all do.

This is an excellent, if rather extreme, example of the difference between **features** and **benefits**. Just because something is blindingly obvious to you (because you work in the business) does not automatically mean that it's obvious to the person you're selling to.

This is why the phrase, 'which means that' is such a useful one. It's a great bridge between listing features and benefits.

In the previous example, the Sales Manager should have said, "The hi-fi features Dolby HX, a graphic equalizer and a SCART socket, **which means that** you get to hear the best, crispest audio, no matter what you are listening to or where you are listening to it."

To give a more relevant example, don't just write on your website and in your newsletters that you offer a "complete bookkeeping service". This doesn't give your client any answer to WIIFM? Instead write, "We offer a complete bookkeeping service, **which means that** you just give us copies of all your purchase orders, receipts and invoices and we take care of everything for you so that you're free to concentrate on running the rest of your business."

Don't use 'which means that' **every** time you mention benefits after features though or else your copy will look repetitive and dull. Alternate it with other words or phrases that achieve the same results, e.g. 'so', 'therefore', 'as a result', etc.

MWR – Most Wanted Response

Copywriting is not something that people do for fun – they do it for a purpose. Most people understand this, but they only have a vague idea as to what the purpose is. This can be a fatal mistake, yet probably the vast majority of websites are guilty of it. They write some copy on their home page, but then just leave the visitor to wander around the rest of their site aimlessly. Maybe the visitor will end up doing what you would like them to do; maybe they won't.

Whenever you are writing copy for any purpose, you should ask yourself the question, "Exactly what do I want the reader to do once they have finished reading?"

The answer to this question is your 'Most Wanted Response' and it should also be the 'A' for 'Action' from the AIDA point. In chapter 8 about designing a website, I suggest that your 'Most Wanted Response' is probably going to be to get every new visitor to the site to contact you for a free consultation. Maybe this is the one that you choose as well, or it could be something completely different.

No matter what your Most Wanted Response is, you should **always** be asking visitors to make it. Ask for it at the bottom of **every** page. Your visitor might not be ready to sign up after reading just your home page – they might want to look around your site a little more. That's OK too. No one is going to punish you for asking them to take a particular action.

It is for those visitors who do want to take time to read more about you before making your Most Wanted Response that you need to ask for it on the bottom of every page of your site. You will never know exactly when each of them will be ready to make that commitment for one reason. For another, not everyone coming to your website is going to arrive on the home page first of all.

Although the above is a highly condensed version of how to write effective copy, by following these five simple rules, it should still be enough for you to write better material than 95% of all your potential competitors.

MONTHLY DEALS/PROMOTIONAL CALENDAR

By using the methods in this book, you will be able to keep your practice in front of potential clients 365 days per year. When they are in need an accountant, many of those who are part of your social networks will definitely have you at the front of their minds. Your marketing will have much greater impact though if you are able to offer something special and time limited to give them a sense of urgency about getting in contact with you. In addition, an offer which changes regularly will keep your content from getting stale and dull.

So in order to make the most of your internet marketing and social media campaign, you need to come up with a promotional calendar, offering some new incentive, ideally on a monthly basis. This will be the cornerstone of all your online promotional activities.

It's good to have the first few months of your promotional calendar worked out in advance so you can slot the first of them into your marketing efforts straight away.

So what are some kinds of promotions that you can incorporate into your marketing calendar? Here are just a few examples:

(a) Offer a free guide to potential clients, such as how they can cut their taxes. It doesn't need to be a massive tome – even ten paragraphs would be sufficient providing that the information is of real benefit to the reader. In fact, they'll probably prefer information which gets straight down to the nitty-gritty rather than something which requires them to wade through pages and pages of irrelevant rambling.

(b) Hold a free seminar one evening where you can host a question and answer session with potential clients. It doesn't need to be anything too grandiose or large-scale. In fact, your potential clients will probably appreciate being able to chat in a smaller, more intimate environment.

(c) Offer a discount on your services during your quietest month to try and get people to avoid the last-minute rush.

(d) Offer a free consultation.

Maybe you are a little stumped as to what you can offer here. After all, accounting is mostly business-to-business and the services that you provide does not change by the season. Also, although your services might be very important to your clients, they aren't going to be as 'glamorous' as many other businesses' products and services are going to be.

In this case, rather than offering a promotion on your own services, consider partnering with other businesses that do have offers which are more 'glamorous' than your own. For these purposes, being the provider of business-to-business services is an advantage, because you already have a network of potential promotional partners in place. They're your clients!

Go through your list of clients and write down all of those that are in the business-to-consumer sector. Restaurants are ideal because they live by their promotions. So are the majority of retailers, plus most other business in the service sector.

Contact all of your potential promotional partners and tell them that you want to run a promotion for a month as part of your online media and internet marketing activities. Ask them if they could provide you with something that you can offer to your network. It doesn't necessarily have to be something really expensive (although that wouldn't be bad!). A free meal for two from a restaurant client of yours would be great. But if that's asking too much, then maybe they could just offer a free dessert with a meal for two, or a retailer could offer a special 'buy one get one free' offer on some selected merchandise.

You should make it clear to your potential promotional partner that you are not asking for this as an act of charity from them. Tell them that you will be promoting the offer heavily across all of your social networks and perhaps on your website too and so they will receive free advertising. If you follow all of the ideas in this book, you could be promoting their business to thousands of people – all of them in your local area. This means that they will all be valuable potential customers for your promotional partner too.

If your potential promotional partner is keen on the idea, you can ask for a little more from them as well. Ask them to mention the promotion on all their social media marketing for the month as well. Chances are that, if they are in a more 'glamorous' business than you and deal with hundreds or thousands of different consumers each month, their networks will be a lot larger than yours. This additional exposure to a much larger social network could be incredibly valuable for you.

If your potential partner figures this out and realizes how much of a benefit this is going to be to you, they might want more from you in return. In this case, you could offer to split the cost of the promotion between you - the additional exposure will almost certainly be worth it.

I am sure that you will find that most businesses will be glad to make a deal like this with you – it saves them the trouble of having to think of a new promotional idea, after all.

Another potential tool in your promotional toolkit is to obtain some low-cost branded promotional merchandise that you can afford to give away for free as opposed to constantly running sweepstakes where people can win something more valuable. This could be a T-shirt or, better still, something related to your profession, such as a branded calculator or something related to money. If you make a Google search under 'promotional gifts accountants', you will find that some companies offer tailor-made items, such as blocks of chocolate in the shape of a 1040 form.

The advantage of making such offers online is that the recipient will need to visit your office to collect them. This gives you the opportunity to try and sell to them in a much more personal way than simply sending them an email. These are the types of promotion that will set you apart from your competitors – putting a human face to a business which is not particularly known for its originality and personality when it comes to marketing activities.

Try to come up with a calendar of three to six months' worth of promotions featuring as many different types of promotions as you can think of. After you have run at least one of each type of promotion, you will have a better idea as to what your potential clients will respond to best. You can then offer additional variations on this theme in future, and avoid those types of promotion which received little response.

So, have you now got your email mailing list, your images, your keyword-rich profile copy and the start of a promotional calendar in place? If so, you should now have all of the basic elements that you need to start putting your internet marketing strategy together.

Let's start off with the Big Daddy of all the social networking sites … Facebook.

FACEBOOK

S AY THE WORDS 'social media' to anyone and the first website that they are likely to think of is Facebook, which has been a global phenomenon over the past five years and is continuing to grow rapidly. At the time of writing, it is well on course to reach over a billion members in the not too distant future.

Assuming that you are between the ages of 13 (the minimum official age for anyone to join the network) and 65, there is a 70% chance that you already have a personal page on Facebook and have a fair idea as to what it does and how it works. If you are one of the 30% that has not yet joined the site, before you read any further, I suggest that you head straight over to **www.facebook.com** and join up. I won't waste your time by explaining how to do this as it is a simple process to sign up and start using it – over 800 million people have figured it out already, after all!

Although most people now have a personal Facebook Profile and know how to use the basic functions of the site, such as posting status updates and photos, sharing interesting links or chatting with friends, there are now several other functions available to all Facebook users that are not as widely known. So let us start by going through each of them in turn:

Facebook Profiles

If you are on Facebook already, then this is probably what you have, and what all of your friends have. Facebook Profiles are for human beings **only**. Some companies and organizations have, erroneously, created Faceook Profiles in the past. Don't be mistaken into thinking that, if it's OK for them, then it will be OK for you as well though. This is against Facebook's Terms and Conditions and so they are perfectly within their rights to close down such pages at any time. And, if they do, then all of the effort you will have put into building your network will have been in vain.

So your Facebook Profile should be for John Smith, the human being, and not John Smith & Associates, the accounting firm.

Always keep this difference in mind when you are deciding what information should be posted to which part of Facebook. The information you post to your Facebook Profile should predominantly be about you, e.g., posting what you got up to at the weekend, a link to the video on YouTube you just enjoyed, pictures of your last vacation, etc. It's OK to mention your business on your Profile page from time to time – after all, it is a major part of your life. However, if you try and make your personal Facebook Profile into too much of a sales tool, you are likely to start alienating several of your friends until they have had enough of your spam and decide to unfriend you. Instead, try and use your Facebook Profile to drive people towards your business Page and ask them to 'Like' it.

Facebook Pages

Facebook Pages are the opposite of Facebook Profiles – they are for corporate entities, brands and organizations as well as celebrities and personalities rather than regular human beings like you and I. Facebook Pages don't have 'Friends' - instead they have 'Fans'. Anyone on Facebook can become a 'Fan' of any Page simply by clicking on that Page's 'Like' button. People don't need to send a 'Fan Request' for approval like they do if they want to become a Friend of yours on your personal Profile page.

If you don't already have a Facebook Page for your business (and today only a small percentage of local businesses have one), you should start one as soon as possible. Most of this chapter concerns how to start a Page for your practice and how to use it most effectively.

Facebook Groups

Facebook Groups is a facility which allows Profiles (but not Pages) interested in a common subject to get together in order to discuss common subjects. Perhaps the easiest way to imagine it is as an online forum that people join to ask questions and inform people about a common subject. There are two ways of using Facebook Groups to your advantage – you can either set up one of your own, or join in the conversation on someone else's.

Used effectively, this can be a powerful tool in your social media arsenal because so few businesses are currently taking advantage of this feature. In addition, you don't need to ask a person's permission to enroll them in the Group. The downside of this though is that, because of this power, setting up a Facebook Group of your own can be intrusive and so can annoy people if they didn't want to be part of it in the first place.

Facebook Events

Facebook Events can be set up by either Profiles or Pages and are used for promoting events that last for a fixed duration. Only Profiles can be invited to such events. Although the majority of people who use this Events function normally use it to promote events such as concerts or parties, etc., I will show you how, with a little bit of lateral thinking, you can use Facebook Events as an effective way of advertising your promotional activity.

Facebook Places

Facebook Places is aimed directly at local businesses – and that means you! Taking advantage of the rapidly growing number of users who access Facebook via smartphones, Facebook Places was established as Facebook's answer to geo-location check-in services such as Foursquare and Yelp, which I describe in more detail in chapter 12.

Facebook Ads

All of the above sections of Facebook are free to use. Facebook Ads, however work in the same way as advertising on any other website – you pay your money to be featured exactly where you want to be featured.

One of the advantages of Facebook Ads is that it is possible to target your advertising tightly against the type of people you would like to attract. This means that you can choose the location of those who see it, their gender, their age, etc., so you aren't wasting any of your advertising budget on anyone who definitely cannot use your services. A second advantage is that is that Facebook Ads get seen a **lot** of times because Facebook is now the most viewed site on the Internet.

The downside, however, is that, unlike someone who has gone to Google and is making a search for 'accountant yourtown', they are not actively searching for your services. They probably just came on Facebook to see what their friends are up to.

Now I will explain each of these different features of Facebook in more detail:

FACEBOOK PROFILES

Facebook Profiles are meant for people and not businesses. However, this does not mean that they are of no use in your marketing activities – quite the reverse in fact.

Although, as we will see in the next section on Facebook Pages, they offer you an enormous amount of marketing opportunities, there is one major downside to them – business Pages are 'passive' means of promotion. Similar to your own website, even if it is the best and most useful site in the world, it is completely useless until someone stops by and visits it.

Facebook Profiles, conversely, allow 'active' promotion on Facebook because the mechanism is in place to go out and use it to attract new potential clients by sending them a Friend request.

Social media is perfect for local businesses because **you** are your product; **you** are the brand. Maybe you find that you are constantly in competition with a large national corporation with a household name and a vast advertising budget that allows them to attract a lot more 'eyeballs' than you can ever hope to do. In this case, you'll be glad to learn that social media is one area where you have the advantage over the national corporations. The Big 4 accounting firms are always going to be faceless entities and real people prefer dealing with other real people.

So to start off your Facebook marketing activity, you should invite as many existing and potential clients as possible to be your 'Friends'. If you are a little hesitant about adding people who you have only met once to your list of friends, then don't be – 'Friends' on Facebook aren't necessarily the same as your 'friends' in real life. 'Acquaintances' would probably be a more accurate term, but it doesn't have quite the same ring to it. While the average person on Facebook currently has around 130 Friends, those people who are actively using Facebook as a marketing tool already will have many more than this – in some cases up to Facebook's maximum limit for a Profile of 5,000 Friends.

There are a couple of major advantages to inviting as many current and potential clients to become a Friend on Facebook as possible:

(a) It is easy to invite all your Friends to 'Like' your Facebook business Page by putting links to it through Profile updates, which will appear in your Friends' streams. This is a powerful and effective way of getting the link in front of them. However, as is the case with all of the most effective promotional methods, it should be used in moderation or else you risk annoying your Friends who could accuse you of spamming. Probably once per month is the maximum that you want to ask your Friends to visit your business Page and 'Like' it in order to avoid incurring their wrath.

(b) As mentioned above, only Profiles are able to take advantage of the promotional opportunities offered by Facebook Groups; business Pages can't use them. So, by having a large number of Friends attached to your Profile, you will be able to invite a lot of potential clients to use this function.

But what about content? It seems as if a lot of people struggle to use Facebook effectively to communicate with their friends. Some people jabber away incessantly, posting dozens of times each day about nothing at all, wishing everyone 'good morning', 'good night' or explaining what they had for dinner. At the opposite end of the spectrum, many other people deliberate so much before whether something is worth posting that they end up posting nothing at all.

Like most things in life, a happy medium is the best strategy. Research has shown that the people who get the most comments and 'Likes' on their posts tend to update their statuses just once every day or two. For maximum impact, Facebook also recommends that people either post late in the evening or early in the morning. This is good news because it means that you don't have to interrupt your working day for your postings to have the best possible chance of being seen and acted upon.

Getting comments and 'Likes' is not just good for the ego; it's important to keep yourself in front of your friends' eyeballs. The main window on everyone's Facebook Profile features what the company believes to be users' 'Top Stories' first of all, with 'Recent Stories' relegated to further down the page.

The 'Top Stories' feed uses complicated algorithms which Facebook called 'EdgeRank' to try and decide which content from which Friends the viewer should be most interested in. Those status updates which get a lot of comments and 'Likes' receive a higher 'EdgeRank' than those that don't. In addition, those Friends regularly posting popular updates are also ranked higher in the streams than those who don't. Furthermore, the posts from Friends you interact with regularly are given more prominence then those of Friends whose posts you intend to ignore.

The net result of all this is that users with a large number of Friends will rarely see content from most of them in their 'Top Stories' feed. This means that, if you are not posting interesting content on Facebook that your Friends interact with often, your postings will become practically invisible to a large proportion of your Friends. In the process, you will lose all of the potential benefits of your relationship with them on Facebook.

In September 2011, Facebook introduced a second, smaller window on the right hand side of the page called the 'Ticker'. The 'Ticker' is completely unfiltered – it shows a constant stream of all updates coming from all Friends in real time. With only the last eight updates shown on the 'Ticker' at any one time though, the updates won't be displayed for long on the Profiles of people with more than just a handful of Friends.

So now you know how often you should update your status and why you should update your status. But still the question remains – exactly **what type** of content should you be posting to your personal Profile?

First of all, **don't** post blatant advertising for your practice – apart from monthly reminders to 'Like' your business Page. You don't want to alienate your Friends who already 'Like' your business Page by posting business related updates twice.

Your Profile page should be personal to you and should show your Friends (and potential new clients) that you are a sociable and likeable individual. You should come across as a three-dimensional person rather than some faceless individual working for a major corporate competitor, where employees are generally kept away from getting too sociable with clients for fear that they may 'say the wrong thing'.

'Saying the wrong thing' might be a worry to you if you are starting to invite potential clients onto your personal Facebook Profile. Perhaps you currently have only your 'real' Friends on Facebook and you are used to posting personal items there which you wouldn't want potential clients to see. Maybe you like sharing risqué jokes and discussing your crazy night out with the boys, or maybe you are sharing pictures of your new baby with the family. In both of these cases, you would probably not want to share this information with people who you have only become Friends with for business purposes.

Up until September 2011, this would have been a real problem on Facebook. However, now there is an easy solution which allows you to post different news items to different 'Lists' of Friends. When this new feature was introduced, Facebook automatically tried to divide up users' Friends into various lists such as 'Family', 'Close Friends' and people in their local area. Sometimes Facebook's guesses were quite accurate, while at other times they were way off the mark.

If you are intending to use your personal Facebook Profile as a way of keeping in touch with both your real friends and also potential business contacts, it's time to utilize this feature by putting all of your Friends on different Lists. You can create as many Lists as you like. I would recommend setting up a new List called 'Prospects' and putting all of your potential new business contacts in there.

Now, when you come to make a posting, you have the option of choosing who will see your posting and who won't. By default, all postings are made 'Public', which means that all of your Friends will see your update, no matter which List they are on. By clicking on the menu next to the 'Post' button, however, you are able to select exactly which Lists will or won't get this update. By using this function, you are now able to continue to be that crazy party animal that your old college buddies know you as while, at the same time, portraying yourself as a sober professional to your future prospects.

If you are stuck for anything interesting to post as a Status Update, have a think as to what event in your day evoked the strongest reaction from you. Did you see or hear something that made you laugh? Or maybe you saw or heard something that made you angry? If something happened that evoked a strong reaction from you, then there's a good chance that it will also evoke strong reactions from other people too.

If you encountered nothing particularly out of the ordinary during the day, then ask yourself what everyone is talking about at the moment. Think of Facebook as the virtual equivalent of an office water cooler which everyone congregates around to share interesting news and gossip. What's the main subject in the news today? What are your own personal views on the subject? Was there something on TV last night that everyone is talking about? Or some celebrity antics? As the old saying goes, stay away from religion and politics for fear of alienating anyone with opposing views to yours, but everything else is fair game. Humor is always a great tool to use if it comes naturally to you – everyone likes people who can make them laugh. But it's not everyone who is able to come up with a humorous take on different situations on a regular basis.

Within reason, don't be afraid of expressing strong opinions – no one is going to have a strong reaction if you just come out with bland 'me too' postings. The most famous names in media are the ones that come out with the boldest statements – some people might hate them, some people might love them, but no one can ignore them. You're not planning on becoming the next Glenn Beck or Jeremy Clarkson, but their popularity and ability to start people debating cannot be argued with.

So consider coming out with updates along the lines of, "I can't believe the government is doing *xyz*. I think they should do *abc* instead." Or, "If I see Lady Gaga in the newspaper one more time, I think I'm going to scream." Don't take these examples too literally though – if it's not something you would say while chatting to your real-life friends, then it will sound fake if you post it to Facebook.

One trick to encourage debate and feedback on your posts which is used by many professional bloggers is to end your postings with a question such as, "What do you think?" Don't do it for everything you post though or else your Friends will soon get tired of it.

When looking for topics to post about, pay particular attention to what's happening locally in your neighborhood. After all, all of your Friends which have the potential to become future customers will live in your local area. This means that anything which affects both you and them is going to be of particular interest – probably more so than the latest events from Washington and London.

As well as making your own posts every day or two, take time to read the top postings in your News Stream to see what your Friends are saying and 'Like' those ones you genuinely did find interesting and comment on their posts when you have something interesting to add to the conversation. In such a way, you will not only be creating a stronger bond with your Friends, but you will also be entering into a conversation with your Friends' Friends. If some of your Friends' Friends look as if they could be potential clients, then invite them to become a Friend of yours as well.

Perhaps you could send them a message in the process thanking them for agreeing with your point of view.

In summary, post often to your personal Profile and engage your Friends. Let your own personality shine through so that potential new clients will see that you are a real person and not some corporate puppet.

FACEBOOK PAGES

As Facebook Pages are specifically designed for businesses of all sizes to market themselves on Facebook, which is the biggest and most important of all the social networks, creating your own Facebook Page is definitely going to be one of the most important elements of your internet marketing campaign. According to a study of 200 accounting firms conducted by World Synergy in late 2011, only 17% of small accounting firms have Facebook business Pages compared with 73% of large accounting firms. As a result, smaller accounting firms really need to catch up with the efforts of their larger competitors.

Fortunately, Facebook now has a user-friendly interface to make starting off a Facebook Page for business as simple as creating a Profile for a person. To start the process, head to:

www.facebook.com/business

There is a lot of information both on the pages inside the business section and also linked from it. Some of it makes for interesting reading and so have a look through it if you have the time and inclination to do so. But don't feel that it is essential to read everything before you get started on creating your Page. It's better to start off with a basic Page and then tweak it as you go along rather than fretting over having the perfect Page to begin with.

Unless you have a medium-sized business with a multitude of different offices, it will be best to choose the 'Local Business or Place' option rather than 'Company, Organization or Institution', as it will be easier to integrate your Page with Facebook Places. This will enable potential clients to find you more easily.

Choose the 'Professional Services' option and then fill in the address of your office (or your main office if you have more than one), and also fill in your phone number. Then continue on to the next step.

The next option is to 'Set Your Profile Picture'. Here you should use the logo that I suggested you get ready in the previous chapter. There, I mentioned that it is best to have a logo which is in a square format. If you have a wide rectangle, either the edges are going to get cut off or else your logo will appear so small as to be unreadable when the 'thumbnail' of the image is produced. The thumbnail image or your 'icon' is featured alongside all of your posts.

This advice is probably best for beginners, but there is another trick that you can use here if you have any ability with a graphics program such as Photoshop (or you have a friend who does). Although the width of your Profile Picture is restricted to 200 pixels, the height of the image can be as much as 600 pixels. That's massive. Therefore, if you can come up with a Profile Picture which is a thin but deep vertical banner, your picture will have a lot more impact than a square.

Once you have uploaded your Profile Picture, continue to the next page.

Step 2 is the 'Get Fans' option, which allows you to 'Invite Friends' and also to 'Import Contacts' from your email accounts. I recommend that you skip this stage for now, because it will probably take you a while to get your Page into a format which you are happy with. You will get the opportunity to invite all of your Friends and contacts to 'Like' your new business Page at a later stage.

Step 3 asks you for your website address if you have one, and also to write a little bit of information which will be displayed on your Page. You only have 255 characters available to you here, which are only going to be enough for one long sentence or two short ones. Of these, only 75 characters are shown without the visitor clicking on the 'More' link, so you will need to get your message over quickly if you want to get the most benefit from this section.

Use this space to sum up exactly what your business is and, if possible, what makes your business unique, or better than your competitors. Maybe your business has been going for decades; maybe you have won some awards; maybe you offer a personal touch that your competitors don't. If something comes quickly to mind, add it in now. Otherwise just leave it as purely factual and you can update it at any time that you might have a 'Eureka!' moment of creativity. Try and follow the rules for good copywriting in the previous chapter to come up with some effective text here.

Once you press 'Continue' again, your Page will be created and you will now be inside the Control Panel or 'Dashboard' for it. Although the basic information will be on your Page already, you still have a bit more work to do to include all of the details which will make your Page a truly useful resource for your customers.

Next, click on the big 'Edit Page' button at the top right of your Page or the small 'Edit Info' link under the name of your business at the top of the Page. This will enable you to makes some changes to the Page 'behind the scenes' and will also enable you to add more detailed information to it.

Familiarize yourself with what the links on the left-hand side of the Page allow you to do. 'Your Settings' and 'Manage Permissions' are for changes that you probably won't need to make any time soon. 'Basic Information' is the important one – go through it and fill in all of the gaps that weren't filled in when you set up the Page during the initial creation process so that your clients know your opening hours, email address, etc.

Here you also have the opportunity to create a unique Username for your Facebook Page. By default, your Page will have a combination of the business name which you gave plus a string of random numbers. No one is going to remember this, so choose a Username that is easy to remember and/or contains your best keywords. A perfect example of a Username would be one along the lines of:

www.facebook.com/Yourtown.Accountant

Moving on down the page, make sure that your address is correct. As long as it is, Facebook will automatically find your location and add it to a map on your 'Info' page, together with the facility for visitors to get driving directions to it.

'Profile Picture' gives you the opportunity to change the one you uploaded during the creation process. If it didn't come out as well as you liked, then you can fine-tune it here. Otherwise there's no need to fiddle with it any more.

'Featured' offers you the ability to put in 'Likes' and 'Page Owners' details. 'Likes' is a bit of a misnomer in this context – after all we are talking about a business entity here, not a human being. So what could your business possibly 'Like'? 'Like' in the context of your Facebook business Page just means the same as 'Useful Links' and the list will appear on the left-hand side of your page, towards the bottom. You can use this facility to put in a link to a professional organization that you are part of, perhaps. Maybe you can also use it to barter with other relevant local businesses, including some of your existing clients if you have some with their own Facebook business Pages already. Are you friends with a local lawyer, for example? Offer to link their Facebook Page to yours if they will do the same and then you will both benefit from the additional exposure.

It is definitely worth adding your own Profile as a 'Page Owner'. As I say time and time again in this book, **you** are the face of your business and you should take every opportunity to associate yourself with it. This is one of those opportunities.

'Resources' gives you some additional information and additional tools to use for promotion. If you have the time and inclination, look through the information here. We will be coming back to this page in chapter 8 where I describe how to build, or improve, your main website. Much of the information linked from here is quite technical though – designed for larger businesses with in-house programmers or marketing budgets that they can spend on hiring outside techies. It's all just 'icing on the cake' though and so there's no need to worry about it.

'Manage Admins' allows you to give access to the Page to someone else. If you have an Assistant who will be updating the Page, then this is where you would add their Profile to the account. If only you are going to be posting to the Page, then you can ignore it.

'Apps' is a big subject. I'll come onto this in a minute.

'Mobile' is a section that you can ignore unless you have a basic cellphone which does not give you internet access. If this is the case and you would like to update your Page status on the move, you can sign up for the option to update your status by SMS. If you have a smartphone, however, there are easier options for updating your status from your mobile, which I will describe in chapter 7.

'Insights' is a useful part of Facebook Pages which will, over time, give you some interesting data about who is visiting your Page, including when they are visiting, what they liked, what they didn't like, plus a whole heap of other information. If you've just set up your Page, then this section won't have any data to display, so leave this too for now and we'll come back to it later.

Last comes the link for Facebook's 'Help' pages. If there was anything regarding the creation of your Page that you didn't understand while you were working through the process in conjunction with this book, here is where you should go in order to find the answers.

APPS

If you went through the above steps, you should now have a perfectly serviceable Facebook Page (or Facebook **Pages** – plural – to be more precise, as I'm just coming on to explain). If you're short on time, money and/or creative skills, feel free to skip over this section on Apps. Although it can take your Facebook marketing to the next level, it's still just an optional extra.

Currently your Facebook business Page looks similar to the Facebook Profile which you have for yourself, the human being. But it actually consists of several different pages:

(a) Your 'Wall' which is like a diary/scrapbook/corkboard, recording all of the interaction that you, or visitors to your Page, has with anyone else on Facebook.

(b) Your 'Info' – the Basic Information that anyone will need in order to learn about your business and contact you outside of Facebook (e.g. your office address, location map, phone number and email address).

(c) Your 'Friend Activity' which shows all of the interaction on your business Page between you and your personal Friends.

(d) Your 'Insights' – statistics which tell you how many people visited your Page and what they did when they got there.

You can see each of these pages listed underneath your Profile Picture on the left of the screen. As mentioned earlier, Facebook gives anyone the opportunity to add some more basic pages to their 'mini-site'. Specifically:

(e) Your 'Photos' – an album which displays all of the photos which you have uploaded in the past.

(f) Your 'Links' – a collection of links to external pages which you have posted in the past.

(g) Your 'Events' – information on past, present and future Events which your company organizes (more on this later).

(h) Your 'Notes' – any long postings which you would like to make in the form of a note instead. Facebook used to restrict postings to a maximum of 500 characters, which meant that Notes were the only way of getting longer messages across. Now, however, the posting limit is a massive 5000 characters, which means that there is not so much need for a separate Notes page. If you fancy blogging though, Notes could be the right place for you to do it.

(i) Your 'Video' – for posting links to videos on sites like YouTube or any that you have uploaded to Facebook yourself. Probably of limited use to most local businesses.

To add any or all of these 'Apps' to your page, go into the 'Edit Page' section, click on 'Apps', then select the 'Edit Settings' link next to it and select 'Add'. Once you have done this, you will see that links to all of these 'Apps' are now listed on the left-hand side of your page, underneath the 'Wall' and 'Info' links.

If you would like to change the order that these links appear in, or change your mind and want to delete any of them, you can do this by clicking on the 'Edit' link while you are in 'Edit Page' mode and then drag and drop the different links into the position you want them to be in, or press on the 'X' to delete the links.

You've now reached the limits of what you're able to put on your Pages through using Facebook's own free facilities. Facebook does have additional facilities for adding more different elements to your Page, but these cost money and can't be set up yourself.

You now have a perfectly functioning Page or, more accurately a 'mini-website' if you have activated several of the Apps and are planning on making use of them all. However, there are some further improvements which you can make if you want to take advantage of all of the opportunities for marketing your business that Facebook offers.

Currently, your Facebook Page is almost identical in look and layout to every Facebook Profile and most of the other business Pages you see. It's functional, it's easy-on-the-eye but, dare I say, it's a little bit boring and lacking in character? Perhaps you've visited some Facebook Pages belonging to big brands and corporations and noticed that they have several different Pages which feature designs different to the standard layouts and wondered how they did it?

Or maybe you think that your Page is not going to be sufficiently interesting to attract a lot of 'Likes' from your personal Friends and potential new clients? Maybe an incentive for them to head on over and click the 'Like' button will do the trick?

But how can you arrange this when Facebook doesn't give you any tools to use unless you pay them big bucks to do it for you?

One way would be to hire some techies to do it for you. But techies don't come cheap and I promised you that this wasn't going to cost you a lot of money. Fortunately, there are several companies producing tools which can transform your Facebook Page into a much more personalized and effective promotional tool. There is a huge variation in the prices that these companies charge for the use of these tools, starting at completely free for a basic service, right up to the level of 'mind-blowingly expensive' (i.e. $2495 per month!). Some of these services require some basic skills with image processing programs such as Photoshop to get the most out of them. Others can be used to create effective pages with just the ability to upload a few photos.

So what additional Pages should you be looking to add to your 'mini site' using one of these services?

The first Page you will probably want to create is a more interesting looking 'home page' or 'landing page' for your Facebook mini-site. By default, all visitors to a business Page go straight to its Wall where they will see all of the recent activity. While it's not a bad page for new visitors to arrive on, it is still a lot better for visitors to arrive at a page which tells them clearly what your mini-site is about and why they should 'Like' it. Without such a page, they only have the 'About' sentence somewhat hidden on the left hand panel to try and figure out what your site is about and why it could be of interest to them.

All of the companies offering these services provide the ability for users to create an interesting looking 'Welcome' page. If you have no skills whatsoever with programs like Photoshop, I recommend you use **www.pagemodo.com** to create your 'Welcome' page. While not as flexible as some of the other services, they offer a wide variety of attractive templates for you to use. This enables anyone who can upload a few photos and type a bit of text to create good-looking and informative pages. Pagemodo is designed specifically for small businesses and is by far the most popular of all these services.

If you do have some basic Photoshop skills, my personal favorite from these services is **www.lujure.com**, which is a flexible tool which can create pages with a huge amount of useful content in minutes through its simple to use and flexible 'drag-and-drop' interface. To get the most out of it though, you will need the ability to create some basic graphics yourself.

Both of these services allow you to create one page for free. If you want more than this, then you need to pay a little extra each month. Pagemodo is by far the cheaper of the two companies, with packages starting from $6.25 per month.

Although both of these services offer the ability to produce a variety of different type of pages, the first one which you create should be a 'Welcome' page. This should introduce your company to visitors and encourage them to 'Like' your Page, ideally by telling them why they should do so.

Follow the instructions that your chosen service gives you carefully in order to produce your first page. Be prepared to spend a little time to create an attractive one. Your first attempt at making the page is probably going to look like a dog's dinner. But, with a little experimentation and a bit of trial and error, you should eventually come up with something that does the job. Refer back to the copywriting tips to write some engaging copy on this 'Welcome' page which asks them to click the 'Like' button in order to receive regular updates from you.

Once you have created your 'Welcome' Page, you should make sure that everyone visiting your mini-site arrives on this page first of all. To do so, go to your 'Edit Page' button or 'Edit Info' link, then select 'Manage Permissions'. Here you will see an option called 'Default Landing Tab' which is currently set on 'Wall'. Change this to the name of the new page which you have created (called 'Meet us' if you used Pagemodo).

Specifically asking visitors to 'Like' your Page is definitely going to have better results than not asking visitors. But the way to **really** increase the percentage of visitors hitting that 'Like' button is to give them an incentive to do so. This powerful promotional method involves two stages:

Firstly, you need to put a 'Fan Gate' or 'Like Gate' in place. This acts as a barrier that keeps anyone who has not pressed the 'Like' button from getting to see the page containing the incentive. Both Pagemodo and Lujure offer the ability to include such a function.

The second part of the operation is to actually offer something of value to the visitor which is hiding behind the 'Gate'. Have a think as to what might make for an interesting incentive which is also relevant to your business. How about offering a report such as 'Ten Top Tips to Trim Taxes Today'? All you would then need to do is to add one more new page to your mini-site giving some ideas for people to reduce their taxes. This can be created simply using Facebook's 'Notes' App, so it's simply a case of your writing up the content.

For other ideas, refer back to the previous chapter where I suggested setting up cross-promotions with some of your clients to run a monthly sweepstakes to win a meal for two at a restaurant, or some similar offer.

Another powerful feature which Pagemodo offers its users is the possibility of creating attractive 'Fan Coupons' which give your visitors something for free or for a discount. These coupons can either be printed by the visitor or else they can contain a 'secret codeword' which clients just have to mention when they come to visit you, or book a consultation with you over the phone. What could you offer potential clients using a 'Fan Coupon' behind your 'Like Gate'?

Get creative here. Wrack your brains to come up with an attractive incentive that will guarantee that visitors to your Page will definitely want to click on that 'Like' button. If they don't, and typically 96% of all visitors to Pages won't, your updates are not going to appear on their streams. And this would mean your losing this one incredibly valuable chance of speaking to them on a daily basis. Once you've come up with a great concept for a giveaway, think about how to use the tools available in order to make it happen.

As well as providing the ability to create 'Like Gates' and Coupons, Pagemodo offers a couple of other useful functions that could also be useful in making your mini-site a real 'Go To' destination on Facebook. One is a contact form enabling potential new clients to contact you directly or ask for more information on your service. The second is a map and location page option which will make it easier for potential clients to find your office.

Lujure has all of these options as well, plus many more besides which you can find details of on their website. Such are the wide variety of options available on Lujure that it can be tricky to decide upon which of them you want to use and which you don't. Avoid the temptation of trying to cram in every single one of their Apps on your Pages though. Otherwise, the pages will end up becoming too cluttered and confusing for your Fans. Ask yourself what you want your Facebook Pages to achieve. If adding another Page or another App is not going to achieve that goal, then it will be better just to leave it out.

The Apps offered by Pagemodo or Lujure should be enough for most local businesses to offer plenty of reasons for their potential new clients to 'Like' and interact with their Facebook Pages. However, there are other services available to anyone wanting to add even more incentives to their offer – if they don't mind paying a higher monthly fee for the opportunity. One of the leaders in offering these advanced services is **www.northsocial.com**, which powers the Facebook Pages of a lot of big name brands due to their offering a slick collection of Apps for their clients to use. Two of the highlights from their App collections which are not included in the services offered by their cheaper competitors are an automated Sweepstakes facility and also a Deal Share facility (similar to the ones I will be describing in chapter 14).

Another option if you are interested in adding even more content to your pages is to have a look at **www.appbistro.com**. This site lists a large number of different Apps from many different producers so you can pick the ones that you think are going to be the most use to you. Although it is usually more economical to get all of your Apps from the same supplier, there's nothing to stop you taking content from a variety of sources.

If you have followed all of the advice in this section, you should now have a slick-looking and powerful mini-site which provides a lot of value to visitors and gives them a good reason to 'Like' you. But creating an effective Facebook Page and then ignoring it takes away nearly all of the advantages that Facebook has over just a regular website – it will lose its powerful ability to proactively engage with your 'Fans' on a regular basis so that they don't simply forget about you the moment they click away from your Page.

To make full use of your superb-looking new Facebook Page, you're going to have to keep updating it with fresh content.

CONTENT

Much of what I posted earlier about content for your Facebook Profile is also valid for your Facebook Page. Posting once either at the beginning or end of each day is a good habit to get into for maximum impact. Posting every second day should be the minimum that you are aiming for.

But where I advised you to be personal and opinionated on your Profile, the opposite is true on your business Page. While you shouldn't come over as too 'buttoned-up' and officious, everything you post to your Page should be directly or indirectly concerned with your business. Save the funny cat video you like so much for your personal Profile.

Below are some suggestions as to what type of content you should be thinking of including in your Facebook updates (and updates to your other social networks which I will be coming onto in the next few chapters). These suggestions are listed in descending order of importance:

(a) <u>Monthly Deals</u>: In the previous chapter, I mentioned how useful it would be for all of your internet marketing and social media activities to regularly be running some kind of a Deal or Promotion to use as 'bait' in your campaigns. Posting about the Deal on your business Page News Stream is one of the main uses of this promotion and so it should be your priority for posting as an update. Something this important should not be posted just once because not everyone checks their Facebook account every day. Instead, mention it throughout the period of the promotion, but not so often that Facebook regulars get sick of the sight of it and unfriend you in order to make it stop. Once a week should be optimum for posting this kind of useful information. Post on different days each week for a better chance that everyone will see it at least once.

(b) <u>Office News</u>: Any useful information that you need to tell your current clients. What are your opening hours during the holidays? Are you going on your vacation next week? Have some of your contact details changed? Have you taken on a new member of staff? Did you just sign up a new, major client? Have you won an award? Have you had an article published somewhere? Every piece of news you have about your practice should be posted to your News Stream. Think of it as your practice's own newsletter which you are compiling one piece at a time.

(c) <u>FAQs (Frequently Asked Questions)</u>: What question did a client ask you today? Is it a question that you find many of your clients asking you? If so, post the question and answer to your Stream. Not only should it be of interest to quite a few potential clients, but hopefully if a few more people see it, they'll take up less of your time asking it themselves. Once you have answered several of these questions, consider compiling all of them onto a new page of your Facebook mini-site. Alternatively, you could use them to create a Note along the lines of, 'Answers to Accountants' Top 30 Questions' which you could offer as the incentive for people to enter through your 'Like Gate'.

(d) <u>Local News</u>: Posts directly related to your own practice are always the best ones to make. But there are sure to be times when you simply don't have anything interesting which is directly related to your practice to pass on to your Fans. In these cases, cast your net a little wider to look for items that will be of interest to them. Follow all your local media's social networks by 'Liking' them on Facebook, following their Twitter Feeds or subscribing to their RSS feeds, as I will describe in more detail over the following chapters. In such a way, you will be one of the first to know whenever there is some breaking local news item that could be of interest to your Fans. Re-share this news or link to the information from your Wall. Add any other local sources of information which could make for good sources of local news, e.g. your local government office, local police, local Chamber of Commerce, Rotary Club, etc. Not only will it be a good source of news for you, but it also cements your position as being part of the local community.

(e) <u>Professional News</u>: Also sign up for all the feeds coming in from your trade association, industry trade publications and the most authoritative websites in your field. When there is some breaking news or developments which are relevant to your existing and potential new clients, then add a summary, your personal opinion if you have one, together with a link to where your visitors can read the entire article.

(f) <u>Ask a Question</u>: As well as giving you the opportunity to post items, links, photos and videos, Facebook also has an option to ask your Fans a Question. To do this, you can easily add a Poll function so that your Fans can vote for their answer. This simple tool is inviting for visitors to your Page to interact with because people love to 'stand up and be counted'. It's also an excellent way to learn more about your Fans' likes and dislikes, helping you to make decisions regarding the future direction of your marketing activities. Facebook also makes it easy for your visitors to share the poll with their friends, which is another way of attracting new visitors to your Page.

(g) <u>Other News Sources</u>: If all of the above ideas **still** don't provide you with enough updates to post something interesting every day or two, then you'll need to look even further afield for relevant newsworthy snippets to add to your News Stream. But how are you supposed to monitor a huge variety of news sources just in case they might mention something that could be relevant to your business and of interest to the visitors to your Page? The answer is by setting up 'Google Alerts' on certain keywords of relevance to you and your Facebook Fans.

To set one up, go to the following page:

www.google.com/alerts

You'll need to set up an account with Google to be able to use this feature. Take the time to set one up now – you'll be using this account a lot as you work through the remaining chapters in this book.

Think of a number of keywords which could lead to finding interesting news and new articles on the Internet such as 'accountant', 'accounting', 'cpa', 'tax return', 'tax rebate', etc., plus the name of your town, city or suburb. Then set up an alert for each of these keywords. Select 'Everything' for 'Type', 'Once a day' for 'How Often' and 'Only the best results' for 'Volume'.

Now, every day, you will get an email giving you the best results for each of those search terms. Chances are that a lot of the results will either be irrelevant or not interesting for your Fans. Fortunately, as each email gives you the full headline and the paragraph containing the keyword, it should only takes a few seconds to scan through each one to see if there is anything interesting there which you can add to your News Stream.

Through these seven sources of potential information, you should be easily able to come up with at least four postings per week which will be of genuine interest for anyone who 'Likes' your Page.

Posting new content every day or two is not the only activity you need to make regularly on your Page though. Check to see if anyone has commented on anything which you have posted previously. If they have, then answer them back, even if it is just to thank them for their comments. Facebook is a vehicle for enabling you to create a dialog with your customers, so make the most of the opportunity.

Over time, you will come to learn what type of content your clients like and what is not so interesting for them by the amount of replies and re-shares you get. This only tells half of the story though. For the other half, Facebook provides you with the tools you need to learn more about the visitors coming to your Page in the form of their 'Insights' data.

INSIGHTS

On the left side of your main Page is a link to 'Insights' (also available as a link from the main 'Edit Info' page). Clicking on this will open up a page of information which gives you a large number of statistics about the number of visitors coming to your site and what they do when they get there.

Information on these pages is not updated in real time – the results can be delayed by up to 48 hours, so if you have recently started your Page and there is nothing much to see on your 'Insights' screen, don't worry – you just have to wait a little.

The first page you see when you enter the 'Insights' area is a broad over-view of what activity your Page has seen over the last week or month. The information at the top of the page gives you the following four pieces of information:

(a) <u>Total Likes:</u> The total number of people who have clicked on the 'Like' button since you launched your Page (also known as your 'Fans').

(b) <u>Friends of Fans:</u> This is the number of people one step removed from your Fans. For example, if you had 100 Fans and each of them had 100 Friends, this figure would be 10,000. It shows you how many people it is possible for your message to reach in the highly unlikely event that every single one of your Fans interacted with one or more of your postings in some way.

(c) <u>People Talking About This:</u> This is the total number of unique Fans who have interacted with your postings during the last week. 'Interacted with' means every time a Fan has clicked on your post-ing and taken some action, whether it is to 'Like' your message, comment on it, open a picture, vote on a poll, etc.

(d) <u>Weekly Total Reach:</u> This is the amount of people in total who will have seen any of your content. It covers all of your Fans who will have seen your content, plus all of their Friends who saw it in their News Streams as well – this is why the number should be higher than your total number of Fans.

Below these key numbers is a graph showing much of the same informa-tion on a weekly basis over the previous month, so you can see at a glance whether your results are improving over time or not.

Underneath the graph is a detailed report on everything that you posted recently, divided up into six columns. The date and the subject of the post-ing are self-evident. The other columns are:

(a) <u>Reach:</u> The total number of unique viewers who saw that particu-lar posting.

(b) <u>Engaged Users:</u>   The total number of unique users who have clicked on the post to read it in more detail.

(c) <u>Talking About This:</u> The total number of Fans who have 'interacted with' the posting, as defined above.

(d) <u>Virality:</u> The percentage of Fans who have interacted with your posting, versus the total amount who saw it.

These figures cover up to the first 28 days of activity on each of the postings.

For 'Reach', 'Engaged Users' and 'Talking About This', you are able to click on the overall numbers in order to 'drill down' to obtain some even more detailed information as to how the overall numbers were comprised:

(a) <u>Reach:</u> Breaks down the numbers into 'Organic' which is the regular way that anyone would see your posting, 'Paid' which is unique people coming from any paid advertising you may have been running and 'Viral', which is the additional number of Friends of Fans who saw it as a result of your Fans' interaction being featured in their own News Streams.

(b) <u>Engaged Users:</u>   Breaks down numbers according to how they interacted with your posting. 'Video plays', 'Photo views', 'Link clicks' are pretty obvious to understand. 'Stories generated' covers the main form of interacting with a posting, such as Liking, Commenting or Sharing. 'Other clicks' is any other form of interaction that a viewer had with the posting, such as clicking on the name of someone who has commented.

(c) <u>Talking About This:</u> Breaks down the most common forms of interaction into the numbers of 'Likes', 'Shares', 'Comments', 'Event RSVPs' and 'Questions Answered'.

These are all the statistics covered from the Insights overview, but you will see that there are more links under the main Insights link on the left hand side of your menu, which lead to yet more statistics. These are:

(a) <u>Fans:</u> A breakdown of the new Fans you have obtained over the period of the report broken down by age group, gender, countries, cities and languages. Beneath the top box is a graph showing you the numbers of new Fans who have Liked your Page on a daily basis plus the number who have Unliked your Page (i.e. they have unsubscribed from any more updates from you). Finally, the 'Like Sources' box tells you how those Fans who Liked your Page found it in the first place.

(b) <u>Reach:</u> More Demographics and Location information as above, but this time it covers everyone who saw any content from you during the period. The graph below breaks down the ways in which the visitors saw your content, divided into 'Organic', 'Paid' and 'Viral', as defined above. Next on the page is the 'Frequency Graph' which tells you now frequently different numbers of viewers saw any of your content during the period. After that is another graph showing the total number of Page Views on a daily basis, plus the number of Unique Visitors who visited your Page each day. Finally, the box at the bottom shows you how many people saw each of your Tabs (i.e. the different pages in your mini-site) plus the links where any of your visitors came from other than Facebook.

(c) <u>Talking About This:</u> More Demographics and Location information, this time for those people who actually interacted with your content in one way or another. The first of the two graphs at the bottom of the page breaks down the number of unique people who have interacted with your postings over the past seven days on a daily basis, while the second shows the number of 'Friends of Fans' who saw your posting each day.

As you can see, there is a vast amount of data that you can find out from Insights. However, while a lot of these statistics are interesting, only a few of them give you information that you can use to improve your performance on Facebook.

Some of the most useful information you can learn from Insights are the statistics which show which of your postings received the **most** Likes and Comments and which of them received the **least** Likes and Comments. Is there a pattern to them? Maybe postings about your local area are getting a lot of Likes and Comments whereas the postings taken from your professional sources are getting very few Likes and Comments. If this is the case, then you know how to change your strategy going forward – more local links and less professional.

Also pay close attention to the number of people who are 'Unliking' your Page, as this is something you should be trying to avoid at all costs. If you made one posting which led to a lot of Fans unliking your Page, try to work out why they might have disliked it enough to never want to hear from you again. Then make sure you never post anything similar to that in the future. Or maybe you find that one day when you got several unlikes was a day when you just had so much of interest to tell your Fans that you posted several times. If this is the case, you will have learned the hard way not to go too overboard with your number of daily postings or else people will think that you are 'spamming' them, resulting in their stopping you from doing it again on a permanent basis.

Another useful piece of information that is buried away at the bottom of the 'Reach' page are the statistics showing how many people viewed each of your 'Tabs' – the word Facebook uses for the different pages of your mini-site. This should give you some useful data as to where most people are going on your site. If you see that few of them are going to the Tabs that you most want them to go to, consider improving the copy on your pages to try and encourage users to go to the Tab or Tabs which will bring you the most benefits.

The above is a very brief overview as to the information which you are able to obtain from Facebook Insights. If you want more details on the data contained here, you can hover your mouse over any of the question marks next to headings to get more information as to what the data means.

Alternatively, it's possible to download an instruction manual which Facebook produced on their Insights statistics from the following link:

ads.ak.facebook.com/ads/creative/insights/page-insights-guide.pdf

My advice to you, however, is not to spend too long checking and fretting over your statistics. Yes, it is worth taking a look at the Insights data once a month or so to find out what your visitors do and don't like. As for the rest of the information on Insights though, if the data you see is not going help you to make changes which will benefit your Page in future, then your available time which you have to spend on your internet marketing is probably going to be better spent on other activities.

I've now come to the end of the section on Facebook Pages. Yes, there was a lot of information there, but your Facebook business Page is going to be one of the lynchpins of your online marketing activities due to the massive amount of users which Facebook has. As a result, it is well worth the time spent on it to make sure that you use it to its maximum effectiveness.

We're not quite finished with Facebook yet though as there are several other functions on the site which you can also use to promote your practice.

FACEBOOK GROUPS

As I mentioned earlier, Facebook Groups can only be set up by Profiles (i.e. human beings) not Pages (i.e. businesses/corporate entities). This means that you can invite your personal Friends to join a Group, but not the Fans of your business Page. This is another good reason as to why it's useful to have a lot of Friends of your personal Profile in addition to Fans of your business Page.

Before you rush ahead and set up a Facebook Group, think long and hard as to the reason why you would like to start one up. It's a powerful marketing tool because everyone who is a member of the Group is going to get a notification every time you post something here, unless they change their default settings. This is as opposed to your regular postings which just go on their News Streams and so can be easily ignored. As the saying goes, 'With great power comes great responsibility', so make sure that you use the power for good and not evil or else your friends could just consider you as little better than a spammer. If they do, the result will be that you could lose a lot of goodwill and, potentially, end up with a lot of people unfriending you.

So if you are going to make use of this powerful tool, make sure you come up with a good reason for the Group's existence which is definitely going to be of benefit to everyone who is a member of it. Perhaps your reason for setting up the Group could be to help your Friends reduce their tax liability for the year. After all, who isn't interested in paying less in taxes?

To start a group, go to your personal Profile page (not the one for your business Page). On the left hand side, underneath your most important pages, there will be a section for Groups that you are already a member of (if someone has already invited you to their Group). Click on the 'More' link and you will be taken to a new page listing all of the Groups you are currently a member of. Click the link at the top of the page which says 'Create Group'.

Once you click on it, you will see a simple form come up that you need to complete in order to start your Group.

The first option is to select a symbol for the Group which will be seen next to the name on all your members' Profile pages. Select one that is relevant to your Group, such as the business card or briefcase icon.

Next you need to come up with a Group Name. Come up with something which is short yet descriptive, maybe something like 'Tax Trimming Tips'.

Now you need to select the Members which you are going to invite to join the Group. Be selective here - if you have Friends who are going to have no interest at all in your Group, then don't bother inviting them as there is going to be no benefit to you and it will just annoy the person you are inviting.

If you have a lot of Friends who you want to invite, it can be difficult to remember them all. There are two tricks to get around this problem:

(a) Before you start this exercise, go through your list of Friends and write down the names of all of the ones you are going to invite.

(b) Go through the alphabet starting with 'a' and going through to 'z'. As you type each letter, the names of your Friends starting with this letter come up and you can just click on each of them in turn.

Once you have selected all of the Friends you want to invite, set the Privacy option to 'Open' – the more people who know about your Group the better. If anyone not on your Friends' list sees it and wants to join, then consider it as a nice little bonus.

After clicking on the 'Create' button, you should now have your third Facebook page, which looks similar to your personal Profile page and also your business Page.

Before you do anything else with your Group Page, click on the 'Edit Settings' button. To make sure that you know about anything that happens in your Group, select the following options:

Notify me when: A member posts or comments.

Tick the box for 'Send me group chat messages'

Save the settings and you will always be informed of any activity in your Group.

Next, look at the options on the right-hand side of your Page and select, 'Edit Group'. The first option you have here is to upload a picture for the Group. Here you can upload either your company's logo or your own personal photo (it's probably best to choose the business version of it here rather than the casual version you used as your personal Profile picture on Facebook).

After this you have the option for changing the Group's name or icon, which probably should not be necessary. After this is the 'Privacy' option allowing you to change the setting from 'Open' to either 'Closed' or 'Secret' – although this is not something that would bring any benefit to you.

Leave the box for Membership Approval as unticked so that anyone wanting to join can do so straight away without having to wait for you to approve them.

For 'Email Address' address, you have the option of setting up a special Group Email address which you can send email to that will be posted directly to your Group Wall. If you think that you could be in a situation where you can only send email and not access Facebook directly, then by all means set it up. Personally I wouldn't bother though.

Finally, use the area for 'Description' to explain to everyone what your Group is for and why they should join it.

At the top of the right-hand side menu is a link to 'See All' of the Group's Members. Here you can make any member of the Group another Admin, which could be useful if you plan on sharing responsibility for the Group with an employee or coworker. Underneath the Members part of the right-hand menu is a link to 'Add Friends to Group' where you can add more of your Friends at some point in the future to the Group if you wish.

Now you are all set up and ready to start posting. Before you start posting though, remember that none of your Friends actually **asked** to be added to this Group, so I strongly suggest that your first message to everyone contains the following information:

(a) Why you set up this Group.

(b) What benefits the Members are going to receive by being part of it.

(c) How they can leave the Group if they don't wish to be part of it (which is achieved by clicking on the 'Leave Group' link on the left-hand side of the Group's page).

Providing that you have shown everyone that they have the opportunity to leave the Group at any time, you can't be accused of being a spammer. However, if you get too carried away with your use of your new Facebook Group, there's still a good chance of your starting to annoy some of your Friends. An endless succession of Notifications can start to become irritating to a lot of users, and so many of them will definitely be using the facility to leave the Group if you don't moderate your usage of it.

To use the power of your Facebook Group most effectively, use it sparingly and make sure that you only post your most useful content here. Once a week is probably enough to keep your name in front of your Members' eyeballs. Use the Group function for just your 'Greatest Hits' when it comes to content. Don't hunt around for something – anything – to post here just for the sake of making one more posting (as you might do on occasions to keep your business Page busy). Make the members of your Group feel as if they are in your 'inner sanctum' of VIPs by giving them content in advance of your posting it to the your business Page rather than after it has already premiered there.

Make sure that you never miss a chance to interact with the members of your Group. Do everything you can to make them feel special and privileged to be a part of the Group by giving them access to useful information that they can't get elsewhere. If you do this, they will see membership of the Group as a definite benefit rather than simply, 'Allowing themselves to be spammed by you'.

OTHER FACEBOOK GROUPS

As well as setting up your own Facebook Group, there is perhaps even more benefit to be had by joining Groups which other people have previously set up. The reason for this is that there should be plenty of new people in these Groups with whom you can start interacting, and **subtly** promoting your business to.

In order to find some Groups that will be useful for you to join, go to the Search box which is at the top of each page on Facebook. Type in the name of your town or city and then select 'Groups' from the menu on the left. Chances are that the results will bring up tens, if not hundreds, of Groups which are running in your local area.

Take a while to go through all of these Groups to see which of them could be relevant to your business, or are very general in terms of topic. If a Group has just a handful of members, then ignore it – it will take up too much of your time to monitor it. In addition, ignore any Group which has been set up for niche interests. If the Group has been set up for vegetarians, or fans of heavy rock music, then even your most subtle attempts at self-promotion will go down like a lead balloon. You could very well alienate people, maybe even some people who could otherwise be interested in your services. After all, vegetarians need accountants too!

Once you have found some relevant Groups, click on the button saying, 'Ask to Join Group'. Once your membership has been approved (if this wasn't done automatically), don't rush in and start posting about how brilliant you and your business are right away. If you did, again this would be blatant spamming. Instead, take a little while to read through other people's posts to get an idea as to what topics are being discussed and a general feel for the Group. In some Groups, you will see that most of the messages posted are from other businesses promoting themselves. If this is the case, you can simply start promoting your business as well. Other Groups will be moderated, however, with blatant advertising frowned upon. In this case, you will need to prove yourself as a valuable member of the Group before you can start to promote your business in a subtle manner.

Check the Group to see what questions people are asking. If you can answer them, or have some relevant comments to make as part of the discussion, then join in with the conversation. Ideally you should be looking to get people to think that you are a useful member of the Group before you start using it to promote your services.

After a while, providing that you have not learned while monitoring the Group that any promotional messages posted here receive a negative reaction, you can start **subtly** promoting your business. This is not something that you are going to be able to do very often – once a month is probably the maximum that you will be able to post a message without irritating people in the Group. Because of this, post your best content, which will be the monthly promotion from your promotional calendar. Pitch the promotional offer so that it comes over as your giving something away for free to the Group – something with a definable benefit rather than it being just an advertisement for your company. Give them a link to your business Page on Facebook and, if you have the relevant Apps installed, get them to 'Like' your Page before they have access to the offer.

Through utilizing this method, you should be able to introduce your offer to many potential new clients.

Also, as you interact with people who are part of these Groups, consider sending Friend requests to those people who look as if they could be good potential prospects for future business, are definitely in your local area and who seem to be approachable. If these people are highly active in these Groups, it means that they are highly active on Facebook in general. As a result, they should make for useful additions to your group of personal Friends so that they will see more of your promotional activities.

As with all your marketing efforts on social media sites, you want to be in a position where, if anyone says to any of your Friends, "I need an accountant, do you know any good ones?", your name is the first one that they think of.

FACEBOOK EVENTS

All of your Facebook activities to date have been aimed at making sure all of your postings get into your Friends' or Fans' News Feeds. This is great because your messages should be seen by the most active Facebook users. However, if your Friends and Fans have a lot of Friends of their own and don't check into their accounts that often, your postings could disappear off the bottom of their News Feeds before they ever get a chance to see them.

Wouldn't it be nice if the most important of your postings remained linked from their home pages all the time? With some clever use of the Facebook Events facility, this is exactly what you will be able to achieve – a permanent advertisement for your top promotion of the month, as described in the previous chapter.

Here's how to do it:

First of all, make sure you are logged into your business Page rather than your personal Profile. However, you should be logged in under your personal name rather than having clicked on the link on the right-hand side of the page called 'Use Facebook as [your business name].

If you have not already added the 'Events' App to your mini-site, go to the 'Edit Page' or 'Edit Info' link.

Click on the link to 'Apps' and then, when you see the 'Events' App listed, first of all check under 'Edit Settings' to make sure that the Tab is Added (if it's not, then add it). Next, click on 'Go to App'. You will then be presented with a form where you can fill in all of the details of your Event.

First of all, click on the 'Add Event Photo' and upload a suitable photo or image here. Again, an image that is roughly square-shaped will be the best.

Next, fill in the 'When?' details using the pulldown menus. Make sure that you also click on 'Add end time' and fill in those details as well.

The exact duration of the 'Event' will depend upon what type of event your promotion of the month is. If it is an Event in the true sense of the word such as an Open Evening or a Seminar, then the start and end times will be the actual start and end times of the event. In this case, make sure that you create the event a couple of weeks prior to it happening to give people plenty of time to see it on their Profile page.

If, however, your promotion is not an Event in the true sense of the word but is rather a more general type of promotion, such as making a free report available, or offering a discount for the duration of the month, then you can make the Event longer. Start it off on the first day of the next month and end it on the last day. In this case, you don't need to create the Event too far ahead of its start date, as people are going to be seeing a lot of it anyway.

Next is, 'What are you planning?' Make the Event name descriptive, but not too long because, otherwise, the full description will be truncated on your Friends' Profile pages as only the first 25 characters or so will be displayed.

After that is 'Where?' Again, if it is a true 'Event', then give the address where the event is really going to take place. If the 'Event' is a long promotion, however, then put in your office address. The more opportunities people get to learn the location of your office, the better. Be sure to fill in the full address accurately by clicking on the 'Add street address' link so that it appears on the Facebook Places map and people can get directions to it.

After this, fill in the 'More info?' box with a full description of your Event (or promotion). Use this opportunity to actively sell the Event to your potential clients. Let them know exactly why it is worth their while either attending the event or taking advantage of the promotion.

Beneath this is the 'Who's invited?' section, with a button to press with 'Select Guests'. Clicking on this will bring up the names and pictures of all your **personal** Friends (not the people who are Fans of your business Page). Tick against the names of everyone who you think might be interested in the Event. Be selective here because everyone you invite will get a Notification of their invitation. If you use **all** of the Facebook marketing methods which I have described in this chapter, then some of your 'real' close friends might start to tire of your ceaseless promotional activities. So better to leave them out.

Now click on the 'Add a Personal Message' link and tell your Friends why you are inviting them. They will see the salesy message which you put in the 'More Info?' section anyway, so make the tone of this message **literally** a Personal Message to make the invitees feel a little special.

Once you are done with this, click the button to 'Save and Close'.

Leave the tick boxes for 'Show the guest list on the event page' and 'Non-admins can write on the wall' as ticked.

Give all of the details one last check over, then click on the 'Create Event' button to add the Event to your business Page and also to have it featured on all your Friends' Event pages for the entire month.

Your Event has now been created. If this was your first ever Event which you added to your business Page, you will see that the Event page has now been added to your business mini-site. This will make it easier to add new events in the future. If you would like to make your Events page more visible, then use the 'Edit' ability on the menu under your profile picture to move it higher up the list.

Next, go out of your business Page and go back to your personal Profile page. Now (or in a few minutes' time) the details of the Event will appear on your personal Events page, which is linked beneath the Ticker on the right-hand side of your Profile page.

Once you see your new Event listed, click on the link to it to make sure that it displays properly. If not, then use the 'Edit Event' button to make the necessary changes. There are also two more useful buttons on this page. Underneath the picture on the left, is a button called 'Select Guests to Invite'. This gives you another chance to send invitations to any of your personal Friends – exactly the same as you did while you were going through the setting up of the 'Event' stage. Even more useful than this is the button on the right called 'Update Fans of [your business name]'. Click on this button now to inform all of your business Page Fans about your Event too.

You've now managed to place a permanent advertisement for free on all your Friends' and Fans' Events pages where your message will be in front of them for the whole month (or as long as you decide your promotion will be running for).

FACEBOOK PLACES

I'm going to cover the whole subject of 'geo-tagging' and 'check ins' in detail in chapter 12. It's a big subject and a useful tool for all local businesses as more and more people use smartphones (such as iPhones, BlackBerrys and Android powered phones) to browse the Internet instead of being tied to a desktop computer or laptop. These smartphones all have the ability to automatically determine the owner's location and so are able to show only local and relevant results to anyone using the facility to search.

Fortunately, Facebook makes it easy to add your business to Facebook Places – so easy in fact that, if you followed all of the instructions to set up your business Page by correctly inputting your business address, then it should have been added automatically already.

It's best to check this though to make absolutely sure. One way of doing so is to click on the 'Info' link on your business Page. You should see a map with a pin showing the exact location of your office if everything went well.

The best way to check that your entry on Facebook Places is correct though is to check it using a smartphone. After all, this is the way that most people using Facebook Places are going to be viewing your business's details. If you don't own a smartphone (seriously consider getting one if you don't – they can boost your productivity dramatically), then ask a friend with one to help you.

While sat in your office, either use the Facebook App which is loaded on the phone or use the internet browser to go to the mobile version of the Facebook site at:

m.facebook.com

On the page that comes up, you will see that you have the facility to make an update which includes a link named 'Check in'. When you click on this, you will see all of the locations near to you which have been added to the Facebook Places database. These will have been added either by businesses setting up their own business Pages as you have done, or by users having 'Checked In' to the place in the past. Hopefully, as you are right at the location of your office, your business should be listed at, or near, the top of the list.

Click on your business's listing to see what information they have about it there and check that it is correct. Also click on the 'Check In' button to tell your Friends that you're there. Click on the 'Like' button as well if it is not already saying that you 'Like' it. Depending on your phone, you may see that there is lot of other functionality to the Facebook Places listing. There is the ability for visitors to add comments to their 'Check In', so ask your good friends to check in on Facebook next time they pass by and say something nice about you!

On some phones, there is also the facility whereby people can take pictures using their phone cameras and upload them straight to the location. Make your Facebook Places listing more attractive by taking some of your offices and adding them to the listing.

While checking on your listing, you might notice some mistakes there. Or perhaps someone had already checked into your business before you created your business Page, meaning that there are now two duplicate entries. This can be fixed.

To do so, it's easiest to go back to your regular computer. Type the name of your business into the 'Search box' at the top of any page of Facebook. Your business should come up now as a suggestion. If there is a duplicate entry, then both your 'real' listing and the other one should both come up. Open up each of them in turn.

In the top right hand corner, you will see a button called 'Edit'. Click on this button to bring up the different fields of the listing and edit any of them which you see is incorrect. If there is a duplicate entry, click on the link at the bottom of the listing called 'Hide duplicates'. Facebook might have flagged up the duplication as being a possibility already, in which case you can inform them that this is true and that the two entries should be merged.

If not, then there is another button next to the 'Edit' button called 'Know the owner?' Click on this button and type your own name into the box and then press 'Submit'. You should receive a message from Facebook shortly after giving you additional instructions as to how you can claim the Page for yourself (and merge it with your official one).

Your Facebook Places listing acts as another free advertisement for you which will be seen by everyone who 'Checks In' on Facebook to any location close to yours. Encourage people who visit your office to 'Check In' to your business to show that your location is a popular one and not some forgotten backwater that no one wants to visit.

FACEBOOK ADS

So far, all of the marketing activities on Facebook which I have described have been completely free (with the possible exception of spending a few dollars a month on Pagemodo or Lujure to enhance the look and potential of your business Page). Facebook would like you to spend a bit of cash with them though in the form of buying some advertising on the site.

There are some definite advantages to buying advertising on Facebook as it can grow your social network a lot faster than simply relying upon it to grow virally (through one Friend introducing another, who introduces another, etc.) However, you need to ask yourself if this is going to be the best use of your limited marketing budget. Personally I would recommend that you hold off for a while before even considering advertising on Facebook and leave it until you have had some success with advertising using Google's AdWords (which I describe in detail in chapter 13) and maybe after you have tried advertising on LinkedIn as well (which I describe in detail in chapter 5).

With Facebook advertising, you can narrow down the number of people seeing your advertisements through selecting only those people in your area who are also owners of small businesses. However, unlike Google AdWords you aren't yet able to target people who are specifically looking for your services.

The primary reason why people use Facebook is to interact with their friends, play games and generally entertain themselves. Most Facebook users do not have business on their minds while they are on the site. Although personal recommendations are 'marketing gold' and it's possible that someone can pop up every now and again to ask, "Does anyone know a good accountant in yourtown?" this is not going to happen every day.

Compare this to Google AdWords where your advertising will only ever appear in front of users who are actively searching for an accountant, or LinkedIn which is a site that is all about business and nothing else, and you will hopefully understand why I believe that advertising on Facebook is going to be much less targeted than either of these other two options. In Facebook's defense, however, at least you are still going to be paying only when someone clicks on one of your ads, even if only one person in a thousand actually does so, and you are still able to target potential clients quite precisely. As a result, it is still a much better investment than buying an ad in your local newspaper, where you would be paying a fixed price even if not one single person responded to the ad.

So if you would like to give Facebook Advertising a try, go right ahead. Facebook makes it easy for you to do so.

It's possible to leap right into creating an Ad by logging onto your business Page and clicking on one of the links on the right-hand side saying 'Advertise Page' or 'Promote with an Ad'. However, it's probably best to learn a little more about the process and your different options first by going to the section of the Facebook site which will tell you all you need to know about Ads. You can find it at:

www.facebook.com/adsmarketing/

I will only go through the basics here as I recommend that you leave Facebook until you have already tried your luck with Google AdWords and possibly LinkedIn Advertising as well. If you have already run successful campaigns on those two sites, creating an advertising campaign on Facebook will be a relatively simple exercise for you. The principles of advertising on Facebook are similar to advertising on LinkedIn and a lot easier to understand than advertising using AdWords.

As a summary though, you are given two options for promoting your business Page:

Facebook Ads

These are pretty traditional ads which run on the right-hand side of user's News Streams.

Sponsored Stories

This is a more subtle form of advertising which can have greater effect, but also needs a bit more thought in order to achieve the maximum impact. It's exactly the same as making a regular posting on your business Page, with the big exception that it will also be seen by your Fans' Friends as well, ensuring that it gets a much wider distribution than a regular posting. For this type of advertising to be really effective, you would need to offer a promotion that would be of interest to a wide cross-section of people. As a result, this is not going to be relevant to the average accounting firm who would normally be targeting a narrow group of people and so I would recommend that you avoid this option.

In their guide to advertising, Facebook suggests that the first step you take when planning your campaign is to decide what you want to achieve with your ad – in other words, you need to decide upon your Most Wanted Response, as described in the previous chapter.

As you will be shelling out quite a bit of cash for every person clicking on one of your ads, I would suggest that your Most Wanted Response should be to get them to visit your website where, if you follow my suggestions in chapter 11, the pages should already be optimized in such a way that they convert as many visitors into new clients as possible. Maybe large brands such as Red Bull and Procter & Gamble, with their massive advertising budgets, can spend serious money just on getting users to 'Like' their Facebook Pages. But your limited funds are going to have to work a lot harder than theirs.

In order to start creating your ad, the first stage is to design it. Facebook ads consist of a small picture, for which I suggest you use your square company logo, with a 25 character headline plus 135 characters of body copy. This is similar to the format for a Google AdWords ad and absolutely identical to the format of an ad on LinkedIn. As a result, by the time you come to advertise on Facebook, you should already have created some ads which have proven to be highly successful in attracting good prospects from your using them on the other networks. There's no need to reinvent the wheel for Facebook – simply repeat your most successful ads here.

Once you have created your ad, move on to the second section which is 'Targeting'. Firstly you need to choose the 'Location' that your ads will be shown in. Select your country first of all if it is not showing already and then select your catchment area either 'By City' and selecting a small radius around it if your catchment area stretches at least 10 miles, or else by choosing 'By Zip Code' and then adding all of the Zip Codes in your catchment area.

For 'Demographics', you should probably leave those as per the default settings because your prospects are likely to come from all age groups and consist of both men and women.

In the 'Interests' section, click on the link which says, 'Switch to Broad Category Targeting'. In the list of options you are now presented with, click on 'Business/Technology'. This will bring up a second menu which will include the option, 'Small Business Owners'. This is definitely the niche you want to aim for because this will be the group of people who make up your most likely prospects.

You can ignore having to make adjustments to any of the remaining categories of 'Connections on Facebook', 'Advanced Demographics' and 'Education & Work' because the default settings give you the widest selection in this area. Providing that you have selected just 'Small Business Owners' in your defined catchment area, your ads will be shown only to those users most likely to be in need of accounting services.

As you prune away at the options, you will see a box on the right come up showing the 'Estimated Reach' of your ads – the number of people to whom the advertising will be shown.

Once you are happy that you are targeting the right audience, you will be asked how much you want to spend per day on the campaign. As with the other Pay-Per-Click advertising networks, don't get carried away here. Select a maximum amount that you can afford to gamble with. Here you will also find Facebook's 'Suggested Bid' for each click. I will cover this subject in more detail in chapter 13, but the bidding process works in an almost identical way to Google AdWords, where there is an auction for the top advertising spots, with whoever is prepared to offer the highest amount per click through for the top spot having their ad shown there.

If you haven't already checked out the chapters on AdWords and LinkedIn advertising, the price of the 'Suggested Bid' could very well come as a shock to you. And remember, you are paying for every single person who clicks on the link to visit your website whether or not they decide to make contact with you. If they spend just a couple of seconds glancing at your website before clicking elsewhere, your money is gone just the same.

Once you have selected your maximum daily budget and your 'Max. Bid', review your ad and then continue on to the billing page to complete the operation. As is the case with AdWords and LinkedIn advertising, you will need to monitor the effectiveness of your advertising on Facebook carefully, by checking the results on your Facebook dashboard. If you take my advice in chapter 9 and set up Google Analytics to monitor what happens once your prospects arrive from Facebook onto your website, it will also be a lot easier for you to accurately determine the success or failure of your Facebook advertising campaign.

OTHER MARKETING POSSIBILITIES USING FACEBOOK

So far I have only mentioned using services which are actually part of Facebook itself (apart from the optional use of services to enhance your business Page such as Pagemodo and Lujure).

There are, however, some benefits to be had through using some of the 'Third Party Apps' which also make use of the Facebook platform. If you've ever played any of the social games such as Farmville or Mafia Wars, or clicked to find out your horoscope, then you've already been using some of Facebook's Third Party Apps.

Most of these Third Party Apps are for entertainment purposes only and so are of little interest to anyone interested in using Facebook as a marketing platform. But there is one that I believe is worthy of adding to your promotional activities.

MARKETPLACE

As can probably be guessed from its name, Marketplace is a classified advertising site, which is looking to compete head-to-head with such free sites as Craigslist in the US, Gumtree in the UK and local newspapers everywhere. The App actually comes from a site called **www.oodle.com**, which is the largest of Facebook's partners in the field of classifieds.

Currently, Marketplace is not as well known as any of the official Facebook promotional tools, but there is a good chance that it will grow as word spreads. At least it means that your competitors probably haven't stumbled across it yet anyway. As it is focused on each user's location, it makes for an excellent tool for promoting local businesses such as yours.

As with most of these additional functions on Facebook, only personal Profiles are able to use the Marketplace – not business Pages. So, to use it, make sure you are on your personal Profile page and use the Search box to find the Marketplace App. If you can't find a link to the Marketplace App, you can also go to **www.oodle.com** and post your ad from there. It will ask you to connect your ad to your Facebook account.

Whichever of these ways you connect to the Marketplace App, once you are inside, you will see listings of the most popular Marketplace items in your area.

To create your own listing, click on the button at the top of the page called 'Post Listing to Marketplace' and a form will come up for you to fill in.

In the first section, fill in the name of your business and also make sure that it has 'Accountant' or 'CPA' in there as well to ensure that anyone looking for an accountant immediately knows that they have found what they are looking for. The location should already be set to your area, but use the pulldown menu to define it further if the default location covers too wide an area. Keep the 'Price' box as empty.

Under 'Category', you can drill down until you get to exactly the right listing you want, which is probably going to be:

Services > Financial & Legal Services > Accounting & Bookkeeping.

The next box is marked 'Why?' You can leave this blank. Then you have a large area to post a message telling people why they should use your services and also the ability to 'Add a Photo'. Here you can upload your logo or a photo of your office building – anything is better than leaving this area blank.

Once you have pressed the 'Post' button, you will be asked to confirm that you allow the App to run (don't worry – it's not going to spam all your friends like some Apps on Facebook can do) and then you will be taken to see your listing.

If you want to make any changes to your ad, then click on the 'Edit' button. It also gives you the opportunity to 'Share' the ad, However, as this will only go to your existing Friends, there is probably not a lot of benefit in doing so as all your Friends should know all about you already. You will notice that your ad is only active for a period of 30 days, so make a note in your marketing diary to renew it once it expires.

*   *   *

So now I have completely covered all of the options available to you for marketing your business on Facebook. If it seems like a lot of work in getting all of the options set up and then keeping your marketing going, there's a reason for it – it **is** quite a time-consuming activity! However, as you will read over the following chapters, it's not going to take much more of your time to work your other social networks at the same time. So the few minutes that you spend on Facebook each day once you have everything set up are going to go a long way.

Quite a few of the activities I have shown you in this chapter are advanced and optional strategies. As long as you are using your personal Facebook Profile and your Facebook business Page effectively, you needn't worry too much about the other options.

> Email us **now** at <u>accountant@informerbooks.com</u> to get our **free weekly updates** in case there have been any changes to any of the information contained in this chapter since publication.

TWITTER

AFTER FACEBOOK, THE other major social network that everyone will have heard of is Twitter. It seems as if every time you turn on the TV or read a magazine, there's someone else twittering on about Twitter.

In terms of size, Twitter is the second biggest of the social networks, currently having around 200 million accounts registered. A lot of these are dormant though – people have set them up at some time in the past – and then not bothered with them again afterwards. So, in terms of active users, Twitter is quite far behind Facebook, but still a valuable marketing tool and one that should be an essential part of your online promotional strategy.

WHAT IS TWITTER?

Twitter is quite different from the other social networks that I cover in this book such as Facebook, LinkedIn and Google+. It is not really a place for friends to interact with one another. Officially, Twitter is called a 'micro-blogging' site; a way of creating your own blog which everyone, anyone or no one can read (depending on how successful you are in promoting it).

A simple way of imagining Twitter is to think of it as an online newsletter which you are writing yourself, one little article at a time. Anyone with a Twitter account can sign up to a subscription to your newsletter and you have the possibility to sign up to theirs as well, but it is not compulsory in the same way that, on Facebook and LinkedIn, both parties have to agree to become 'Friends' before they start exchanging information with one another.

The other big difference between Twitter and the other social networks is the maximum length of each posting, or 'Tweet' as they are known on Twitter. On Facebook, LinkedIn and Google+, you can write paragraphs in your postings if you like. On Twitter, however, you are restricted to a maximum of 140 characters, which is really only enough for one sentence at a time. It is possible to Tweet longer pieces of information through including a link in your Tweet. This requires more interaction on the part of the person reading your Tweets though, which readers are probably going to do only if the subject is of particular interest to them. As a result, Twitter is most effective for sending small bursts of information rather than sending more complicated messages.

SETTING UP YOUR TWITTER ACCOUNT

Setting up an account on Twitter is a lot simpler than setting up a business Page on Facebook.

To start the process, just go to:

www.twitter.com

Fill in your **business name** (not your personal name), email address, choose a password and click the 'Sign Up' button.

On the next screen you see, you will be asked to confirm the details, or make any changes that might be required. Here you will also be asked to choose a Username. Try to choose one that is obviously associated with your business, but also try and keep it as short as you can. Note that your Username will display using a mixture of upper and lower case letters, so use this to make your Username more legible. For example, instead of making your Username 'johnsmithcpa', you can make it 'JohnSmithCPA' – much easier to read.

The site will immediately tell you if your first choice of Username is available. If not, then it will suggest alternatives which are. Once you are happy with your Username, click on 'Create my account'. You will receive an email to the address which you gave on the 'Sign Up' page. Click on the link in the email to confirm that your email address is correct.

You now have your Twitter account set up and will be run through a few steps to get you up and running by finding some people to Follow. Let's skip through these steps for the moment until we have our account properly set up and looking professional. You can come back to it at any stage.

You should now be at a rather empty and bland looking page which gives you several different options for getting started on Twitter. Click on the links underneath 'Set up your profile' or click on the link at the top of the page called 'Profile'.

First of all, upload a photo to replace the default icon they use of an egg. If you are marketing a practice which features several partners, I would suggest that you use your logo here. If your business is just yourself, I would recommend using your business photo to make the account look more personal.

Next, fill in your location. This is important for all local businesses as it will allow potential clients to find you more easily.

If you already have a website, then fill in the address in the section marked 'Web'.

Finally, fill in the details of your Bio explaining what your business does and why people should be interested in you. If you did not include your most important keywords like 'accountant' or 'CPA' in the Name of your business, make sure to include them in this Bio section. As with all Twitter-related matters, brevity and conciseness is important in the Bio, as you can only use a maximum of 160 characters.

Before finishing off setting up your profile, click on the tab called 'Design'. Currently the background and image and the colors used on your Twitter Profile are the same as for everyone else who has signed up for Twitter and couldn't be bothered to change it. So keeping it the same could mark you as being an amateur or a half-hearted user.

You will see that Twitter offers a selection of Themes which you can use. Unfortunately, most of these are a bit too twee for business use. Another option is to change the design colors. I recommend your avoiding this option though unless you have a good eye for color as it can be quite difficult to come up with a combination of colors which are both easy on the eye and legible everywhere. Instead click on the link called 'Check out Themeleon'. Ignore the 'Themes' and 'Patterns' sections and go straight to the 'Layout' option. Look through the 'Top Palettes' options until you find a combination of colors which you like. It also helps if the colors are similar to the ones that you use in your logo to keep your branding consistent. The colors in these palettes have been carefully chosen to be complementary to one another and so you can be sure of not accidentally ending up with an eyesore.

Once your Theme has been saved, you should now have a professional looking page on Twitter. So what are you going to do with it?

ENGAGING WITH EXISTING CLIENTS

It seems to me that most personal Twitter users (i.e. those who aren't using it to promote their products or services) have an 'all or nothing' relationship with the network. A lot of people sign up for the service because they've heard the hype and wanted to see what all the fuss was about. Because Twitter isn't the same Friend-to-Friend kind of network as Facebook, they don't get the same kind of instant gratification, so find themselves in a situation where they're 'talking to themselves' and soon give up.

Others, conversely, particularly those who use their smartphones a lot, can get into Twitter in a big way, Tweeting many times per day and using Twitter as their primary social network – even more so than Facebook.

If your existing clients use Twitter a lot more than Facebook, then you're going to want to reach them on Twitter as well as, or instead of, on Facebook. So how do you find them?

Firstly, click on the link at the top of your page marked 'Who To Follow'. If you keep your contacts in any one of the listed email programs – Gmail, Yahoo!, Hotmail/Messenger, AOL or LinkedIn, it is a simple exercise to find them on Twitter so that you can start Following them here.

But what if all your contacts' email addresses are on Outlook or Outlook Express? If so, it's still possible to add them, but a little more complicated.

First of all, you need to save your contacts' email addresses as a CSV file. To do so, open up Outlook/Outlook Express and select:

File > Import and Export > Export to a file > Comma Separated Values (Windows)

Then, navigate through the folders on Outlook/Outlook Express to find your Contacts file and save it somewhere where you will find it again easily.

Next, if you are not already using one of the accounts that Twitter can automatically check, then go to **mail.yahoo.com** and set up a new email account there. Once you have set up the account, click on the Contacts tab at the top and select 'Import Contacts'. Now click on the icon marked 'Others'. Tick the box marked, 'A desktop email program' and use the 'Choose

File' button to locate the CSV file which you just created. Complete the operation and you will end up with all of your Outlook contacts copied onto Yahoo!

Why choose Yahoo! and not one of the other programs such as Gmail? This is because there is another trick you can use while you are at it. Yahoo! is the one program which also allows you to import the email addresses of all your Facebook Friends into the account as well.

Once you have all your contacts' addresses added into Yahoo!, go back to Twitter and click the 'Search contacts' button to see which of your contacts are already on Twitter. Now you can go through all of the ones who you think might be interested in Following you on Twitter by Following them on your Twitter stream.

As I mentioned above, just because you're Following someone on Twitter doesn't mean that they are automatically Following you back. They will, however, receive an email to say that you are now Following them and so hopefully they should return the favor and Follow you back.

Although you should be able to find a lot of your Friends through their email addresses, you won't have email addresses for the Fans of your business Page on Facebook. Make sure you post an announcement on your Facebook Page to say that you now have an account on Twitter and ask everyone there to Follow you if they have a Twitter account.

OBTAINING FRESH CONTENT

These days, you hear Twitter mentioned a lot while you are watching the news on TV. This is because Twitter is an excellent tool for journalists to use. By making a simple search, a journalist can track down people actually at the scene of a breaking news item on the other side of the world and can obtain firsthand, instant information as to what is really happening there. A good journalist will sift through a large quantity of Tweets to find some new angle or piece of information which he will then pass on to his viewers or readers.

In order to provide interesting and relevant content for your Facebook Fans and your Twitter Followers, think of yourself as performing the same role as a journalist by sifting through information coming from a variety of sources. Then select the information which you believe will be of interest to your Fans and Followers and add it to your streams. In such a way, your Fans and Followers will come to value your content, as they should discover interesting and relevant information from you that they might not get from any other source. Many of them are likely to pass the information on again to their Friends and Followers, giving you additional exposure and growing your Follower list virally. If you didn't Tweet anything else but heavy-handed sales messages to your stream, then your Followers will soon get tired of hearing from you and either start to ignore your Tweets or, worse still, will unfollow you. Experts disagree as to the right ratio of sales messages versus other useful information. Some people believe that one sales message in five Tweets is acceptable; other people think that as much as 1 in 15 is a better ratio to ensure that Followers really value your content.

So how do you use Twitter to discover some useful new sources of content?

As a local professional, there should be two types of news that you want to keep abreast of and which your Followers should also be interested in hearing – **Local News** and **Professional News**. Let's look at Local News first.

To find out all that's happening in your local area, go back to the 'Who To Follow' option in the top bar of Twitter. You will now see a Search box on the page (in addition to the one on the black bar right at the top of the page). Into this Search box, type the name of your town or city. You should get around twenty recommendations for top Tweeters in your local area. Which of these are likely to be Tweeting news of interest to your local community? All of the local media outlets will definitely be relevant, as will any government bodies – city hall, the local police department, etc. If there is one local sports team that the vast majority of people in your area support, Follow them as well. If you're not sure as to whether someone is going to be of use to you or not, click on their names and check out their most recent Tweets. If there is nothing there of particular interest, then don't bother with them. If there is, then add them too.

Click the Follow button for each of the accounts which should have some interesting local news that you can use. After you click on the Follow button, a couple of new suggestions will come up on the right-hand panel of the page with suggestions of people who are 'Similar to' the account which you just followed. Check these suggestions out as well and, if they are relevant too, then add them as well. Go through this exercise until you're Following everyone who you think can provide you with some interesting nuggets of local information and until Twitter has run out of any more suggestions for you.

Once the Local News channels have been taken care of, move on to the Professional News category. This needs a little more lateral thinking than the Local News category. Start off with the channels that you, personally, use to get all of your professional news. Twitter is so popular now that nearly all media makes heavy use of Twitter today. Start with your trade publications, then your industry bodies, then important sources of information such as the IRS/Inland Revenue. Next add your main national competitors. It should be **very** useful for you to keep an eye on what they are talking about. Who else is going to be Tweeting about accountancy matters? Producers of accounting software packages certainly will, for example. Once you have exhausted all the obvious ideas for accounts to follow, go back to the Search box on the 'Who To Follow' page and type in keywords associated with your profession, e.g. 'accountant', 'accountancy', 'taxes', 'bookkeeping'. Again, add all of the accounts which look as if they are going to provide useful information to you and your Followers.

As you did when you were compiling your list of Local News providers, check the 'Similar to' suggestions every time you start Following anyone from the main list to maximize the total number of suggestions.

By now you should have plenty of potential news sources to start off with. You can carry on adding others over time as you come across them.

Head on back to your Home page on Twitter to see the results of your activity. Your 'Timeline', which is the default view on your Home page, will now be full up with updates from all of the sources which you started to Follow. If you leave the page for a short while, grab a coffee and come back to it, then you'll probably see Twitter informing you that another mass of Tweets has arrived for you to look at.

At first, this can seem quite intimidating. How can you possibly keep up with such an overload of information? Once you calm down though, you'll see that the 140 character limit forces everyone to be concise, with the result that you are just seeing headlines, usually with links included for anyone who wants to find out more information. This makes your Twitter feed easily 'scannable'.

Have a look down your streams now. A lot – probably most – of the Tweets you're reading are not going to be of much interest to either you or your Followers. Unfortunately, a lot of people using Twitter mistake quantity for quality, which makes a lot of their Tweets not far off being spam. However, chances are that, among the trash there are a few pieces of treasure – useful pieces of fresh news and facts which will be of interest to pass on to your Followers, so making your own stream of value to them in the process. Pay attention to topics which are being Tweeted from more than one source. If several people are Tweeting the same news, then this could mean that it's of interest to a lot of people, so well worth considering passing on to your Followers as well.

How often should you be Tweeting (or Retweeting)? In the chapter on Facebook, I suggested only posting once every day or two so as not to irritate too many of your Fans there. As you will quickly learn after spending a bit of time on Twitter though (if you have not already learned), people on Twitter tend to be a lot more active than those on Facebook, with a lot of them posting ten times per day or more. As a result, you shouldn't feel too worried about posting too often **as long as you always have something interesting to post about.**

Passing on information with Twitter is simplicity itself. When you hold your mouse over an interesting Tweet from someone you follow, you will see that a link comes up saying 'Retweet'. Click on this and confirm that you want to share the Tweet with your own Followers and it's off in less than a second. Followers receiving the Retweet will see it coming from you, but it will also mention the original source of the Tweet. In such a way, you are rewarding those accounts you Follow by exposing them and their message to a wider audience. If you are providing useful information to your Followers, then hopefully they in turn will Retweet your content to their Followers too and you will start to get your name better know and pick up new Followers as well through this method.

Using Twitter to find and then pass on interesting news – both Local and Professional – to your Followers is fine for starting a dialogue with them. |Don't forget, however, that you didn't sign up to Twitter just to become a 'citizen journalist'. You signed up to advertise your business to new and existing customers, so don't neglect your own news over that which is happening locally or professionally. All of the content you post to Facebook should also be Tweeted via Twitter. To save you having to copy and paste postings from Facebook to Twitter, or vice versa, I will tell you how to speed up the process dramatically in chapter 7.

LOCATING NEW CLIENTS

If you've been following the process so far, you should have promoted your new Twitter account to your existing Friends and customers, and also come up with an excellent source of information to pass on to them. That's all well and good, but am I right in thinking that the main reason you bought this book was to find some **new** customers? So here's how to do it.

Firstly, let me provide an overview as to how the system works, then I will go into details.

In summary, your plan of attack should be to Follow as many potential clients as you can find on Twitter. A proportion of these (20-30% is quite normal) will be flattered that you have followed them and will Follow you back in return. When they check to see what you have Tweeted in the past and realize that you are providing a service in their local area, as opposed to just being a spammer, they should see that there is a real value in following your account. In such a way, it's possible to get hundreds of potential new clients Following you and reading your marketing messages without your spending a cent – all it takes is a bit of clicking.

As you are a local business though and everyone outside your catchment area is going to be irrelevant for you, how do you just concentrate on those who live locally?

There are several ways to locate local Twitter users. Here's how to find them:

Who To Follow Search

Repeat the operation you made when looking for local sources of news (i.e., click on the 'Who To Follow' link at the top of the page and then put your home town in the Search box). Quite a few of their suggestions will probably be ones that you are already Following. Fill in the gaps by Following all of those which you didn't bother with during your news gathering operation, providing that they are all based inside your local area. But don't stop there.

Some of the users that you might just have added could be local companies or organizations who are marketing to a national or international market. Don't bother with them as most of their Followers will be outside your catchment area. Many, if not most, of the accounts which come up though are probably only going to be of great interest to your local community though, e.g. local news outlets, government bodies, retail outlets, police departments, etc. Therefore, you can assume that most of their Followers are local people, which also make them potential clients – so start Following their Followers as well.

Just one of these accounts can deliver you several thousand potential new clients, so click away until your fingers are sore. It might seem like an awful lot of work but put that in context with how much you would have to pay to get in front of each of these targeted people. To get the same kind of exposure as you're getting with each click of the mouse here on Google or Facebook, you'd probably be paying a buck or two for each pair of eyeballs you're getting in front of on Twitter for free. So don't see it as a chore – see it as an investment.

Twitter's Advanced Search function.

Go to Twitter's Advanced Search function, which you will find at:

www.twitter.com/#!/search-advanced

You can leave all of the fields blank apart from the one headed 'Places'. The default distance from your location is set at 15 miles. If you live in a densely populated urban area, you might want to reduce this distance. If you live out in the wilds and cover a larger area, feel free to enlarge it.

After you hit the 'Search' button, you will see the latest Tweets from everyone who is posting from within your local area. How does Twitter know where people are Tweeting from? A great many people Tweet from their phones - the 140 character limit was actually set because this is the maximum amount which they could fit into a Tweet sent by SMS. Since then, the smartphone revolution has taken off in a big way and it's easier than ever for people to Tweet from their iPhones and Android phones. In addition to this, Twitter is also able to tell most users' locations from the IP address which they are posting from.

In such a way, you can use this function to reach only people who are local. OK, so they might just be in your location temporarily on a visit, but still most of them will be residents. Go through all of these people who have been Tweeting and add them as Followers. If any of the people you find there are obviously not going to make for potential customers (e.g. teenage girls who only signed up to Twitter to keep abreast of what Justin Bieber is up to) then leave them out. In general though, better to Follow someone who is irrelevant to your marketing strategy than to miss out on the chance of a potential customer by not Following.

'Industrial Espionage' Search

You must know who your local competitors are. Check to see if they already have a Twitter account set up. Don't Follow their account directly If they have so as not to alert them to the fact that you are now starting to use Twitter as a useful marketing tool, but **do** start to follow all of their Followers. It's OK, they will never figure out what you're up to – unless they bought this book too! These Followers in particular should be absolute solid gold, because several of them are likely to be your competitor's existing clients.

With your Twitter account, you have the opportunity to send a private message (again limited to 140 characters) to any other Twitter user. How aggressive are you prepared to get in your hunt for new clients? If your answer is "very", then you have the possibility to contact your competitor's Followers offering them a special deal in order to try and encourage them to move over to you. Beware though, if your competitor finds out what you've been doing, then he can use exactly the same strategy against you! So think twice before leaping in with this strategy.

As well as your direct competitors, have a think as to who else's customer list you would kill to get your hands on. How about the law firms covering the same areas as you? How about the local golf club with all of its affluent members? Or the most exclusive and expensive restaurant in town? With a little bit of lateral thinking and a little bit of effort, you should be able to introduce yourself to the vast majority of the best potential clients in your area over time. OK, so not all of them will be interested enough to start Following you. But, at the bare minimum, everyone who you start Following will get an email to their Inbox with your Bio on it telling them that you are now Following them (unless they have taken the trouble to change their Settings so they don't receive an email alert).

Twellow

Twellow.com is short for **Twitter Yellow** pages and does pretty much what it says on the can. Register on the site using your Facebook and Twitter accounts and Twellow should automatically discover your location. Once it has, one click will bring up all of the other Twitter users in your location – and there's likely to be a lot of them. You can Follow all of them right from the Twellow site rather than having to go back into Twitter each time, making it simple to start Following large numbers of local users quickly. Another advantage of using Twellow to find local people to Follow is that everyone is ranked according to their number of Followers. This means that, if you start at the top of the list, you will be starting with the most influential Twitter users first.

There are other websites that offer a similar service to Twellow, but none of them seem to have as large a database as Twellow has.

By using some or all of the methods above, you can start Following a vast amount of people in your local area in the hope that many of them follow you back. But, before you decide to spend this weekend adding 10,000 people, just slow down a little.

Unfortunately, not everyone is as discerning as you when it comes to choosing who to Follow, because there are many people who use Twitter for nothing more creative than spamming. You might have encountered some of them already when some people started to Follow you within minutes of you starting off your account. Once you receive a notification, you excitedly click on the details to see who they are, only to find out that a link on their profile points you to a porn site or a 'Get Rich Quick' scheme.

To limit the effects of these spammers, Twitter introduced a rule whereby no one can Follow more than 2,000 more people than they have Followers themselves. This means that, if you have 8,000 Followers, you can Follow 10,000 people, but if you only have one Follower, you can only Follow 2,001.

In order to ensure that you don't fall foul of this rule, I suggest that you add new people to Follow in blocks of no more than 1,000 at a time (even 1,000 clicks at a time is going to be tiring for your fingers!) Once you have added your first 1,000 people, leave it a week to see who Follows you back and who doesn't. If you have had an average level of success in attracting people to Follow you back, then you might get 250 of them as Followers. Don't feel too bad about the 750 people who ignored you – a lot of them have probably abandoned their accounts and so it wouldn't be worth having them as Followers anyway. However, you don't want all these 750 unresponsive people taking up valuable 'space' on our Twitter account, so it will be better if you stop Following them. But how do you quickly go through 1,000 people and separate those who are Following you now from those who aren't?

Fortunately there are several options that make this exercise a lot easier. Most of the sites which allow you to automate this task deliberately make the process quite a laborious one unless you pay a monthly fee to speed up the process. But there is one good, free service, which again is twellow. com.

Once you are logged back into Twellow, click on the 'Following' link to bring up a list of everyone you are currently Following, exactly as you would see directly on Twitter. At the top, you will see a yellow button named 'View Non-Mutuals'. Click on this and you will get a list of all the Twitter accounts which you are Following who are not Following you back. You can now easily go down the list and unfollow everyone on the list, with the exception of those accounts you want to stay signed up with to get your news items.

Get into the habit of using this facility on Twellow to clear out your non-followers once per week and adding another 1,000 or so each time to re-place them. You should make a note of the sources for new people to Follow which you have already used so that you don't keep going back over old ground.

It will probably take you several weeks – or even months – before you have exhausted all of the possibilities for new potential clients to Follow in the hope that they will Follow you back. By the time you have finished the exercise, however, you should have built up a Following of many hundreds, if not thousands, of Followers, making your Twitter account an incredibly valuable resource.

Following such a large number of people does present a new problem though. If you follow 1,000 people and all 1,000 people Tweet six times per day, if you assume that they are all asleep at night, it would mean that you received one new Tweet every 10 seconds. How can you possibly sift through that lot looking for some interesting news to Retweet? It would take you all day!

Fortunately, there is an easy solution for this problem too. Underneath the main 'What's happening?' box on your Home page where you post updates, there are five links, the last of which is 'Lists'. Click on this and you will see a link called 'Create a list'. Use this facility to set up three different lists:

Local News
Professional News
Key Contacts

Set the Privacy on all these lists as 'Private' so you don't give any useful tips to a potential competitor.

Once you have created these three lists (feel free to create more different categories if you think that they could be of use), go to your list of accounts which you are following. On the right hand side of every entry, you will see a button featuring an icon of a person's head and shoulders. Clicking on this will reveal a new menu, one of the options being, 'Add to list'. Clicking on this will bring up a box allowing you to add them to any of the lists which you have created. Go through all of the accounts which you are Following in turn until you have all of the useful ones added to one of your three lists. Don't bother adding anyone whose activity on Twitter you're not really interested in reading about.

Now, rather than having to wade through your entire stream every time you want to search for some news items, or want to check what your real friends or existing clients are up to, you just need to select the appropriate list from the menu. This will speed the exercise up greatly.

In chapter 7, I will be talking about social media tools such as TweetDeck and HootSuite. All of these tools have the facility to divide the people that you are following into groups, which is a useful alternative way of separating the 'wheat from the chaff'.

Maybe you have this fear though that, by not monitoring what those people you are following are Tweeting about, you might miss out on a great potential lead. What if they are Tweeting messages like, "Does anyone know a good accountant in [yourtown]?" Wouldn't it be terrible if, after all your hard work in finding these potential clients, you missed them when a new client could be there for the taking?

Fortunately, you can sleep easy because there is a service which can take care of guarding against this possibility in the form of Twilert. Twilert is a service that can send you an email which will tell you if someone in your local area is enquiring about your services.

It's easy to set this up. First of all, head off to:

www.twilert.com

Sign up for the service using either a Google or Twitter account then input the email address to which you would like the alerts to be sent to. The system should automatically work out which time zone you are in, but you can change it if it is wrong.

Move on now to Step 2, which is to create your alerts. Click on the link for 'advanced search options'. In the box marked 'Search for', put your most important keyword. In the 'Send when' box, type in 'Every day at xPM'. Select a time just before you regularly spend time on your social media activity every day.

Next, go down to the 'Location' area. In the 'Near' box, type in the name of your town or city. Use the 'Within' box to select the radius. Once you're done, click on the 'Create this Twilert' button and your alert will be set up. Repeat the exercise for all of the keywords on your list to make sure that you don't miss out on anything. Also create alerts for the full name of your company, plus the Username for your Twitter account, starting with the '@' symbol, such as @JohnSmithCPA.

You will see all of your different alerts listed in the 'Manage Your Twilerts' area of the page, which allows you to edit or delete them, or to turn them off if you need to do so at some point in the future.

With these alerts set up, you need never have to worry about missing out on any important leads and can respond to anyone who might be in need of your services.

ADDITIONAL INTERACTION ON TWITTER

So far I've talked a lot about Following and being Followed in this chapter, but I have not talked much yet about interacting with other people on Twitter – just about reading each other's Tweets.

Twitter is a lot more than a broadcast medium though – it's also a medium for conversing with other Twitter users, in exactly the same way that you would communicate with them using email or by sending them text messages.

So how can you use this facility to help you with your promotional activity?

Thank You Messages

One simple use of the facility to communicate with your Followers is to send them a thank you message once they have started to Follow you. To do so, bring up your complete list of Followers, then click on the names of them. This will bring up their full details on the right panel. Below their details, you will see a button with an icon of an envelope. Click on this and you will see a form come up which allows you to send them a message. As with most things Twitter-related, you're limited to 140 characters, but this should be enough to send them a simple thank you message along the lines of:

Thanks for following me. If you're in [yourtown] and you're ever in need of a CPA, please contact me for a free consultation.

I would suggest, however, that you only send these 'thank you' messages to Followers who you think could have good potential of being potential clients at some point in the future. I also suggest that you don't send these messages to 'power users' who are Following thousands of people already, because some people find these 'thank you' messages to be annoying. If you send them to people who aren't Following too many people yet, then they should not be too tired of receiving them.

Contacting Anyone Needing Your Services

In the section above, I suggested that you arrange daily alerts to inform you about anyone in your area talking about accountants. It might not happen often but, when it does, you've just found yourself a red-hot prospect. You should send the prospect a message as soon as possible introducing yourself before they find an accountant through some other means.

Increase Exposure by Starting Conversations

Identify which of the Twitter accounts you are Following have large numbers of Followers. It could be the local newspaper, the local chamber of commerce or it could be a local golf club, depending on what type of clients you specialize in. Watch their Tweets for something which you can comment on, or ask a question about. Most people and organizations with a Twitter account are delighted to get feedback from their Followers. As a result, there is a good chance that they will answer you providing that you've said something interesting (and they don't have so many Followers that people inundate them with comments and questions). If they reply to you, then your Twitter address will appear in their stream and will be seen by all of their Followers.   As the question to which they answered is not included in their stream, several people are likely to click on the Tweet so that they can understand the whole exchange. In doing so, they will see your profile with a link allowing them to Follow you. It's all good exposure.

Use this facility in moderation or else the important Twitter account you're constantly questioning could get tired of answering you. Instead, alternate your questions between several accounts with useful Followers and you should be getting regular exposure to a lot of useful new people.

As a Direct Means of Communication

I don't recommend that you actively do it yourself, but some people are using Twitter as a replacement for email or text messages due to its immediacy with people using Twitter from their smartphones. As a result, you might get some contacts sending you direct messages via Twitter. By default, these messages are visible to everyone as they appear on both your timeline and that of the person you are in communication with. If someone is asking you a general question and you are happy to share it with a wider audience, then simply reply to it. It strengthens your position as a useful source of information on all matters related to accounting.

Sometimes though, you will not want everyone to see your response. Twitter gives you the opportunity to make a message private by starting the message with the letter 'd' and then the person's Username.

Personally though, I think that it is a lot safer to send confidential information to people using either email or text message. Former congressman, Anthony Weiner, lost his career when he accidentally left the 'd' out of a supposedly private message, thus releasing a picture of his nether regions to his public Twitter feed. As this rather extreme example shows, accidents can happen and the results can be highly embarrassing when they do.

ADVERTISING ON TWITTER

As of summer 2011, Twitter had just started accepting paid advertising in the form of 'Sponsored Tweets'. These, however, are only sent to Twitter users who are already following your account, so the only difference between a paid-for 'Sponsored Tweet' and a free 'Regular Tweet' is that the sponsored version will appear at the top of the Followers' streams so it doesn't get buried as easily.

The 'Sponsored Tweets' are currently aimed only at the large corporate market, with an average campaign purportedly costing somewhere in the region of $120,000. On Twitter's page about advertising, the minimum level of campaign that they mention is $5,000.

Although there is a good chance that Twitter will make some more affordable advertising packages available at some time in the future, this is unlikely to happen any time soon – at least not at the price levels which will be affordable to the average local business. As a result you can forget about paying to increase your exposure on Twitter any time soon. However, with all of the options available that I have mentioned above that are available to anyone for free, is there really any reason to want to pay for the privilege?

*   *   *

So that's my guide as to how to get the most from Twitter for your business. Very few businesses are currently using Twitter to its full potential by Following many of the people in their local areas. With a little time and effort on your part, you can use this ability to expose your business to a lot of potential new clients – and it's not going to cost you a dime.

Email us **now** at **accountant@informerbooks.com** to get our **free weekly updates** in case there have been any changes to any of the information contained in this chapter since publication.

LINKEDIN

COMPARED TO FACEBOOK and Twitter, which both seem to be in the news every day, at first glance LinkedIn can appear to be a bit of a 'poor relation' in the social media stakes. Additionally, with 120 million registered accounts as of late 2011, the number of users is substantially less than are registered with Twitter and the network has only around 15% of the number of Facebook users.

However, what LinkedIn might lose in terms of quantity, it more than makes up for in quality – to an extent where LinkedIn is probably going to be the most useful site of all to business professionals such as accountants.

The reason for this is that LinkedIn is purely a business networking tool – none of those 120 million signed up for the site because it will help them keep up with their favorite celebrity's latest antics.

Ready to start accessing hundreds of well-targeted potential new customers? Let's jump straight into it:

CREATE YOUR PROFILE

You should be quite an expert at setting up your profile by now, so just follow LinkedIn's detailed instructions for setting up your account. Fortunately, LinkedIn has a category for 'Accounting' so choose that one and it will be easy for potential clients to find you.

During the second step of the operation, LinkedIn asks you if you would like to search your email contacts to find people you already know on LinkedIn. You most definitely do want to do this, so don't skip this step. Unless there is anyone on your contact list that you specifically **don't** want to connect with on LinkedIn, then add everyone you can. As you will see as you work through this chapter, successfully using LinkedIn as a promotional tool is all about casting your net as wide as possible to create the biggest network you can as fast as you can.

After having the opportunity to connect with everyone who is already on LinkedIn, you have the opportunity to invite everyone in your address book who is not yet on LinkedIn. Invite them – not all of them are going to sign up, but chances are that some of them might do and they all give you additional promotional opportunities. If you have a list of email addresses elsewhere, then add them here (or come back to this exercise later so that it doesn't slow you down now). If you have most of your email addresses on Outlook, or have a lot of Friends on Facebook, then use the trick of importing them via Yahoo! that I mentioned in the previous chapter on Twitter.

You will now be asked to choose a Plan Level. Although there are some benefits to becoming a Premium Member which I will describe later, for the moment, let's just start with a free Basic account.

Your account is now set up (although you will need to confirm your email address by clicking on the link in the email which LinkedIn sent to you to complete the operation).

Now that you have your account set up, your first task is to fill in your profile details, which you can do from selecting 'Profile > Edit Profile' from the bar at the top. You will notice that LinkedIn asks for a **lot** of information compared to either Facebook or Twitter. It is basically asking you to input your entire resume/CV as your profile. Avoid the temptation of bypassing this step now and 'coming back to it later'. If you don't complete it, you are going to be missing out on an incredibly valuable tool for increasing your visibility and using this highly targeted method of discovering a lot of excellent potential new clients. So, grab a coffee, relax and start to fill in all of the details.

Fortunately, LinkedIn will 'hold your hand' and guide you through the process of setting up your account one step at a time. First of all, it will ask you to put in all of the places which you have worked during your career and then ask for details of where and when you studied.

Once you have input all of the details of your education, it will ask you for your skills. 'Accounting' will probably be the main one you want to enter here. As you start to type though, the system comes up with some other suggestions, such as 'Financial Accounting'. Consider adding more relevant skills here that your potential clients might be searching for, such as 'Bookkeeping', 'Tax Preparation', etc. The more relevant skills you can add in this section, the more often your profile will appear when potential clients are searching for your services.

Now that the basics are set up, go down the profile filling in the rest of the details necessary to complete your profile by clicking on the '+ Add' links in each section.

Start by adding your photo. In chapter 2, I recommended that you select a professional picture as well as a personal one for using on your profiles. LinkedIn is one case when you should upload your professional photo rather than your casual one.

Carry on working your way down the page. Leave the 'Recommendations' and 'Connections' for the moment – I will be covering them in detail a little later.

Next add a summary section, which contains two parts, 'Professional Experience & Goals' plus 'Specialties'. The first section should be a summary of what makes you unique and qualified in your position. Don't write a long, rambling essay here – bullet points with a sentence or two for each summarizing your major skills and achievements work best. Again, imagine you are writing your resume/CV – what would you write in the introduction to get a recruiter interested in you? If you are struggling in this section, read some articles on how to write a good resume/CV to get some more advice as to what it will be useful to put in here and what to leave out.

After this comes 'Specialties', which are more detailed versions of the 'Skills' that you added earlier. Think of these as keywords that people might use to find you with if they were looking for specific skills that they need to hire.

Continuing down the page, we come to the 'Experience' section. This should already have details of the companies which you have worked for during your career, but clicking on the 'Edit' link provides you with the opportunity to 'flesh out' the bare bones information which is all you have at the moment. Put in the website address of your own company if you have one and fill in its location so that potential clients can find you easily. Next add a brief 'Description' covering your key responsibilities and achievements in the form of bullet points, as you just did in the 'Professional Experience & Goals' overview earlier. Complete this information for all of the companies you worked for previously as well because it all adds to your professional image.

Next is the 'Skills' section. You should have filled in three of these earlier, but this section gives you the opportunity to add up to a maximum of 50. Come up with as many of them as you can think of which are still relevant to you so that your name comes up for a large amount of searches from potential clients looking for your skills.

Following on comes the section for 'Education'. Again, fill in the empty sections with any relevant information. Add your extra-curricular activities here as well – they all make you look like a well-rounded person.

You're getting towards the bottom of the page now. Fill in the 'Additional Information' section with all of the relevant entries. You certainly want to mention your company's website here if you have one, and also your new Twitter account which you recently started. Fill in all of your interests outside work - 'Groups and Associations' you are a member of and any 'Honors and Awards' which you have received. Don't be afraid of 'blowing your own trumpet' too loudly here – it's your resume/CV and so you're not expected to be modest!

'Personal Information' is one of the most important sections here. You want to make it as easy as possible for any potential customer to get in touch with you. People on the Internet have short attention spans and so, if someone wants to call you and your number isn't here, they could well move straight on to the next choice on their list rather than take the trouble to send you an email. Always remember that, on the Internet, your competition is only a click away. Fill in the details of any Instant Messenger program which you use regularly as well.

In the section for address, I suggest that you put your **business** address. For one reason, you don't want people turning up at your home thinking that it's your office. For a second reason, you need to guard against identity theft. By the time you have completely filled in your profile, a potential fraudster will have much of the information they need to impersonate you. For this reason, don't give them the final missing pieces by telling them where you live and your exact date of birth. Fill in your birthday by all means, but never fill in your birth year – either here or anywhere else online, unless the information is completely protected. LinkedIn does give you the option of restricting the information to certain people, but it's still safer not to fill in this section at all. Marital status is probably another field that's best to leave blank, especially if you are female.

Underneath is a list of 'Contact preferences'. By default, all eight of the options are selected. You might want to edit this section by removing such options as 'Career opportunities' or 'Job inquiries' in case some potential clients think that you're doing so badly that you're ready to start working for someone else again!

You have now filled in all of the default sections, but there is also the facility on LinkedIn to 'Add sections'. Click on this to bring up a list of all of the boxes which you are able to add to your profile. Many of these will be irrelevant to your needs, but there could be a couple of useful ones.

'Certifications' should be a relevant one to add. Include details of your CPA or ACCA certification here so that everyone visiting your profile can see that you are a qualified professional.

'Courses' could also be relevant if you have taken one or more courses that are relevant to your profession. If so, add this section to your profile and complete the details. If you want to highlight any 'Honors and Awards' which you have received, add this section too. Have you written any 'Publications'? If so, add this section to your profile as well because it all helps to show that you are at the top of your field. Go through each of the boxes in turn to see if they are going to be relevant to you. If they're not, then don't bother adding them.

You're nearly done now in completing your profile. Have a look as to how it reads and how it is laid out. Is everything in the right order? Are there some elements which you would like to increase visibility of, or you think should be given less prominence? If this is the case, LinkedIn gives you the opportunity to move any of the sections around as you wish. To do this, just hover your mouse over the title of any of the sections, then drag and drop it to a more suitable position.

Once you have completed all of these sections, your profile should be looking very impressive. Maybe too impressive?

GETTING RECOMMENDATIONS

If you bought this book off Amazon, then chances are that you would not have taken too much notice of my back cover blurb. After all, I'm hardly going to be unbiased – of course I'm going to say that it's absolutely wonderful and the solution to all your problems! Chances are that instead, you paid a lot more attention to the customer reviews in order to get an unbiased opinion as to how good (or bad) the book really is.

People reading your profile will be thinking in the same way. People are used to everyone singing their own praises in their resumes/CVs and so are likely to take everything you say with a pinch of salt. This is why your profile is going to have a great deal more credibility if you can obtain some recommendations from previously satisfied clients.

By now you should have uploaded all of your contacts' email addresses to the site and started connecting with them, so you should have a fair few connections already. If you have **not** already done this, then please do this now as you can't move on until you have done so.

Now go to the section in your profile called 'Recommendations' and click on the link called 'Ask for a recommendation'. This will bring up a list of your previous positions, with a link next to each of them saying 'Ask to be endorsed'. Click on this link and you will see a template message that you can send out.

By clicking on the address book icon in Step 2 – 'Decide who you'll ask' – you can ask as many of your contacts as you like to make a recommendation just by ticking against their names. It's worth ticking against everyone who you have done business with at your company as not all of them are going to respond.

In Step 3 – 'Create your message' – LinkedIn has already written a short template message for you to send to all your contacts asking for a recommendation. I would suggest changing this message though. The template message only **asks** the recipient to make a recommendation. I am sure that you will get a lot better response to this exercise if you first offer the recipient to write a recommendation for them, and then ask them to provide you with one in return.

Something along the lines of:

Hi,

I have recently joined LinkedIn. I have always enjoyed the professional relationship that we have had together and would be happy to write a recommendation for you if you would like me to do so.

If I was to do this, would you be happy to write a recommendation for me in return?

Thanks in advance for helping me out.

If the contact replies to you saying that they would be happy to do this, then you should write a recommendation for them first. This doesn't need to be an essay – a short paragraph of three or four sentences will be enough (after all, few people like reading massive amounts of text on webpages – they prefer to quickly scan through information). But once you have written a recommendation for a contact, then you should be able to guilt them into writing one for you in return.

If you get a lot of contacts responding that they are happy to write you a recommendation, then don't spend too long trying to come up with a totally unique recommendation for each of them. Come up with a standard recommendation and just amend it slightly for each person so that it is not too impersonal.

LinkedIn suggests that everyone on the site aims to have three endorsements as part of their profile. After this number, the 'law of diminishing returns' kicks in. If anyone viewing your profile is not convinced that you are a reliable professional after reading three recommendations, then another dozen is probably not going to make much difference. So, once you have three recommendations, you can consider the exercise to be complete. Until that point, keep badgering your closest friends to help you out with this.

Once you have your recommendations in place, your profile should now be complete and looking impressive. Take the time to look over the complete version once more just to check. If you were a potential client looking for your services, would you hire yourself? If you are still not 100% sure, then go back to your profile and tweak it a little more to make sure that it shines.

Now that your profile is perfect, it's time to put it into action by starting to introduce yourself to a lot of potential new clients.

NETWORK, NETWORK, NETWORK

It's best to think of LinkedIn as one vast virtual cocktail party or business mixer. Many of your existing contacts are at the party – and so are a large percentage of all the other professionals in your local area. LinkedIn provides you with an opportunity to get your 'super virtual business card' (i.e. your LinkedIn profile) into the virtual pockets of a vast amount of people from your home and without having to drink gallons of cheap wine.

You've probably heard of the trivia game, 'Six Degrees of Kevin Bacon'. LinkedIn works in a similar way. So are you ready to play, 'Six Degrees of Thousands of Potential New Customers'?

Let's start with the 'low hanging fruit' first of all. On your LinkedIn home page, you will see a box called 'People You May Know' giving three potential new connections. Click on the 'See more' link to see 200 suggestions as to 'People Who You May Know' which are based upon your contacts' contacts as well as people in your local area.

Some of these people you may already know, so definitely click on the 'Connect' button to invite them to join your network. A lot of people you won't know, however. Some of them could make for potential customers; some of them probably won't as they will be living too far from your location or else they will be working in a position where they will not have responsibility for hiring accounting firms.

LinkedIn can punish people using the service who are too aggressive in trying to make new contacts. Upon receiving an invitation, recipients can click a radio button saying, "I don't know this person" and send the information back to LinkedIn. Most people won't do this – they will simply ignore the invitation completely if they don't want to make a connection. However, if five people click on the "I don't know this person" link and report you, then you will only be able to add new people to your network if you know their email addresses. And this would bring your network building activities using LinkedIn to an abrupt end.

So rather than trying to contact all and sundry, only invite those people who you think would benefit from your services to join your network. At the bottom of everyone's profiles, there is a box listing what reasons the person would like to be contacted for. Only send a Connection request to those people who have asked to be contacted regarding 'business deals'.

When sending an invitation request, you are asked to choose an option marked, "How do you know this person?" Although it's a bit cheeky, you will get a better response if you select, "We've done business together".

The more Connections you add to your network, the wider your network will become and so LinkedIn will suggest more and more 2nd and 3rd degree contacts. As a result, adding Connections on LinkedIn is not a one-time operation. It's something that you need to keep coming back to. I would suggest checking for new suggestions on a weekly basis in the first few months of building your network. Every time you keep coming back to this exercise, you will get another 200 suggestions which you can keep on adding. Certainly not everyone who you invite to Connect with you is going to accept the invitation, but a lot of them will and so your network will grow rapidly.

OK, not all of these people that you have added are going to be potential clients because a lot of them will be outside your local area and, the more often you repeat this exercise, the more tenuous the 'real' link back to you will have become. There is an easy way to tell how well you are doing in getting useful contacts through this method. If you click on the 'Contacts' tab at the top of the page, your LinkedIn address book will come up. On the left hand side, you will see that a number of filters are available. The one that is most useful for local businesses is the 'Location' filter. Hopefully a lot of these contacts will be in your local area. These are the ones that are of value to you and the ones which you should be focusing your marketing activities towards.

But it's still something of a 'machine gun' approach to finding new contacts – spraying bullets almost randomly in the hope that a few of them at least will hit their targets. This can be a rather dangerous strategy, as you are more likely to accidentally hit someone who complains to LinkedIn that they don't know you and that they don't want to know you. Fortunately, there is also a 'sniper rifle' option to locating contacts on LinkedIn which is a lot more effective at finding just those potential new clients in your own catchment area.

To take advantage of this powerful function, look in the top right of your screen to find the Search Box. Click on the link marked 'Advanced'. Here you will access a page allowing you to search for people using a massive amount of different filters. The only one which we are interested in though is the Location settings.

Here, firstly select 'Located in or near' next to the Location field, then choose your Country and your Zip/Postal Code. Finally, select an appropriate radius for your search using the 'Within' pulldown menu. Unless you live in the middle of nowhere, it's best to select the search radius to be as narrow as possible – you're going to be presented with more potential contacts that you can handle, so best to concentrate on those who live right on your doorstep.

Click on the 'Search' button to bring up the results. The first thing you will probably see is that LinkedIn bring back a **lot** of search results – many thousands unless you live somewhere obscure. You will then see an overview of each of the contacts in your local area.

The first contacts to be listed are your existing contacts, so you can skip through them. After this will be a list of all your '2nd degree contacts' – people with whom you have a mutual contact already. These are the people you should be adding to your network pronto as they are all good prospects because you know that they are definitely local to you. As you hover your mouse over each entry, four options will come up.

There are two ways of approaching each of these potential contacts – one is to 'Get Introduced'; the other is to 'Add to Network'. You should be able to tell from each person's description as to how hot a prospect they are. If they are an employee of a big corporation, then they are probably of only moderate interest to you. In this case, you might just as well use the simple 'Add to network' option. However, if they look like a hot prospect, such as a small business owner, then you might want to go to a little extra effort in order to make sure that they respond to your request. You can find out who is the mutual contact which you and the prospect have on their profile summary as the contact will be listed at the bottom as 'In Common'. If one of the 'shared connections' which you have is a good friend of yours, you can consider using the 'Get introduced' facility to highlight the fact that you both have a mutual contact, which could assist you in making the connection.

Once all of your '2nd degree contacts' have been listed, LinkedIn goes on to list everyone else in your local area to which you only have a '3rd degree contact' or an even less tenuous relationship. Unfortunately, LinkedIn doesn't let you connect with these people because they don't give you the contact's name and they don't provide you with a free way of getting in contact with them either. Only the person's position and company is listed. This is to stop people from getting too carried away in expanding their network too rapidly.

LinkedIn also puts another barrier in place to stop you getting too carried away in trying to add every single person in your local area to your network. LinkedIn only shows you the first 100 results in your area … unless you give them some of your hard earned cash to show you some more.

For now, I would suggest that you leave your credit card alone and spend a while growing your network using the free methods which I have covered above. The more contacts you are able to get inside your local area for free, the more '2nd degree contacts' will turn into '1st degree contacts' and the more '3rd degree contacts' will turn into '2nd degree contacts'.

After a month or so of growing your LinkedIn network as much as you can using all of the available free methods (including the LinkedIn Groups method which I will cover in the next section), **then** it will be time to consider investing in one of LinkedIn's premium services. Although I am naturally tight-fisted when it comes to spending money on marketing, used in the most penny-pinching way possible, all of LinkedIn's premium services still offer an incredibly cheap way of getting valuable new contacts.

Rather than taking the cheap option in this case, I recommend your signing up for the top of the range package, which they call the 'Executive'. At $99.95 per month currently, this might seem expensive. However, there is going to be little benefit in making this exercise more than once, so it is only going to be a **one-time investment**. I do not recommend signing up for more than one month, because you will not be seeing any more contacts in the second or subsequent months than you will see in the first.

By buying a one month's subscription to the Executive package, you get to increase the number of people whose contact details you can find in a search from 100 people to 700 people. This means that, for $99.95, you have the possibility of adding an additional 600 highly targeted local people to your network – that works out at less than 17 cents per potential contact. Compare this to the price of getting someone to click on one of your advertisements on Google, Facebook or LinkedIn's own ads, for example, and you will find that this kind of money is chicken feed in comparison.

So sign up to the Executive package, connect to every potential contact who you are not already connected with and then, at the end of the month, cancel the package and go back to the free service. Once you have 700 local connections from your searches, it's not possible to gain any more and so leave it there. Just continue with the other methods of gaining new contacts which you can continue using week in, week out – *ad infinitum*.

Want even **more** potential leads? Here's yet another trick. After you've built up quite a nice little list of contacts, scroll down them all by clicking on the 'Contacts' list and see who you have in there. Look to see who from your list would have similar types of contacts to the ones that you are look-ing for – such as the owners of small local businesses. Ignore the ones that just have a handful of contacts listed – you're looking for contacts that are using LinkedIn actively and have amassed 100 or more contacts of their own already. Go through all of their contacts and send invitations to them as well. All of this person's contacts will be '1st or 2nd degree contacts' so you will be able to send invitations to every single one of them and a great many of them are likely to be useful contacts in your local area again.

LINKEDIN GROUPS

LinkedIn Groups is similar to Facebook Groups, but it is going to be a **lot** more useful to you because the function is used more on LinkedIn than it is on Facebook. In addition, because it is more professionally orientated than Facebook, LinkedIn Groups can deliver you with a lot more targeted prospects.

To make the most of your LinkedIn Groups, you're going to want to join as many of them as you can find that are going to be relevant to your business in your location. To get started, look down the boxes on the right hand side of your Home page until you see a box called 'Groups You May Like'. Click on the 'See More' link to get a full list of recommendations.

Do you see any there which are worth joining? Chances are that there will be quite a few. Click the 'Join Group' button for each group that you find that looks like it will contain some useful contacts. Click on the 'Similar groups' link to bring up suggestions of more relevant Groups which you can become a part of. Go through all of the suggested and similar Groups until you are sure that you aren't missing out on any useful ones.

Next use either the search box on the left hand side of the 'Groups You May Like' pages, or select 'Groups' from the main search box at the top of the page and type in the name of your town. Once again, join any Groups which seem even slightly relevant and have the possibility of yielding even just a handful of well-targeted new prospects.

In order to stop spammers, many of the Groups you will join will likely be 'Closed' which means that you have to apply for membership and wait for a human being to approve your application. Providing that you have filled in your profile, you shouldn't have too much problem in getting approved though (and if you do, you probably didn't want to be a member of that Group in any case!)

Click on the 'Groups' tab at the top of the page and select 'Groups You've Joined' for a listing of all of the Groups you have applied to join (both ones which have accepted your membership and ones where your membership is still pending).

Click on the tab at the top called 'Members'. Bingo! It's Contact Klondike time!

Compared to the 'People Who You May Know' method of finding potential new leads, which offers you 200 choices, and the 'Location Search' method where you can only get access to 100 potential new leads, LinkedIn is very generous with the number of fellow Group members you are able to contact. Here you are able to contact a massive 500 of them for each Group. Multiply 500 potential new contacts by each of the relevant new Groups you were able to find and you should be talking about thousands and thousands of potential new contacts here.

Generally, anyone who has signed up to a Group should be as interested in networking as you are. As a result, it should be pretty safe to invite them to Connect with you without them reporting back to LinkedIn that 'I don't know this person'. LinkedIn actually encourages this networking among Group members by having a special option on the Invitation Request for Group Members wanting to connect with one another.

Because of this, I would recommend that, if you are able to find some relevant Groups in your area, making Connections via Groups is probably going to be your best option for rapidly expanding your network to targeted people who will be interested in Connecting with you. As a result, I would recommend you use this method before trying the others (apart from adding people you already know in real life, obviously).

OK, once again, the laws of diminishing returns will probably kick in after a while as more and more of the 500 potential new contacts on your list are ones who are already part of your network. However, you should already have literally thousands of contacts as part of your network before you run out of anyone new to invite by the time you get to that stage.

If you decide to pay the $99.95 for a month's Executive level service, then you get access to more potential new contacts via the Groups as well. Also you are able to filter out current contacts through using the 'Advanced Search' filters to look inside each Group you are a member of in turn.

Another word of caution before you go too crazy and send out invitations to 5000+ people in one marathon contact-making session. LinkedIn could have some anti-spam countermeasures in place to stop anyone from sending out too many invitations in a short amount of time, which again could lead to you only being able to make future contacts if you know their email addresses, so proceed with caution. Rather than trying to complete the entire exercise of sending invitations out to every member of every Group in one day, it's probably better to go through the members of one Group each day sending invitations. Again, be selective as to who you invite – if there is little chance that someone could prove to be a useful prospect, then don't try and Connect with them.

Hopefully, by now you have realized what an amazingly powerful tool LinkedIn is for getting 'linked in' with a vast number of local professionals who are exactly the type of prospects you are looking for in order to market your practice. OK, you are not going to sign up **every single** local prospect on LinkedIn – many people probably signed up to LinkedIn for a while and then lost interest in it. Other people will be more selective about who they allow into their network and may not accept new connections if they don't know the person in real life. But a large proportion of them will accept your invitation, and your network will continue to grow until there are hardly any useful contacts left in your local area who is on LinkedIn that you have missed out.

After a few weeks or months of growing your network on LinkedIn, you should have amassed a network of hundreds, if not thousands – the majority of whom should be hot prospects for being potential future customers. Usually it would cost thousands in advertising to build up such a comprehensive list of prospects – and you've managed to put it together for free (or a maximum of $99.95). What's more, they aren't complete strangers either – by accepting your invitation, they have actively chosen to have some kind of a business relationship with you.

The cap on the maximum number of connections which it is possible to have on LinkedIn is 30,000, so you don't have to worry about reaching the upper limit any time soon. Another good thing is that, until someone joins your network, they can't tell exactly how many contacts you already have exactly. Once you reach 500 contacts, LinkedIn will just give the number as 500+ whether you have 501 contacts or 29,999. This means that you don't have to worry about new invitees seeing what a massive amount of contacts you have already and ignoring your invitation because they are worried that you are just a spammer.

ENGAGING WITH YOUR CONTACTS

I've talked a lot now about how to use LinkedIn to create a large network of highly targeted contacts. But now that you have your network, what are you going to do with it?

The short answer is – the same as you're doing on your Facebook business Page and your Twitter account, which is to provide your contacts with interesting and relevant content about your offers, your business, your local area and your profession (probably in that order). When you go to your Home page on LinkedIn, you will see that it's not too dissimilar from your Home page on Facebook. There's a box at the top where you are invited to tell all your contacts 'What's on your mind?' and, beneath this, there is a stream featuring Updates from all your contacts – pretty standard stuff.

I covered the process of deciding what to post and what not to post in the section on Facebook Pages, so I won't repeat myself here. If you need a refresher course already, then go back and read it again.

How often should you post? For Facebook I suggested that you post once every day or two; on Twitter, several times each day. On LinkedIn I would suggest that you should post only as often as you post on Facebook, namely once every day or two. So why is this?

One of the downsides to LinkedIn is that it does not get the same level of engagement as you find with Facebook and Twitter because of its more serious and professional nature and the fact that most of the people in everyone's networks are going to be work contacts rather than 'friends' in the true sense of the word. Because of this, people on LinkedIn are a lot more subdued in their activity than on other social networks – people aren't going to be posting links to funny cat videos and risqué jokes here because it would not be appropriate. This makes the News Stream on LinkedIn pretty dull compared to the ones on Facebook and Twitter.

If you have a look down your News Stream, you probably won't find a lot of original postings on there. The vast majority of the information you see will be:

(a) Notifications that one of your contacts in now connected to someone else.

(b) A repeat of someone's Twitter stream (it is possible to connect your Twitter stream to your LinkedIn stream – this is something I will describe in more detail in chapter 7)

(c) Postings from recruitment consultants (LinkedIn is an incredibly useful tool for recruitment consultants and so they tend to be most active on the network).

As I said, it's nowhere near as interesting as your Facebook and Twitter News Streams are likely to be. And, because it's quite dull, most people don't bother to check in to LinkedIn as often as they would the other social media networks. Although it's still a good idea to post your news to your LinkedIn News Feed, chances are that a lot less people are going to see it than they will your postings on Facebook and Twitter.

Because of this, you will have much better engagement if you try and add your best prospects to your other networks where there is a lot more chance of them seeing your marketing messages. To do this, click on the 'Contacts' tab to bring up the full list of everyone you are connected with on LinkedIn. Next, use the Location filter to find all of your contacts in your local area and click on each of them to bring up a summary of their profile in the right hand panel of the screen. This will bring up each contact's email address. You should add this address to your database, whether you keep this on Outlook, Yahoo or one of the other email programs. After you have added all of the new addresses which you have acquired from LinkedIn to your email list, you should go back to Facebook and Twitter and use the automatic services to invite them to join your networks there as well. In chapter 7, I describe using a free CRM (Customer Relationship Manager) program called Nimble which can automate a lot of this process for you.

Using this method, you have the best of both worlds. LinkedIn is a great way of locating highly targeted potential new leads in your area, but not such a great way of spreading your marketing message to all these contacts. By adding them to your other social networks which they will interact with more often, however, you avoid the potential downside of only communicating with clients using LinkedIn, which is that, most of the time, the messages which you will be sending to your contacts on LinkedIn will be falling on deaf ears.

Although this lack of engagement on LinkedIn is based on my own personal experience - your mileage may vary. So it's worth keeping an eye on your News Streams to see what's going on there to see if a decent number of your contacts really are posting new updates there (and not just copying over their Twitter posts). It's also worth taking a look inside your Groups on a regular basis to see if there are any interesting discussions going on. In all likelihood though, you'll probably find most of the activity involves little more than people spamming one another, and so there are probably better ways of spending your time than wading through all of the entries here on a daily basis.

LINKEDIN TODAY

I have a suspicion that I'm not the only person who thinks that LinkedIn is a bit dull compared to the other major social networks. I'm pretty sure that LinkedIn themselves do as well.

For this reason, in early 2011 they launched a new feature called 'LinkedIn Today' which they hope becomes your own personalized daily newspaper based upon what other people in your business are sharing on LinkedIn. The idea is that a lot of people with LinkedIn accounts will log in each day just to read their most important daily news.

You can see what LinkedIn thinks you should be interested in by clicking on the 'News' menu tab. Do you see much there that you think could be of interest to your Facebook Fans, Twitter Followers or LinkedIn Connections? If you took my earlier advice and set up Google News alerts and have started following the most relevant and useful Twitter accounts for your area and industry, my guess is that it probably is not going to inform you of any important pieces of news that you won't find out faster via Twitter. As a result, you can probably ignore this element of LinkedIn.

LINKEDIN ADVERTISING

As is the case with all of the social media networks, LinkedIn offers a facility for you to pay to advertise your message to a highly targeted audience. LinkedIn knows a lot about each member of the site as a result of the wealth of data on each of them contained in their profiles - much more than people tend to give out on either their Facebook or Twitter profiles. This would enable you to advertise to people just in your local area in the same way that it is possible to target prospects on Facebook and through Google AdWords. However, as is the case with advertising on both Facebook and using Google AdWords, it's not cheap. The minimum price for anyone clicking on an ad on LinkedIn is $2 and the minimum daily spend is $10. So that's $300 per month – more than you are likely to spend for a Google AdWords campaign where you can be sure that everyone clicking on an ad is actively searching for your services at that time. Compared to this kind of expenditure (which is still only going to get 150 people to click through to your profile or website), the $99.95 for the Executive level membership which will allow you to potentially add hundreds of more connections to your network is looking like an excellent investment once more.

LinkedIn does have one major advantage over all of the other advertising methods I describe in this book though due to the fact that it allows you to target prospects by individual job types, including the owners of companies. If small business owners in your local area are where the majority of your revenue comes from, then it might be worth $2 per click in order to reach this market, which can be quite difficult to pinpoint using other alternate marketing methods.

To launch a LinkedIn advertising campaign, click on the 'Home' button and select 'Advertise on LinkedIn'. Then click on the 'Start Now' button to begin putting your campaign together.

Give your Campaign a name – this is only for your reference, so anything will do. You will then be asked to choose where the ad will lead to when someone clicks on it. I suggest that you send prospects to your own website rather than to your LinkedIn profile, because your website should be better optimized for selling your services than your LinkedIn profile. After all, your LinkedIn profile is really only a resume/CV covering your personal career to date rather a page which is set up to actively sell your practice.

Next you get to choose an image. The maximum size of the image is only 50x50 pixels, which is absolutely tiny. As per my advice regarding your Twitter image, here I would suggest putting your professional photo if you work on your own, or your company logo if you are marketing a larger practice.

Next comes the copy for the ad. Here you have 25 characters for a title and 75 characters for the main copy. This is almost identical to the space you have available for Google AdWords. I go into a lot of detail about writing perfect ads for AdWords in chapter 13 and so take a read of the advice there for creating good LinkedIn ads as well.

Personally, I would recommend leaving LinkedIn advertising until you have had some success in running Google AdWords campaigns to start with. With no minimum daily spend there, plus the ability to buy clicks for well under $2, it will be a lot cheaper to learn from your mistakes on AdWords before you raise the stakes by advertising on LinkedIn as well. Once you are confident that your AdWords advertising is a cost-effective means of promoting your business, then you can try LinkedIn advertising as well. By this time, you should also have fine-tuned your ad copy so that you can go straight with your winners on LinkedIn.

Once you have written your ad, click the button to bring up the 'Next Step'.

Here is where you get to choose the targeting for your ads. It's vital to target as narrow a group as possible here because, at a minimum of $2 per click, you can't afford any wastage at all. Start with the 'Geography' field. Click on the plus sign next to the name of each continent to drill down to first your country, then your state and finally your city. If you live somewhere fairly obscure where LinkedIn does not show an option there is, unfortunately, not a lot you can do other than selecting a wider area and specifying the exact area that you cover in your ad copy in the hope that no one clicks on it if they aren't going to be a potential prospect for you.

Once you have selected your geographic area, click on the 'Job Title' box to bring up the options here. One way of targeting is to type in a specific job title. Chances are though that this will be too narrow and your ad will appear in hardly any searches at all. As a result, it is better to click the radio button named 'Select categories of job titles'. Here you have two options, either Job Function and/or Seniority. If you target larger corporations in your business, you can select, 'Job Function > Finance'. Then you will need to also click on the Seniority box and choose only top level management who would be in a position to choose whether or not to work with practices like yours.

If you are more interested in small business owners, however, the selection process is easier. You can ignore the 'Job Function' box completely and select just 'Seniority > Owner'.

As you narrow down your selection, a box in the top right hand corner of the page will give you the Estimated Target Audience that your ads will be displayed to.

Once you are satisfied that you have the targeting for your ads, click on the 'Next Step' button to set up the financial part of the campaign. LinkedIn offers two different opportunities for paying for ads. You can either pay a fixed cost for every 1,000 impressions (the number of times that the ad is displayed) or else you can Pay-per-click, which is exactly how Google AdWords work. Pay-per-click is the recommended method, because you only pay whenever a prospect actually clicks on one of your ads and goes through to your site, so there is less wastage this way. You are then asked for a maximum price you are prepared to bid for each of the ads. As I previously mentioned, the minimum you can bid is $2. However, depending on how competitive the market is for your chosen niche, LinkedIn might recommend you bid substantially more than this. Personally I would still start off with just $2 to test the water first of all, no matter how high a price LinkedIn suggests you bid. If you find that your LinkedIn advertising is producing good results, you can always increase the budget later.

As well as the maximum bid for each click you receive from a prospect, you are also asked to give a maximum daily budget, which can be no lower than $10, but can be as high as you like. Again I would advise you to err on the side of caution here – even just $10 a day can add up to $300 over the course of a month, which would make it probably the most expensive form of advertising that I describe in this book. Note that, the daily spend you are specifying is your **maximum** spend – it could be a lot lower than this. If you have selected just a small group of people to display your ads to and have set your bid lower than the recommended amount, your ad will be displayed less and so you will probably get less than the five clicks per day at $2 each, which would be required to reach your daily budget. Until you are sure that you are getting some good prospects via this means of advertising, this is not necessarily a bad thing so that you can test the success of LinkedIn advertising for less than $300 per month.

Finally, under the last option of 'Show My Campaign', select 'Continuously'. You can switch your advertising on or off at any time and so there is little point in choosing to end your campaign on a specific day.

Click on the 'Next Step' button, which will take you to the fourth and final part of the operation, which is to complete your billing information. You will be charged $5 as a set up fee, which will be then credited to your account.

Once your account is set up, you can access your LinkedIn Advertising dashboard where you will see the results of your campaign coming in. The information on the dashboard is pretty basic compared to the multitude of options you get on a Google AdWords dashboard, but the basics are there to show you how many times your ads were shown and how many were clicked upon. Make sure that you check your dashboard regularly, particularly in the first days and weeks after your have launched your first campaign so that you can see exactly what results you are achieving and how much the campaign is costing you.

Although you know exactly how many people clicked on your ad, there is no way that you can use the dashboard to show how many visitors from LinkedIn went on to complete your Most Wanted Response. It is possible to set this up using Google Analytics, however, which I describe in detail in chapter 9. Although setting up such a monitoring system is a little complicated, it is highly recommended to do this if you are going to be spending a substantial sum of money each month advertising on LinkedIn as it is the only accurate way to see whether or not you really are getting a good return on your advertising investment here.

*   *   *

So this is my guide to getting the most out of LinkedIn. To summarize, LinkedIn has the major advantage of making it simple for users to make connections with a vast number of well-targeted local users. However it has a major disadvantage in the fact that few LinkedIn users check the site on a daily basis compared to Facebook and Twitter.

Therefore, to get the most from LinkedIn, I suggest using the network only to make initial Connections with new prospects and then invite them to join your other social networks as well, and/or your company newsletter. If you are able to do this, you will be better able to keep in contact with them and thus get the best of both worlds.

Email us **now** at **accountant@informerbooks.com** to get our **free weekly updates** in case there have been any changes to any of the information contained in this chapter since publication.

GOOGLE+ AND OTHER SOCIAL NETWORKS

GOOGLE+ IS THE new kid on the social media block, having only launched in June 2011. Google+ is Google's second attempt at creating a social media network. Their first attempt, Google Buzz, was poorly received and so it failed to take off.

If any other company attempted to launch a new social network so late in the game, with Facebook having such a huge share of the market, they would almost certainly be doomed to failure. However, with Google being such a 500-pound gorilla in the area of internet marketing and communications, with their products being used by the vast majority of internet users on a daily basis, they are the one company that has the possibility to make it work.

At the time of writing (late 2011) Google+ seems to be taking off, slowly but surely. It has been well-received by the 'early adopters' who like to play with all the shiny new tech gadgets and its user base has grown in less than six months to over 50 million. That's pretty impressive compared to how long it took the other social networks to get to this figure, but still means that Facebook has 16 times as many users as Google+ does currently.

As a result, I would say that Google+ is an optional extra to your internet marketing and social media campaign at this stage, although it's worth keeping an eye on the network in case it becomes really essential at some point in the future.

If you would like to start using it, here's a quick guide to the essentials:

CREATING A PROFILE

If you have used any Google services in the past (e.g. you have a Gmail account, or you took up my suggestion in chapter 3 about signing up for

Google Alerts to keep abreast of all the latest news, etc.) then you will already have a Google account. If you don't yet, then it's well worth signing up now as you will definitely need one later on to take advantage of the multitude of useful tools and services which Google offers to internet marketers – most of which are free.

Your Google account in the past has probably been pretty anonymous. Google Accounts gives you the opportunity, after you have logged into Google's system, to create a public profile. Your public profile on Google is another way for prospects to find you so it is well worth completing, even if you decide that it is not worth the effort of taking part in Google+. This public profile fleshes out the account information which Google already has on you and turns that information into a fully-fledged social network entry, the same as you now have on Facebook and LinkedIn. So follow the instructions that you are given to fill in all of the required fields and to add a photo, etc.

Although you now have a public profile for Google, you are not a member of Google+ yet. You can have a public profile on Google without being part of Google+, but you can't be a member of Google+ without some kind of a profile, even if you have just the basic information completed.

To sign up for Google+, look for the black bar at the top of your screen. On the left hand side, you will see a link called '+You'. Click on this, fill in any additional information that you are asked for and then click on the 'Join' button.

You should now be inside Google+. But your profile will only have your most basic information on it. So click on the link called 'Complete your profile' to fill in all the optional missing details.

At this point, it's worth saying that this profile is going to be for you, the human being, rather than your business. So use your friendly personal picture rather than your professional one. Google+ asks for a tagline – one sentence which describes yourself to everyone visiting your profile. Here I would suggest that you mention that you're an accountant and also mention your hometown, as this will make it easier for people to find you. Feel free to add any other personal information which you're proud of – your kids, your pets, your hobbies, etc. Add details of your business under 'Employment' and 'Education' as well here.

You still haven't filled in your full profile yet – there's a lot more information that can be added to make your profile 100% complete. Click on the 'Edit Profile' button to fill in the last of the gaps. Fill in all of the information that you are comfortable in giving out. If there is some information that doesn't seem relevant such as your 'Relationship' status and who you are 'Looking for', then leave it out (or else you could have some serious explaining to do to your spouse!). It is good to fill in all of the various ways in which you can be contacted at Work though so any potential client who comes across your profile can contact you immediately. You can set the level of exposure for each of these fields across the Web on an individual basis. To obtain maximum exposure, it's probably best to set most of these as 'Anyone on the web'. For your email address and other sensitive information (such as your Home number) it's probably better to set this to 'Your circles' so it's safe from the prying eyes of any spammers or potential stalkers.

It's definitely worth adding your current location on the map on the 'Places lived' section, again so that people can find you more easily when performing a search. Places where you have lived in the past are not so important.

On the right hand side of the page, you will see a link called 'Links'. Click on this one. This will bring up a little box with a couple of options. If you have your own website, then click on 'Add custom link' and input the name of your business and also the website address. Then click on the link called 'Manage connected accounts' and then the 'Connect an account' button.

This will bring up a list of all of the major social networks which you can connect to, including the most important ones of Facebook, Twitter and LinkedIn. Go through each of these in turn adding the details of your account there so that anyone who finds you on Google+ is also able to add you to their networks on the other social media sites as well.

Your Profile should finally be complete now (if it's not, you can go back and add more detail to it at any time). It might seem like a lot of hassle to go through and fill in all of the fields, but it is a worthwhile exercise. If you plan on using Google+ to its maximum potential by going out to hunt down potential new contacts, then a fully complete and 'human' looking profile will show potential contacts that you are a real person who has something serious to offer them. Most spammers can't afford to spend much time on creating profiles as they usually don't last long before they are spotted and deleted.

USING GOOGLE+

If you have been working through every chapter in this book in order, by now you should be an expert in using social media, because this will be the fourth account that you will have set up. So I won't go through every step of the operation in detail.

Initially, you will have no Friends on Google+. Once again, the way to resolve this is by using your database of email addresses to send invitations to connect. If you have a Gmail account, this process is simple. Google+ also offers easy uploading options for Yahoo!, Hotmail and Outlook if you have a lot of addresses there. You will notice that one option which is conspicuous by its absence is the ability to invite your Friends over from Facebook. Facebook and Google are bitter rivals and so Facebook is not going to make it easy for you to 'jump ship'.

There is a way around this though which I covered in detail in chapter 4 on Twitter, which involves importing your Facebook contacts into Yahoo! and then importing your Yahoo! contacts into Google+.

Once you have imported addresses into Google+, it will show you which of your contacts are on the network already and which aren't. You should definitely connect with all those who are already using Google+. They might be paying closer attention to the posts they receive on Google+ than those on their other social networks. Probably though, most of your contacts will not yet be on Google+. You have the option to send invitations to everyone else to come and sign up for Google+ themselves. It's up to you as to whether you want to do this or not. If they're happy enough on Facebook, Twitter and/or LinkedIn and you are reaching them there without a problem, then there is probably no great benefit in reaching them on Google+ as well. It will take up too much of your time to come up with separate postings to make on each of the social networks and so there is a chance of 'overkill' if your contacts are following you in four different places and they see all of your messages four times.

Once you have added all of your existing contacts into Google+, you can start to use it as a tool for finding and engaging with potential new contacts, in a similar way to how you found them on Twitter and LinkedIn. The search box at the top of the page allows you to search for people by their names or by keyword. To hunt down potential new contacts, make a search under the name of your town or suburb.

You would have thought that, with Google being masters of internet search, you'd be able to use a variety of filters to quickly locate all of the other Google+ users in your local area. Unfortunately though, you would be wrong. As you will see, the search is not clever at all, throwing back every result with yourtown in it, whether it's the profile of 'Mike Yourtown' or someone who was born there but moved away decades ago. So, to use the analogy that I used in the previous chapter on LinkedIn, it's a 'machine gun' approach to finding potential new contacts rather than a 'sniper rifle'. I can only assume that making it not so easy to track down every single potential new contact in your area is a deliberate attempt on Google's part to stop people using such a powerful tool for building up their address book in such a way.

As a result, I would suggest that you use this tool in moderation rather than connecting with hundreds of people in one go and risking incurring the Wrath of Google. It would be better to add just a few new potential contacts each day or each week in order to avoid setting off any potential alarm bells.

Once you have a few friends signed up, your home page will start to fill up with their postings. At first glance, it will look similar to your home page on Facebook, with your friends sharing information about their daily lives, pictures, links to interesting articles, videos, etc. You will also be using your Google+ account in pretty much the same way you have been using your **personal** Facebook Profile – there are no special tricks to learn unique to making posts on Google+, so just follow the same information on what and when to post on Facebook here as well.

Google+ was launched around the concept of being able to share certain pieces of information with certain groups of people, which Facebook also introduced in August 2011. Google+ achieves this through the use of 'Circles'.

Whenever you connect with anyone on Google+, you are invited to 'Add them to a Circle'. There are four Circles set up for you by default (all of which can be changed, renamed or deleted). These are 'Friends', 'Family', 'Acquaintances' and 'Following'. I'll come on to 'Following' in a moment.

By dividing up each of your contacts on Google+ into 'Friends', 'Family' or 'Acquaintances', you are able to keep your personal life and business life separate by just posting the relevant pieces of information to the relevant groups, exactly how I suggested in the chapter on Facebook by creating and using Lists there.

With Google+, you choose which Circles receive which of your postings by clicking on the 'Add circles or people to share with' link at the bottom of each message. If you want everyone to see what you are posting, then select either 'Circles' to send it to all of your contacts, 'Extended Circles' so that all your contacts plus your contacts' contacts can see it, or 'Public' so that anyone at all who might stumble upon it can see it. If, however, you want to restrict your information to certain circles (e.g. business information to your 'Acquaintances' or pictures of the kids to just your 'Family') then just select that particular Circle from the drop-down menu.

The 'Following' Circle works in a similar way to the 'Subscriber' function of Facebook and the 'Follower' function of Twitter. Your 'Followers' here are people who have added you as a contact but you have not added them back. Similarly, you can Follow people as well as you do on Twitter and you will see their postings if they set them to 'Public', but they won't receive your postings in their regular News Streams. As for your 'Followers', their posts will appear in a separate area of your site called 'Incoming', but they will not appear in your main News Feed unless you choose to add them into one (or more) of your Circles.

On the left hand side of the page is a list of all your Circles. You can add and rename as many of them as you like and have need for to compartmentalize all your contacts. Clicking on each of the Circles brings up just the postings from people inside that Circle, making it easy to filter postings from different groups.

This will make it easy to keep an eye on useful pieces of news to share with your networks. Remember how on Twitter I suggested that you set up one Group for Local News and another for Professional News? The same exercise is simplicity itself on Google+. You just need to set up one new Circle for Local News and another for Professional News and add the sources to the relevant Circle. Then you just need to click on the relevant Circle whenever you're looking for some new interesting content to post.

GOOGLE+ FOR BUSINESS

So far I have only described the process for setting up personal accounts on Google+. In November 2011, Google+ launched their pages for business, however - in exactly the same way that Facebook offers business Pages in addition to Profiles for human beings.

Setting up a Page for your business on Google+ is very simple - a lot easier than the procedure for setting one up on Facebook.

To start your business page, make sure that you are signed into your personal Google+ account and then either click on the link on the right hand side of your home page saying 'Create a Google+ page' or go to:

www.google.com/+/business/

You will first be asked to select a category, for which the 'Local Business or Place' option is the obvious choice, unless you have multiple offices.

Next you will be asked to select your location by checking that the country is correct and then inputting your phone number. Google+ asks for this so that they can check whether they already have details of your business on their Google Places database, which I describe in more detail in chapter 12.

If your business is not already listed with Google, complete the information which is requested. When asked for your business name, it's a good idea to put your main keywords here, as in 'John Smith CPA - Yourtown Accountant', as this will help your page to be found by anyone making a search. Then fill in your address and check that it is correct by previewing the map which Google will automatically generate.

For 'Category', choose 'Professional Services' and choose 'Any Google+ user' when you are asked for whom the content is appropriate for. Once all of this information has been added, click on the 'Create' button.

Your account will now be activated and so you can start to fill in all of the other details on your profile in order to make it more useful and attractive. Most of the suggestions that I made regarding the elements for your Facebook business Page apply to your Google+ business Page as well when it comes to choosing a Profile photo to use on your Page, etc. Google+ also asks for a tagline, but here you are limited to just 10 words, so you have very little space available to 'sell yourself'. If you did not use your main keywords for your business name, then you really need to add them here. If you did, then add more keywords in the Tagline, such as:

"Offering accounting and payroll services to businesses in Yourtown, TX"

Once you have chosen your Profile photo and created a Tagline, click on 'Continue'.

On the next page, you have the opportunity to tell all of the Friends you have added to your personal Google+ account about your new business Page. If you already have several Friends there, then this is worth doing.

Your business Page is now up and running but, before you do anything with it, you should click on the 'Profile' tab at the top of the page and then click on the 'About' section. Here you should click on the 'Edit Profile' button and write a more detailed description of you and your business in the 'Introduction' and add all of your 'Contact info' below it as well. You also have the opportunity to add 'Recommended links' to all of your other social networks and also to upload some more photos.

There is currently no option to get really creative with your Google+ business Page as it is possible to do with your Facebook business Page through using services such as Pagemodo and Lujure. This means that your Google+ Page can look quite bland. One of the only ways of personalizing your Google+ Page is through the use of five photos which appear at the top of your Page, so try and find five good photos (preferably square-shaped) to feature here to try and make it look a little more interesting.

Another way in which Google+ is similar to Facebook is that it is not possible for business Pages to go out and start adding people to their Circles. As is the case with Facebook, only personal Pages are allowed to do this. So the only way to actively go out looking for potential new clients is to add them as personal Friends first and then invite them to start Following your business Page as well. Once someone has started Following your business Page, you are allowed to add them to one of your Circles. As with personal Pages, you can create as many different Circles as you like to differentiate between different types of contact. By default, Circles are set up with 'Customers', 'VIPs' and 'Team members' options.

Google+ business Pages were just launched as this book was going to press. My first thoughts are that they are a little underwhelming. Although they have the basic functionality of Facebook's business Pages in that you can post news about your business, plus photos, videos, links, etc., they don't really offer anything new currently. There are also a lot of functions which Facebook offers that Google+ doesn't (yet at least). As well as there being no way of creating custom pages, it is also not possible to get a custom name for your page - each Page is identified only by a 20-digit string of numbers, which no one is ever going to remember. In addition, it is against the terms and conditions of Google+ to offer any contests or sweepstakes, which it is possible to run on Facebook. There are also no analytics yet for Google+ as Facebook offers with their Insights, although Google+ is saying that they will start to offer this facility at some point in the near future.

The net result is that Google+ for businesses looks very much like a 'work in progress' at the moment and that it will take a while before it really has the potential of becoming a serious challenger to Facebook's business Pages.

So is there really any advantage in starting a Google+ page for your practice at the moment? Actually there is.

Google's great strength is that they completely dominate the search engine market. As I will describe in more detail in chapter 11, getting your practice listed on the first page of Google's search results is going to bring you a great deal of extra business and should be one of the most important elements of your internet marketing strategy.

Although Google is always quite secretive about how exactly they compile their search engine rankings, they have already dropped a fair few hints that businesses with Google+ Pages are going to have an advantage over those without one. As a result, even if you set up a Page for your business on Google+ and do very little with it, it could still be worth the half an hour or so that it takes you to set up an account here just to give your practice a little extra boost to its visibility on Google.

So that was a brief introduction to Google+. It's definitely not yet at the stage where it's an essential part of your internet strategy and, if you're already starting to feel swamped by the amount of work it looks like it's going to take to keep on top of the three essential social networks, Facebook, Twitter and LinkedIn, then definitely don't bother with this one.

Another reason why I think it is probably a little early yet to add Google+ to your social media campaign is that Google+ is not yet integrated to any of the tools which I will describe in the following chapter. This means that it is not possible to automate the process of posting there yet. As a result, you have to post all of your updates separately to Google+, making it a more time consuming network to post to than the other ones.

Such is the power of Google due to its domination of the search engine market, together with the number of people using its services such as Gmail, etc. that it is worth keeping an eye on this social network. While it is unlikely to be toppling Facebook from its throne as king of the social networks any time soon, there could very well be a time in the not too distant future when Google+ does become an essential part of every business's online marketing activities.

OTHER SOCIAL NETWORKS

But what about some of the other social networks which you might have read about? What about MySpace? What about Friendster? Hi5? Google Buzz? Orkut, etc.?

The social network business is a fickle one. MySpace was the dominant network until it was eclipsed by Facebook in 2008, but it has been in terminal decline ever since. Many of the other social networks that you might have heard of never achieved a 'critical mass' of users in the first place (e.g. Google Buzz), or else only became popular in a few countries outside the US and UK (e.g., Orkut).

Social networks only make for useful marketing tools if there are significant amounts of other people using them and people use them on a regular basis. If you are spending time posting to a social network that no one uses any more, or never joined in the first place, you're just wasting time which can be better spent elsewhere. Social networks is an area where the 80/20 rules most definitely applies, so just concentrate on the top three or four networks which are going to provide 80% plus of the potential maximum results.

Email us **now** at **accountant@informerbooks.com** to get our **free weekly updates** in case there have been any changes to any of the information contained in this chapter since publication.

SOCIAL MEDIA AUTOMATION TOOLS

I F YOU IGNORED my advice at the start of this book about quickly reading through all of the chapters first to get an overview of the entire process before putting it into theory, you are probably finding that it's a time-consuming and frustrating exercise to keep going from Facebook to Twitter to LinkedIn (and perhaps to Google+) and back again checking what your contacts are saying and posting interesting new content to them.

If this is the case, I have some good news for you. You don't have to do it like this anymore. There is a **much** easier way to keep on top of all your social media accounts – and this is through the use of social media dashboards.

There are several different systems which do more or less the same thing, which is to create a single window into which you can plug in your accounts on all of the different social networks, allowing you to see what your contacts are posting at a glance and to post back to them.

Imagine how much quicker and easier this is going to be rather than having to go to three or four different websites each day and then copy and paste your postings from one network to another. Now you can post just once and send the same content to all of your networks at the same time – or just some of them if you want to vary your content according to the individual network.

CHOOSING THE RIGHT TOOL

Most of these applications come in two varieties – a 'desktop' version which requires you to download a program, or a 'web based' version which you can use through your regular browser. If you always work from the same computer (maybe you have a laptop that you take to work and bring home each evening) then the 'desktop' version will probably be better for you. You can run it all day in a separate window on your computer without having to wait for it to refresh every time you want to check it. If you use more than one computer (maybe you have one computer in the office and another one at home), then you would be better off with the 'web based' version.

Although there are many different systems to choose from, the most popular social media tools are:

www.hootsuite.com
www.seesmic.com
www.tweetdeck.com

You only need one of them, so which one is best?

The short answer is all of them and none of them. All of them will do the most important tasks which you want them to do and there is not a huge amount of difference between them. If you are already using one of them, then I would certainly advise you to stick with that one rather than start to working your way up the relatively steep learning curve which comes with any of them.

If you have to choose one of them though, then here are my thoughts as to the pros and cons of each one.

If you aren't terribly technically minded, I would suggest that you start with one of the web based versions first of all as they tend to have less 'bells and whistles' which you probably aren't going to use, but will make it that little bit harder to figure out the basic functionality which you will need.

HootSuite is currently only available as web based application – there is no desktop version of it (yet, anyway).

HootSuite is personally my least favorite of the three. The main reason for this is that the there is no 'at a glance' view possible in HootSuite which will allow you to see your Feeds coming in from Facebook, Twitter and LinkedIn all at the same time. You have to click each tab in turn to see each one. In such a way, to my mind, it's not that much more useful than having different windows of your browser open because you need to wait for each window to refresh every time you switch between them anyway.

Another minor gripe about it is that you are only allowed to follow five different accounts using the free model. OK, this is probably enough for most people because you will only need to follow your personal Facebook page, your business Facebook account, your Twitter account and your LinkedIn account. However, if you then add a Foursquare account (see chapter 12) a personal Twitter account and maybe, if they add it at some point in the future, a Google+ account, then you are going to need to pay for the same features that you get for free on the rival systems.

This is a shame as otherwise it is a very nice program – easy on the eye, not too difficult to figure out what does what, and it offers all the other functionality which you need.

TweetDeck's web based application is new although the desktop application has been around for a while. In fact it's so new that it's not completely available yet for every browser (although this could well have changed by the time you read this). Currently, if you want to use the TweetDeck web based application, you need to be using Google's Chrome browser (which isn't such a bad thing to do as it is lightning fast – which is why I use it personally).

Personally I think that TweetDeck is the best-looking of the web based applications and makes the best use of all the 'on screen real estate'. The interface has been deliberately left clean and simple, and so it is probably the easiest of the three to get to grips with.

TweetDeck has a couple of useful columns that the other two web based applications don't have. One is the 'Home' column which pulls all your feeds from both Twitter and Facebook into one column, so you don't have to hunt around between the columns to keep abreast of everything which is happening. Similar to this is the 'Me' column which brings together all of the alerts you get from both Facebook and Twitter. Another nice little touch is that each piece of information is color-coded according to its source – Twitter content is the default black, Facebook is dark blue, and Foursquare is a mid-blue.

TweetDeck would be my favorite of the web based application were it not for one major missing elements – LinkedIn doesn't work with TweetDeck – yet, at least. The desktop version of TweetDeck does include LinkedIn, so hopefully they are working on incorporating it into the web based version (it could even be available by the time you read this, so it's worth checking their site to see how they're getting on).

So this leaves **Seesmic** as my favorite of the three options because it offers the 'at a glance' functionality of TweetDeck, but also has the advantage of incorporating LinkedIn. It's not the prettiest of the three and it lacks both the 'all in one' 'Home' and 'Me' columns of TweetDeck and the color coding as well. It does the job though.

So these are the web based application. As I said earlier, the other option is a desktop version. Because HootSuite doesn't offer a desktop version, you just have two to choose from.

The good news regarding the desktop version of **TweetDeck** is that the major omission from the web based version, namely the option to get LinkedIn updates, is included here. The bad news is that a lot of the good stuff in the web based version is missing from the desktop version – there's no 'Home' column, no 'Me' column and no color-coding.

But there is an even bigger problem than that – you can't separate the incoming stream for your Facebook business Page from your Facebook personal Profile. You can post from the two of them separately, but not see which posting to Facebook went to your personal Profile page and which went to your business Page. For me that's another deal breaker.

So once again Seesmic is the default winner for me with **Seesmic Desktop 2**. Sadly, it too is not perfect – there is no facility here for scheduling posting in advance so, if this is something that you are going to need to do sometimes, you are going to have to go to the web based version just to do this.

Seesmic Desktop 2 should have everything else you're going to need though – a 'Home' column that includes absolutely everything that anyone posts to any of your News Feeds (although no 'Me' column), separate Facebook business Page columns – and a whole lot more besides through a whole host of 'plugins' which can add yet more columns of content to your Desktop. Some of these, such as Yahoo!, Google Reader and Gowalla, you might have heard of, but a lot of them are pretty obscure. This huge array of options is both a blessing and a curse for Seesmic Desktop 2. It's great to have such flexibility, but it will probably take you quite a while to figure out what everything does and how to set the system up just the way you want it.

So have you decided which one you want to use? OK, let's get it set up and learn how to use it.

USING YOUR DASHBOARD

Better grab a coffee – this might take a while!

Although the details of each of the three dashboards are different, the principles are quite similar. Usually you will need to register an account first. The advantage of doing so is that, once you have set everything up once, you'll be able to use the same settings everywhere that you log into the service.

Once the program is open, you then need to add your different accounts. To do this, you will need to log into Facebook, Twitter and LinkedIn separately. Once you have logged into each of them once though, you shouldn't have to do it again.

Once you have added them, each of your accounts will appear as a different option on the left hand of the screen. Now click on each of them in turn to add each stream as a panel to your main display. It won't take long before you have too many panels to fit on your screen and so you will have to scroll the page horizontally to see everything. Rather than opening every single sub-menu as a panel which will be displayed all of the time, be a little selective – you probably won't get so many private messages via Twitter that it's worth keeping a panel open just for them. It will be easier just to click on them when you see you have something new.

Once you have opened all of the panels that you want visible at all times, position them how you would like them. You'll probably want the most active panels such as your Twitter account next to the menu on the left of the page, and the less active ones such as LinkedIn on the right. By clicking and holding the top of each column, you can then 'drag and drop' each panel exactly where you want it to go (you might have to go to the settings menu for each column before you can do this, depending on which of the programs you're using).

That's the basics set up already. Now, instead of having to keep opening up Facebook, Twitter and LinkedIn several times each day to keep abreast of what's happening in your personal world of social media, you can keep your dashboard running in the background all day and take a look at it whenever you have a spare moment.

But an even bigger advantage of using a social media dashboard is the fact that you can easily post to as many or as few of your networks as you like at the same time. At the top of the screen, you will see the area for making a posting. Either below or to the side of it, you will see buttons for each of your networks. Click on all of the buttons of the networks to which you would like to post to. For Facebook, you will need to click on the little symbol at the side of the Facebook button to bring up a menu where you can choose exactly where you want your posting to go to or not. You can post to your personal Profile, your business Page and, on TweetDeck, you also have the option of posting to a Group if you are a member of one.

At the time of writing this book, Facebook had only recently introduced the facility to add personal Friends into different lists and the social media dashboards had yet to catch up with this functionality. As a result, currently any postings you make on Facebook will be made publically. Hopefully the developers of the dashboards are adding functionality into them so that in future it will be possible to make postings just to 'close friends', 'family', etc. However, for the moment, if you don't want to make a posting here to everyone, you will need to open up Facebook and post from there instead.

Once you have selected which networks you want to post on, just start typing. Remember that Twitter only has a limit of 140 characters – a lot shorter than either Facebook or LinkedIn. Depending on your settings, you will be unable to post more than 140 characters if you have the Twitter button selected, or else your posting will be split into two or more parts when it is posted to Twitter. Avoid the temptation of doing this just to save you time. With Twitter displaying Tweets in reverse chronological order, your Followers will read the second half before the first and it will look terrible. In this case, it would be a lot better to spend a couple of minutes longer on the exercise and post your full version just to Facebook and LinkedIn where you are not so restricted on the number of characters and then go back and try and cut it down as much as possible to fit it on Twitter. People are much more used to seeing short messages on Twitter but, it can look a bit lazy and out of context on either Facebook or LinkedIn.

If you are incorporating a link into your message, then there's a good chance that it will take up nearly all of your 140 characters with just the URL (website address) alone. All of the dashboards have the facility to shorten links for you so they just come out as something like bit.ly/sEr-WGw instead of a long original address. Make sure that you use this function by clicking on the 'link' option rather than just copying and pasting it in the main box for the posting.

That was easy compared to having to go to three different sites to make a simple posting. However, be warned that it is **so** easy that it is very possible to make mistakes. Recently there has been a spate of people working for sober and serious organizations accidentally posting some very unsober and not at all serious messages to all their business contacts when they thought that they were just sending them to their closest friends. Once a message has been sent, it will appear in all of your Followers' streams even if you find it and delete it later and it can lead to a lot of embarrassment.

There are two solutions to this potential problem - the first is that you (or whoever is taking care of your internet marketing on your behalf) only ever uses your social media networks professionally so there is never a risk of you accidentally posting something that you don't mind the whole world seeing. The second option for those people who do want a personal stream where they can 'let their hair down' and say whatever they want is to keep that profile totally separate from the professional streams on the dashboard so that they have to completely leave the program every time they want to say something a little risky.

As I mentioned while listing the advantages and disadvantages of the three different systems, many of these dashboards have the facility to schedule postings in the future. This can be an incredibly useful feature for anyone who wants to keep in regular contact with all of their Friends and Followers, but only has time for their social media activities once per day (or perhaps even less).

Let's say that the only time you have to check your social media accounts is after you finish work at 6.00pm but you want your Twitter Feed to be active throughout most of the working day. The solution to this problem is to spend a while deciding what you would like to post the following day. Take a look at your News Feeds to see what interesting news you have that you would like to share with your audience as well as any important announcements that you would like to make. The most important of these, you will probably make immediately (as 6.00pm is a pretty good time to make a posting anyway because a lot of people will have finished posting for the day). The remainder you can spread throughout the following day. One suggestion for a good posting schedule is as follows:

9.00am – People will be logging onto their work computers at the start of the working day. Not many people will have started posting yet and so your information will be one of the first postings they read.

12.00 noon – Lunchtimes should be a good time to reach a lot of people as they check through their social media accounts while having a sandwich at their desk.

3.00pm – People are starting to wind down for the day and so more people will have chance to check their accounts to see what has come in earlier.

As I mentioned earlier, you should always have some sort of offer running every month to get people to contact you. As this is the most important piece of information that you want your prospects to see, you can't run the risk that it will get lost in people's streams and so you want to repeat it. Once a week is probably ideal, giving you four opportunities for people to see it each month. Once a week is not so often that it will drive those people who check all their streams regularly so crazy that they unfriend you as they become tired of your 'spamming'. For maximum impact, don't post the offer at the same time on the same day of the week always. Instead, post it on a different day of the week and at different times of the day (as above) to make sure that you have the best possible chance of even the most causal social media user seeing the message at least once. Again the scheduling option is ideal for this so you can promote the offer for the entire month and then you don't have to worry about forgetting it.

So these are the basic functions and advantages of using social media dashboards, but there is a lot, lot more that you can do with them. The frontrunners in dashboard developers (the three that I mentioned earlier) have been striving to offer as much functionality from the dashboard as it's possible to get on each individual site. In some cases, they offer even more than the social networks' own sites themselves. With a lot less 'on screen real estate' at their disposal, a problem which they tried to solve by making each panel as narrow as possible, they have needed to find shortcuts wherever they can. The result is that it might not be apparent at first glance as to what you can do with each of the dashboards.

One way to learn how to use all of the features of your dashboard is to go through the 'Help' section of the developer's website. In some cases, they have video tutorials on the site. If not, then head on over to **www.youtube.com** and make a search under the name of your dashboard, Chances are that someone will have produced a 'How To' guide that will help you out.

Another alternative is to go through all of the menus clicking on every link in turn to see what options are under each of the main menus. It's also worth clicking on, or hovering your mouse over, new postings which come in, as this can often reveal new options for interacting with that posting (e.g. on Twitter you have the option of Retweeting a posting, replying to the sender, etc.). It might take a little trial and error but, after fiddling around with the dashboard for a while, you're sure to pick up all its tricks in no time at all, meaning that you rarely have to go back to the individual social network sites.

One of the options you probably want to hunt down quickly is to turn off the pop-up messages you get every time you receive a new posting, which comes as a default on many of the desktop dashboards. As you grow your list of Friends and Followers, you will probably be getting several updates a minute, which will soon start driving you crazy and will distract you from the rest of your work.

NEWSGATHERING AND LISTS

In chapter 4, I described how useful Twitter can be for finding useful news, both local and professional, which you can pass on to your Friends, Fans and Followers in order to provide a useful service to them and give them another reason to pay close attention to you.

In the same chapter, I also suggested making Twitter Lists – one for local news and another for professional news – so that you don't have to wade through a long list of irrelevant content coming in from all of the people that you are Following just to find a handful of useful items which are worth posting or Retweeting.

Dashboards make following lists even easier. On twitter.com, you have to open each list individually. On most of the dashboards, however, you can display all of your lists side-by-side, making it even easier and quicker to find the most interesting 'news nuggets' at a glance.

My favorite of the programs, Seesmic Desktop 2, has another function which is a great help in finding current news from sources which either don't have a Twitter account, or are a bit lazy in keeping it updated in the form of a plugin for Google Reader.

Google Reader is the leading 'RSS Feed' Reader. RSS (standing for Really Simple Syndication) is a format for creating feeds of fresh web content in a standard format. Over the past decade, it has grown in importance until it has now reached a point where virtually every news resource on the Web, plus all of the main blogging platforms including WordPress and Blogger, automatically make their content available in the form of an RSS Feed. If you check the pages of your favorite online news channels, you will probably find a link marked 'RSS' or featuring the RSS icon, which consists of an orange square with a couple of curved white lines on it. Most often this link is found on the top right of a webpage, but sometimes it can be found elsewhere.

If you would like to obtain news through RSS feeds, first go to the Google Reader page, which you can find at:

www.google.com/reader

If you have an account for Google already, either for Gmail or Google+, then you just need to log in. If not, then it's time to open an account with Google now as you will need one later.

There are several ways to now start filling Google Reader full of useful news feeds. One way is to go to all of the sites that you can think of which are going to offer news items which should be of interest to your Friends, Followers and Fans. Then, look for the orange RSS icon or the link to 'RSS' and click on it. It should then ask you whether you want to subscribe to the feed using Google Reader. You do.

If the link doesn't ask you whether you want to subscribe using Google Reader, you can add the RSS Feed from inside Google Reader itself. Click on the large red 'Subscribe' button and then you just need to copy and paste the URL of the Feed into the box and it will be added.

You can also use this same box to find more useful feeds. Type in the name of your town to come up with suggestions for local news and then type in terms like 'accounting' or 'cpa' to find sources of professional news. Once you have added a fair few sources, you can click on the 'View all recommendations' link to come up with even more ideas for useful news sources to monitor.

When you look at the Google Reader home page now, it should be full of interesting news. It's probably going to be more useful for you to divide out the local news and the professional news, which you can do by creating separate folders for each in the 'Subscriptions' part of the left hand panel and then dragging and dropping each link into its respective folder.

Now you can go back to Seesmic Desktop 2. Click on the little 'gear' item to bring up the 'Options' list and add your Google Reader account to your dashboard. Now you can position it alongside your Facebook, Twitter and LinkedIn feeds so that you can, once again, find plenty of useful news items to share with your Followers. Items from your Google Reader feed will also appear in your 'all in one' Home panel as well.

In such a way, you should have no problem now in finding plenty of useful content on the Web to share with your Followers. Now your only problem is going to be trying to choose just the best of the best to share with everyone. Avoid the temptation of sharing absolutely everything you find with everyone. If you subject them to a barrage of Facebook and LinkedIn postings and Tweets, it doesn't matter how interesting the links are, your audience will quickly tire of them and unfriend or unfollow you.

Your goal should be to become one of the best sources of information around for both your local community news plus professional advice so that people start to pay attention to your streams. In such a way, when you drop in the occasional post or Tweet which sells your business to them, they are actively reading your content compared to other businesses which provide no benefit to them other than constantly trying to sell to them, which people will start filtering out.

NIMBLE SOCIAL CRM

Hopefully I have by now managed to explain why the dashboards are useful and timesaving tools which will make your life easier and avoid your having to monitor three or four different websites at the same time. Although some of the options come with the ability to merge all of your different feeds together so that you can see everything in one place, these dashboards still don't offer a great deal more functionality than you get from working Facebook, Twitter and LinkedIn separately though.

Let's remind ourselves as to what the big picture of a social media campaign is at this point – it's to turn strangers into friends, friends into prospects and then prospects into clients. You should never forget that, ultimately, your marketing is not about posts or streams – it's about **people** and all your marketing activities depend upon your communication with them.

Nimble CRM (**www.nimble.com**) takes a lot of the functionality of the web based social media dashboards I described above and takes them one step further, by focusing on the people that you interact with on your social networks rather than on the social networks themselves. As well as the ability to combine all your feeds from each network into one stream, and to post one message to all of the networks at the same time, Nimble has a unique feature. This is to take all of your Friends, Fans and Followers on all three of your networks, plus your contacts stored on Gmail or Outlook (if you upload them to the system in the form of CSV files) in order to form an incredibly detailed address book containing all of the information which they have made public on any of their profiles.

If you take the time to keep your Nimble contact lists updated, it can become an incredibly powerful resource for keeping tabs on your current and (hopefully) future clients. Through using the system, you can find other social networks that the prospect is a member of. Perhaps you only have them as a LinkedIn contact at the moment but guess that they will see more of your marketing activities if you could add them to Facebook and/ or Twitter. In addition, Nimble also allows you to see their recent activity on the social networks, plus any recent correspondence which you have had with them all in one place.

In such a way, when you want to make direct contact with a prospect to talk business, you have all of their contact information in one place and can also learn quite a lot about them. This is going to make it that much easier to start a relationship with them. It's a fact of life that people like dealing with people like themselves. Joe Girard is, according to the Guinness Book of Records, the world's greatest salesman of all time. One of his tactics for quickly showing empathy with his customers was by keeping a collection of photos in his pocket book, such as him with his children, him with his dog, his classic car, fishing, golfing, etc. During the course of his conversation with clients, he would find out about their interests and pull out the appropriate photo, showing to the client that he was 'just like them', sharing the same interests.

By checking a prospect's social media stream, you should be able to find out a large amount of information on them. Is he crazy about a particular sports team? Is she a cat person? Is he a keen fisherman? Has she recently had a second child? You can learn all of this information by checking their recent activity on the different social networks.

Use this information in a subtle manner - you don't want the prospect to think that you've been stalking them after all! But by taking an interest in their lives and learning what is important to them, it will allow you to connect with your prospects a lot quicker than someone who knows nothing about them at all.

Nimble also has a useful 'Export' function which allows you to save all your contacts' details as a CSV file which you can then move over to other database programs such as Outlook or a mailing list database (which I will talk more about in chapter 10). Combining all of these functions together makes for an incredibly powerful tool by following this system:

(a) Import all of your contacts from your existing mailing lists and social media accounts.

(b) Tidy up the database by merging duplicate entries.

(c) Find other social networks your contacts are on and add them there.

(d) Export your cleaned up and expanded database into your mailing list program.

This is the core of Nimble's functionality, but there is a lot more that you can do with the system, such as planning communications in advance using the built in Google Calendar function. It's worth going through their tutorials to see everything that you can do with this useful tool.

At the time of writing, Nimble is still pretty new. One advantage of its being new is that it is currently a free service. Hopefully it will stay that way for small users and it will only be larger companies which need more functionality that will have to pay for it. The downside to still being new is that it doesn't offer the same amount of functionality as the more established dashboards. One major missing element is that there is no support at all on the system for Facebook business Pages at the moment. It's not possible to post from Nimble to your business Page and nor is it possible to import details of Fans into it. Nimble also lacks the possibility of scheduling postings in advance. It also doesn't automatically 'push' new incoming messages to your streams – you need to hit the 'Refresh' button every time you want to update it.

As a result, I recommend that you currently use Nimble alongside your regular social media dashboard so that you get the best of both worlds. Use your favorite dashboard such as Seesmic or TweetDeck for monitoring your streams and posting to them, while using Nimble for the all important task of managing your contact lists.

MOBILE DASHBOARDS

As I have already mentioned, the rapid rise in the number of people using smartphones is changing the way that people are using the Web. Owning a smartphone gives you most of the functionality of a desktop computer right in your pocket or purse so that it's always to hand.

This portability and convenience provides an excellent way of using otherwise wasted time. Maybe you commute by train, or find yourself waiting in lines, eating alone in a restaurant, waiting for the commercials to end on TV, etc. Now you can use all this previously wasted time to keep in touch with what's happening on your social streams and making quick postings as soon as the thoughts enter your head.

As well as the web based and the desktop versions, all three of the main companies offering social media dashboards, HootSuite, TweetDeck and Seesmic, also produce mobile versions which run on an iPhone, Android or Blackberry. You can download any of them for free at your regular App Store.

Once again, there is little to choose between the three different applications – they all have pretty much the same functionality. Personally I think Seesmic once again trumps the other two as a result of having additional features, but TweetDeck's interface looks absolutely beautiful. Feel free to check them all out and see which one you like best. Just because you are using Seesmic on your main computer doesn't mean that you have to use it on your smartphone as well, because you will need to add all your feeds in again and get up to speed with a completely different interface anyway.

Frustratingly (there always seems to be one frustrating omission from the different applications) none of these smartphone applications currently supports LinkedIn (although this could well change by the time you read this). LinkedIn does have its own smartphone application which you can use, but it still means that you are not able to monitor, and post to, all three of the social media networks at the same time.

All of these three mobile applications allow you to follow your Facebook and Twitter streams and repost or Retweet those links that you find interesting. As easy as the developers have tried to make this though, I still find it a little fiddly to post much from a smartphone (maybe it's just my jumbo sized fingers which are the problem though!) As a result, I prefer to use my smartphone to just look for interesting content and then 'favorite' or 'bookmark' anything that looks interesting to read and repost once I am back at my main computer.

One handy little application which I use every day for such a purpose is called My6Sense, which you can download for free at the iPhone App Store or Android Market (unfortunately there's not a BlackBerry version out yet). In many ways, it works the same way as any of the other mobile dashboards in that you can read your Facebook and Twitter streams, make postings to both of them at the same time, reply and Retweet, etc. But there are another couple of useful features which makes My6Sense unique. One of these is the fact that you can link your Google Reader account to the My6Sense application and so you can read all of your RSS Feeds here as well. But what **really** makes the application special is the fact that it rather cleverly learns over time what content should be of interest to you, and which content is probably not.

This can be a useful way of dealing with the 'information overload' that you could well be feeling if you have taken all my advice and signed up to all of the relevant information sources for your local and professional news. There's simply so much news being generated each day, but much of it can be only marginally interesting and a lot of it can be little better than spam.

You need to spend a while interacting with My6Sense before it starts to become really useful as it 'learns' what type of content is interesting to you and which you will just scroll on by. It's not infallible – it will still throw up articles which are of no use to you and fail to spot some articles which could be of interest. As a result, it is not a complete replacement for going through all of your feeds. However, if you are getting thousands of messages every day and can't possibly spare the time to even glance through all of them, then My6Sense is a good compromise. If you just look through their top 100 recommended links from the past 12 or 24 hours, then you should get 80-90% of the most useful content which you will need.

By using My6Sense, you will eventually create the equivalent of your own personalized newspaper – one that only shows you the topics and articles which you are most likely to be interested in – one which is constantly updated in real time and one that you can carry around with you in your pocket everywhere you go, so you can read it any time you have a spare five minutes.

My6Sense currently only works on smartphones – at least in its full version. While this has the advantage of the portability and convenience I mentioned above, it can be a pain to repost the content which you find (especially as, once again, there is no support for LinkedIn on My6Sense).

The way to get around this problem is by using a simple service called Instapaper (sign up free at **www.instapaper.com**). Instapaper allows you to create bookmarks for webpages on any device – your computer, smartphone, iPad, etc., which you can retrieve from anywhere. My6Sense allows you to save any link to Instapaper with just one click.

Combining these two services allows me to keep abreast of all the news that is relevant to **me** (and only me, with no irrelevant articles to wade through each day), saving the ones that I want to share with my audience to Instapaper. Then, when I am back in front of my computer, it's simplicity itself to share them to all my social networks by copying and pasting the link over and writing my unique, individual comments on them. By scheduling my postings over the next 24 hours, as I described earlier, all my postings for the following day can be set up in just a few minutes because I have already selected the most interesting articles during otherwise wasted parts of the day.

*   *   *

In summary, although it might take you several hours to set up your social media dashboards on your computer and on your smartphone, plus a few hours more to find your way around all of the options until you've fully got to grips with it, it's an excellent investment in time. Once everything is set up, it can reduce the amount of time it takes you to keep abreast of all your streams and make a whole day's worth of postings in less than half an hour.

> Email us **now** at **accountant@informerbooks.com** to get our **free weekly updates** in case there have been any changes to any of the information contained in this chapter since publication.

BUILDING OR IMPROVING YOUR WEBSITE

IF YOU'VE READ any internet marketing books written at any point since the dawn of the World Wide Web, you will have found that at least half the book is devoted to the importance of having a website including as many bells and whistles as the designer can convince you to pay for. Yet here I am nearly halfway through the book and I've hardly mentioned websites at all.

So what's going on?

As I mentioned in the introduction to this book, I stated that websites are perhaps not as relevant to the needs of local businesses as most 'internet marketing gurus' claim them to be.

Ask yourself **why** your clients or potential clients would need to come to your website. They might need to:

(a) Find your contact information so that they can set up a meeting

(b) Find your address so that they can locate your offices

(c) Find out your working hours

(d) Find out a little bit about you to check that you are an experienced professional who can help them solve their problems

But what else are they going to need from it? Are they going to read all your news and your blog entries? Probably not – it might be important for you, but your existing and potential clients are probably not going to care that much. So why spend a lot of time, effort and money creating an 'all-singing, all-dancing' website which no one is ever going to use on a regular basis?

This is why I have been focusing so far in this book on using social media. On each of the social networks, you are able to give potential clients most of the important information about your business that clients are going to need without ever having to visit your website. But, more importantly, by using the tactics which I have gone through so far, you can use the social networks to **actively** go out and hunt down potential new clients rather than **passively** crossing your fingers and hoping that, one day, someone happens to stumble upon your website.

OK, so it would be going too far of me to say that you don't need a website at all. Twitter, for example, doesn't have much of a profile page where people can find out everything that they are going to need to know about you. Also, many of the tactics I will introduce in the remaining chapters involve sending potential new clients **somewhere** on the Web, even if it is to the simplest of pages.

In summary, your website is not the 'sacred cow' that a lot of people might tell you it is. If you already have a website, but are worried that it's 'not good enough' then I'm going to reassure you that it probably is – or at least it will be with a few little tweaks here and there. If you don't have a website yet, then it's worth putting something simple together – something that you can either do yourself for free or at little cost. I am certainly not proposing that you spend hundreds, maybe thousands, of dollars to create a fabulous looking website. Let's keep things simple (and as cheap as possible).

CHOOSING A PLATFORM

If you don't have a website already, then there are several options available to you ranging from free up to an investment of several hundred dollars, or a **lot** of time in trying to figure out how to do it yourself if you have no experience of creating websites in the past. Unless you specifically enjoy 'messing around with computers' and are interested in learning how to create websites as a hobby, I would advise you not to try to teach yourself the finer arts of putting a website together. There is a steep learning curve involved in figuring out how to create good websites and, if you only intend to create one relatively simple site for your business (which is all you really need), then the time you spend learning the process will probably be better spent on your other internet marketing activities.

Below I run through several different options for creating simple sites ranging from completely free through to an investment of several hundred dollars per year. In each case though, the more you spend, the better the results will be and the more flexibility you will have in making them exactly the way you want them to be.

Central.ly

If you have no skills at web design, very little money and would like a web presence up and running in less than an hour, then Central.ly could be the solution to your problem.

Central.ly (**www.central.ly**) allows anyone to sign up for free and create what they call a 'social media website', which is designed as a single page where you can pull all your social streams together in one place.

The site has not been around too long and this shows from the cutting edge designs that it's possible to create using the tools which are at your disposal. If you look through examples of sites that other people have made using the system, you will see that most sites are created around one huge photo with a minimum amount of text on it, giving a modern feel to the pages. Most of the pages look more like album covers than traditional websites.

Once you have signed up for the service, you can start creating your page. The possibilities that you're presented with in terms of colors, fonts, positioning, etc. are virtually endless. The site's WYSIWYG (What You See Is What You Get) editor is so simple to use that you can knock up a simple page in a little over ten minutes. However, such are the infinite number of possibilities available that you'll probably want to spend quite a lot longer than that fiddling with everything to get it just right. It's just as easy to create a hideous looking site as it is a fabulous looking one.

If you aren't terribly gifted artistically (be honest with yourself) then get someone who is to take a look over your site and make some suggestions as to how it could be improved. Look through the many examples of sites other people have made using the system to take ideas from them. You don't need to copy them right down to the final details, but it can be a great source of inspiration. You will probably notice as you go through the examples that, the simpler the sites, the better they look. Just because you have the ability to use every color and font under the rainbow doesn't mean you'll have a good looking site if you do!

Central.ly makes it incredibly easy for anyone to design their site by holding the user's hand through the process, one step at a time. Start off by giving your home page a title and some text and uploading a logo if you have one. Then, choose the Theme you would like to use for the background. Next you have the opportunity to add more pages to the site. You can incorporate your Twitter and Facebook business Page News Streams directly into the site, add your location using Google Maps, a contact form and even a newsletter signup form for MailChimp (which I will describe in detail in chapter 10). The 'Custom Page' option allows you to create additional pages as you need them, so you can create an 'About Us' page plus a 'Services' page. The final section allows you to choose different fonts and colors for your text and a different color for the info box.

Once you have set up your site, take a look at the dashboard which gives you some simple statistics which show the number of visitors coming to your site from the different social networks.

The main concept behind these 'social media websites' is that you really don't need much of a website these days because its people's social media streams which is where everyone is most active. As a result, you just need to refer them to your website once and then they can sign up to one of your streams and keep the contact going from there.

This is true up to a point, but there are many disadvantages to having a Central.ly site as your main website. Although you are able to add as many custom pages as you like to your site, Central.ly is optimized for small amounts of copy on each page – one paragraph maximum.

As a result, it is difficult to use Central.ly to actively sell yourself to potential visitors and, for a website, this is a major negative. Your website could be a very effective marketing tool with a bit more time and effort put into it. Unfortunately, few of the promotional methods which I describe in the remainder of the book can be implemented with a Central.ly site because you need to be able to add elements to the HTML (the code which generates most websites) in order to make them work. Central.ly does not use standard HTML, which limits your possibilities for adding additional elements to it.

Most importantly, a Central.ly site will be a practically invisible as far as the search engines such as Google are concerned, because Google will see the site as being just one page. Also, as I will describe in detail in chapter

11, Google needs lots of text to read if it is going to give your website a high ranking and Central.ly is not designed to create sites which contain a lot of text on each page.

As a result, I would say that Central.ly should only be considered as a 'last resort' for anyone who needs a bare minimum web presence in a hurry. If you do decide to go down this route, however, then it is worth paying for an upgrade. This currently costs $9 per month (which is pretty expensive compared to the next option in this section). This will get rid of the Central.ly logo on your page and will also allow you to host the page under a domain name of your choice rather than the regular address, which is along the lines of **central.ly/yourname**.

Weebly/Webs.com

Weebly (**www.weebly.com**) and Webs.com are good intermediate choices for anyone who needs more flexibility than can be offered by Central.ly, but doesn't have the technical skills to build a website themselves or the budget to hire someone else to do it for them. The main reason for this is that they offer a set of simple 'drag and drop' tools similar to Central.ly, but also offer the ability to design a fully-functioned website that can take advantage of most of the promotional methods which I describe in this book, including the ability to optimize your site for search engines.

As is the case with Central.ly, the permutations for creating different websites using either of these two systems are practically endless. Although millions of websites have already been produced using these tools, the chances of two sites coming out the same are zero because of the infinite number of possibilities.

Once you have signed up, you will be asked to choose from a basic template which will be the bedrock which you build your site upon. It's worth spending a good amount of time choosing which template you are going to use. Both Weebly and Webs.com have a variety of templates to choose from. As there is so little to choose between these two services, you are probably better off taking a look at the templates offered by both of the sites and going with whichever of the companies offers you the best template.

When choosing a template, bear in mind that there is a lot of flexibility to modify the template once you have chosen it. So don't get too hung up on the colors, fonts, etc. – it's just the general layout of the pages that you will need to keep (although you can keep changing templates as long as you like until you find a template and a combination of styles that you are happy with). Be prepared to spend a fair while getting your first page to a state that you are pleased with because, once you have the first page to your satisfaction, it should take no time at all to create all the other pages of your site. As I will show you later, you're only going to need a relatively basic site to accomplish all that you need it to do, which either of these systems will easily be able to create for you.

Due to the amount of options which are available for creating and altering pages, the process can be a little intimidating for the beginner. Fortunately both Weebly and Webs.com come with simple yet detailed instructions which guide you through the whole process. So read through them if you find yourself getting stuck at any time during the creation process. Even once you are happy with the results of your site building, make sure that you go through each of the settings filling in each of the fields. Both of these sites offer a fabulous selection of 'bolt on' extras which will help make your site look more professional and also enhance the possibilities of the site ranking highly on Google and other search engines. It's all there for you to use, so don't ignore some major benefits which they offer just for the sake of saving yourself five minutes before making the site live.

One of the attractive functions that both of these sites offer is the fact that they both automatically generate dedicated mobile versions of the sites, i.e. scaled down versions of the website which are automatically formatted to be easily read on smartphones. As I will describe in more detail at the end of this chapter, this is becoming an increasingly important feature of sites today due to the growing number of people accessing websites via their smartphones, particularly for local businesses.

As I mentioned at the start of this section, the basic services for both Weebly and Webs.com are free, including the vast majority of the tools necessary to create a good looking site. However, there are some important reasons as to why it's worth spending a relatively tiny amount of money each month to upgrade to one of their premium services.

The first reason is that the free versions of both sites have a label at the bottom saying that the site was created using a free website builder. Even if you are a bit of a cheapskate (like me) who tries to spend the least amount of money as possible, it's probably not a good idea to advertise this fact to your clients! The second major reason why you will probably want to upgrade is that it is the only way to get the site hosted under your own domain name. With the free version of the site, your domain name will be something like **yoursite.weebly.com**. Again, this does not look very pro-fessional compared to having a site under your own unique name.

Of the two sites, Weebly offers the best prices, costing just $3-5 per month depending on how long you sign up for, and this covers absolutely all of their premium services. Webs.com works on a sliding scale – the more services you want, the higher the price. Currently their 'Enhanced' pack-age, at $7.50 per month is the cheapest one which offers the possibility of using your own email addresses. This is something that you are definitely going to want to use as, again, it looks unprofessional to use a Hotmail or Yahoo! account for your main business correspondence. So, as you can see, Weebly is definitely the cheaper of the two options, although even an expenditure of $7.50 per month is tiny compared to the expenses involved in creating and then hosting a purpose-built site.

Weebly and Webs.com are not the only players in town when it comes to providing simple 'drag and drop' interfaces to make it simple to create good-looking, fully-featured websites. Many of their competitors, how-ever, produce sites which are not coded in the usual language of the Web (called HTML), but instead use a rather fancy program called Flash. Flash can produce some impressive animation work, so many web designers love to use it because it looks impressive and so allows them to charge their cli-ents much more than they need to pay. Flash is a major negative for users like you who just want to offer a simple site for your visitors though. For one reason, search engines like Google are not able to read the words of your copy and so your site will not rank highly. Secondly, Flash sites take a lot longer to load than regular sites. By the time there is something for visitors to look at, if they're on a slow connection, they could have given up and clicked over to your competitor instead. Finally, Flash doesn't work on iPhones at all and the other smartphones can often struggle with it as well. So don't use any Flash on your site as it could cost you quite a few potential clients.

In summary, the Weebly/Webs.com option is the best one for the hobbyist who is happy to settle for a relatively basic and probably quite plain look-ing site at minimum expense. While producing a basic site is quite simple, however, adding more advanced features to the site can prove to be more difficult than with one of the more advanced methods of creating websites.

WordPress

If you have absolutely no technical skills and don't have the time or inclination to spend a minimum of a couple of weekends learning them, then this is not for you. Move along now please; there's nothing for you to see here! Either rewind to the last section (Weebly/Webs.com) or fast forward to the next one (Elance).

If, however, you don't mind rolling your sleeves up and getting your hands dirty, and want the most fully-featured, flexible and totally free website creation program with which to create the perfect site of your dreams, WordPress could well be the right tool for you.

WordPress started off in 2003 as a simple and effective free tool for bloggers. The software is 'open source', which means that it is free to use and anyone can do pretty much whatever they want with it. Because of this reason, thousands of people have tweaked and improved the basic code and shared it with the rest of the community, which has made for a constantly evolving and improving product. After so many years of these tweaks and improvements, WordPress now rivals, and in most cases, exceeds similar commercial software solutions and is now used by millions of websites, from the most humble bedroom blogger to Fortune 500 companies.

There are two quite separate WordPress options – WordPress.**com** hosts your website on WordPress's own servers, whereas WordPress.**org** is just a site from which you download their software. Once you have downloaded it, then everything from that point is pretty much down to you – you need to get your own hosting, install it and customize it yourself.

So which one is better? Well WordPress.com is a lot easier for beginners as it can be quite a headache to find a hosting company and then set up your software. However, if you go down this route, then you are once again restricted to only the themes which WordPress provides. There are quite a few to choose from but, to my mind, they look a bit too 'bloggy' in the main. By this I mean that the templates are mainly designed for bloggers who update their sites regularly with new entries and don't have so much need of a proper multi-page site like you will need. As a result, you will probably struggle to find a template which fits your needs. And, although it's not so difficult to customize the sites, it's not nearly as simple as it is to use Weebly/Webs.com. Therefore, WordPress.com 'falls between two stools' – you're better off going for either the simpler option of Weebly/

Web.com or else going the whole hog and getting stuck into WordPress. org.

The WordPress.org software is a lot more flexible than the WordPress.com system. Due to the fact that it is open source, thousands of companies have used its basic functionality to create enhanced themes with. Some of these are available for free; others are available to buy at a reasonable price ($30-100 seems to be the going rate). You can find a vast number of themes to choose from at the following link:

www.wordpress.org/extend/themes/

Alternatively, make a search under 'wordpress themes' or 'wordpress templates' for a vast number of options for themes that you can buy and modify to your own requirements. With so many tens of thousands of themes to choose from, you'll surely be able to find one that you like. In fact, your problem is probably going to be on deciding which of the many options to choose from. Just don't spend too long going through the options – any website is better than no website, after all.

Unfortunately, choosing your theme is the easy part. There is a fair bit of work to do in order to get your theme up and running and modified to your needs. It's beyond the scope of this book to go through each of the steps involved in installing and modifying a WordPress theme as it would take the rest of the book to go through the process for all of the different variations. If you do decide to take this option, there are various resources on the web which will help you to learn how to use your theme, including many useful videos on the subject which you can find at WordPress. tv. Several of the companies selling themes also offer the facility to set everything up for you for an additional price. This is an option well-worth considering if you don't want the hassle of trying to learn how to do everything yourself.

Fortunately, once you have WordPress installed and you have found your way around the system, it becomes simple after that. As WordPress is, at its heart, a blogging platform, it has a sophisticated CRM or 'backend' function which makes it simple to create and update different pages.

Another useful feature of WordPress is that there is an excellent free plugin available for the platform called WPtouch. With just a few clicks, WPtouch can create a professional-looking version of your site which is optimized to be read on smartphones. This avoids the cost of having to buy and create a separate version if you want to make life as easy as possible for your visitors.

In summary, WordPress.org is an excellent choice for anyone who is looking for a low-cost way of creating a professional-looking website. However, they have to be prepared to put in a fair bit of work in setting it up in the first place.

Elance

If you have been reading through all of the above options thinking that it all sounds like a lot of time and effort and thinking that it would be a lot easier just to pay someone else to do it as long as it doesn't cost a small fortune, then you are probably right. If your business is going pretty well at the moment, then why spend several hours or days trying to put your own site together when you could get a professional to make it for you in a lot less time? If you follow all of the advice in this book, your website should bring you a lot of new business over the next twelve months and beyond, so it could be false economy to try and create a website too cheaply.

Most people would probably prefer to get someone else to do it for them, but they are afraid about how much it would cost. Maybe you have called around a few local web designers to find out their charges and have found it to be a pretty costly exercise – particularly if you are living in a major city.

But what if you could find a way to get someone to build you a website which probably isn't going to cost you a great deal more than it would to buy a WordPress template and figure out how to build it yourself? Well now you can, by using Elance.com.

Elance takes advantage of the Global Village that we are all now living in. Do you really need to employ a web designer who lives just a few miles from you when you can communicate with anyone in the world these days for free via Skype or a variety of other tools?

Elance puts tens of thousands of professionals all over the world at your disposal. And, because there are so many of them, it's a buyer's market, allowing you to hold a 'Dutch auction' where web designers compete in order to offer you the lowest prices.

To check on what Elance can do for you, head to **www.elance.com**. There is a wealth of information on the home page of Elance explaining the whole process to you. So look through it all and watch the videos if you need any more information after reading my write up.

Think of Elance as a giant virtual marketplace where buyers and sellers of services meet up. There are two ways of finding the right person to make your website – either you can go around everyone offering the service asking them if they want to build a site for you, or else you can advertise the fact that you're looking for someone to build a website for you and ask people to bid for the job. Or you can use both methods (which is probably the best).

Although there are many ways for someone to build a site for you, I recommend trying to find someone to create a WordPress site for you using a custom theme as there are several advantages in this:

> (a) You're not paying someone to reinvent the wheel. Tens of thousands of man hours has gone into getting WordPress to the stage where it is today, so why bother with a less advanced system?

> (b) When you tell someone that you want them to create and install a WordPress site for you, they'll understand exactly what you want, avoiding any potential confusion (and possibly extra time and expense if the supplier didn't understand your requirements properly).

> (c) Creating and installing a WordPress theme is the most popular job advertised on Elance, so you'll have the widest number of potential companies to choose from for the job.

To advertise your requirements, click on 'Describe Your Job'. To make sure that you are giving potential suppliers all of the information they need to bid on your job, click on the link marked 'Open Description Assistant'. You should see a template come up called 'WordPress Themes' as this is such a popular job.

Work your way down the list of questions filling in all of the fields, giving as much information as you can think of to save any confusion further down the line. Where it asks for the 'purpose of the WordPress website', choose 'Informational/Online Brochure'. For the number of pages, see the next section in this chapter. If you have seen any websites that you like the look of – maybe that of another accountant that's not a competitor of yours on the opposite side of the country – then put the link to their site where it asks for any websites that share a style you're aiming for.

Where the form asks if you need help with coding and installation, select the option offering both 'Design and Code' so that, once the job is finished, you have nothing to worry about.

Where it asks, 'What is the work arrangement?' choose the 'Fixed Price' option – otherwise you could be in for a nasty surprise. Where it asks for your budget, select the 'Less than $500' option. As you are only going to need a relatively simple site, the total should be lower than $500, but it's better not to set your price too low in case you're not impressed with those designers who put a bid in for your low offer. It would be better to pay $499 for an excellent site than $299 for a terrible one.

I would suggest selecting '7 Days' for the duration of the ad as this should be more than enough to find a good supplier. You will probably find one quicker than this, but you can always take the ad down once you have found someone that you are happy with.

Once your ad is live, you will start to get offers for the job. Don't rush into accepting the first offer you get as you might get a better one a couple of days later. Don't just go for the company offering you the best price either – Elance gives you a lot of information on each supplier. Check how much business they have done in the past on Elance and whether their previous clients have given them good reviews. If less than 90% of their previous clients are satisfied, then this should be a warning. Also check out their online portfolio to see if they are producing the type of work you like the look of. If it looks bland or amateur to you, then wait for a better offer.

Elance offers another way of matching you up with the ideal supplier other than just placing an ad and crossing your fingers, hoping that a great company makes you an offer. If you would like to choose a company to perform the work for you, then go to the 'Search Contractors' link and type 'word-press themes' into the search box. You will find thousands of contractors listed who can do the job. In order to narrow down the options, use the filters on the left hand side to make sure that you are only dealing with the 'best of the best'.

Use the 'By Feedback' filter to choose only those suppliers that have an average five star rating from their previous clients over the last 12 months. Use the 'By Reviews' filter to choose 'At least 15 Reviews' to make sure that their good reviews came from a large number of satisfied clients. Finally, set the 'By Hourly Rate' level as low as you dare. You should still find some good companies that are willing to work for you even for $10 per hour or less. Once you have narrowed down the options to a manageable number, click on the link to the companies' portfolios to have a look at their previous projects. Do you see any examples there that you like? If it all looks a little underwhelming, then move on to the next option. Once you find someone who is creating websites that you like the look of though, invite them to pitch for your business. You might have found the company that you're looking for.

After a few days, you should have found at least one good contractor that you would like to work with and so you can then use the system to award them the job. You will then be required to place the agreed amount in an escrow account held by Elance on both parties' behalf, which gives the contractor peace of mind that you have the money to pay them.

The contractor might want to set some 'milestones' into the agreement so that they don't have to wait right until the end of the job to receive a cent. A set of 'milestones' could look something like the following:

$150 upon the submission of four concepts for the site.

$150 for the first working page of the site.

$150 for completion of the job, uploaded onto your own server.

As each of these 'milestones' are achieved, you would release the appropriate amount to the contractor's account. In such a way, both you and the supplier each have a great deal of protection so that neither of you can end up getting cheated by the other.

If you are not happy with the work that the supplier has performed for you, give them the opportunity to improve it. If the worst comes to the worst, Elance will arbitrate, but this should be a very rare occurrence. Once you are happy with the work, give your supplier some good feedback in order to give future clients of theirs an idea as to what to expect from them.

In summary, Elance is a highly effective tool for getting a professional website produced without the need to do anything other than detail exactly what you want from them and then to get your credit card out. If you can afford a few hundred dollars then this is probably going to be your best option rather than spending many hours trying to do it all yourself.

Professional Dedicated Service

Does Elance **still** sound like it's going to be too much hassle for you? Would you still rather pay some more money and get someone else to take care of the whole process for you?

If you are not on a tight budget and just want to get a good site up and running as quickly as possible with the least amount of effort, then help is at hand in the form of several companies that offer accountants like you the complete service from start to finish.

These companies understand your business and, through the economies of scale afforded them by providing similar websites to a large number of accountants all over the country, they are able to offer you additional elements for your site which would cost you an absolute fortune if you were to hire a company to build them just for yourself.

All of these companies cover pretty much all of the essential features which I describe later in this chapter. Most of them offer a lot more in addition, such as a large number of downloadable forms, financial calculators, guides, the facility for clients to upload large files to you securely, newsletter mail-outs and a whole host of other benefits.

There are well over a dozen of these companies to choose from, all of which provide a similar service, although the number of 'bells and whistles' that each of them offers varies tremendously from one to another.

In addition to a wide range of different services that these companies offer, they also differ greatly in their charges. Because of this, it really does pay to shop around and consider all of the options carefully if you are interested in hiring one of these companies to handle the whole website creation process for you.

Some of these companies require a set up fee, which can range from $250 - $1500 in order to create a site for you in addition to regular monthly fees. Others forego the set up fee and charge just a monthly fee, which starts around $50 per month and goes up to around $120 per month.

Having looked through all of the different options in this field, two stand out in my opinion:

www.cpasitesolutions.com – no set up fee and then from $49.50 per month

<u>www.emochila.com</u> – no set up fee and then $69.95 per month

In the UK, my recommendation would be **www.accountantwebsmiths. co.uk** – no set up fee and then from £55 per month.

With any of these companies, you will start off by choosing from a variety of templates and then the company will modify them to make the site personal to your own firm. In such a way, you don't have to worry about ending up with a 'cookie cutter' site which looks identical to hundreds of others. If you prefer, they can create a completely original site design for you, but this increases the price quite considerably. These companies claim that they can have your site up and running in as little as 48 hours.

So can you simply hand over your money to one of these companies, sit back and simply wait for them to create the perfect website for you? Not quite. Although the sites I have seen from these companies look nice and contain all of the elements necessary for a site (plus quite a few optional extras which are 'nice to haves' not 'need to haves') the copy that they produce definitely has room for improvement. They don't follow all of the rules from the section in chapter 2 on copywriting. In addition, they don't follow all of the rules for search engine optimization that you will read in chapter 11. I have also seen little in the way of social media integration from them either.

As a result, in order to get the most effective website possible, I would suggest that you are still better off writing your own copy and asking them to ensure that the site is optimized for search engines (and Google AdWords) as per the advice that I give in the remainder of this book.

Obviously the cost of the service is going to end up being a lot more expensive over time than getting a site built for you on Elance for a low one off fee. However, if you are clueless about even the basics of creating and updating a website, the peace of mind knowing that it is possible to call a professional to add new elements to your site is probably going to be worth the price of the monthly fee.

CHOOSING A DOMAIN NAME

Once you have decided which of the above options you are going to use to build your site, you need to decide what you are going to call it.

This is not as simple an exercise as it might sound because your website address (or URL) is important to two different types of visitors:

(a) Your clients

(b) Google and other search engines

Unfortunately, what they want from an address ideally are complete opposites. Your clients are going to want an address which is short and easy to remember. For them, something like **johnsmithcpa.com** would be ideal. Google, on the other hand, wants a URL which contains lots of keywords that people would be using to try and find your site. It would prefer **johnsmith-cpa-business-accountant-yourtown-yourstate.com**. But no one is going to be prepared to type that out whenever they visit your site (not to mention the fact that you'd probably need an extra-long business card to even fit the name of it on there in the first place!). You will also probably want to use a professional email address which includes your domain name rather than having a Gmail or Hotmail address (e.g. **john@johnsmithcpa.com**). So it would look terrible if you had a long, descriptive domain name.

There is no ideal solution to this, unfortunately, and the best that you can aim for is a happy compromise, so you would probably be better to come up with a halfway house along the lines of **johnsmithcpa-yourtown.com** or just forget about trying to please Google and use other methods to try and rank highly in the listings.

Actually, there **is** a way that you can have the best of both worlds if you're prepared to go to a little trouble, and that's to register **two** domain names. One would be your ideal short URL, like **johnsmithcpa.com** while the second one would contain your best two keywords, like **yourtown-accountant.com**.

You would use the short address on your business cards, any signs that you have and for your **john@johnsmithcpa.com** email address. However, your long address is the one that your website is actually hosted under – the one that Google should hopefully find and list highly in its rankings.

The trick is to link the two together in such a way that your visitors aren't inconvenienced by being transferred from one domain to another. Many domain registrars have the facility to forward one domain to another without your having to pay any hosting fees. If they can do this and can also provide you with the opportunity of having your own email address too, this is the perfect option.

If not, then you will have to find hosting for the website (see below for more information). The 'website' for your short domain only needs to consist of a single page with a few lines of code on it.

To find the code, just make a Google search for 'javascript redirect' or else type in the code below:

```
<HEAD>
<SCRIPT language="JavaScript">
<!--
window.location="http://yoursite.com";
//-->
</SCRIPT>
</HEAD>
```

Just change **yoursite.com** for the URL of the site you want to forward your visitors to. Now, when anyone types in your short website address, they will be instantly transferred to the real address that your website is hosted under without even realizing that the transfer ever happened, unless they pay close attention to the address in their browser.

Before you get too set on a particular domain though, you need to make sure that it is still available. Go to **www.godaddy.com** or search for 'domain names' on Google to find other options. Here you can try out different options to see if your chosen name is available. If not, then try and come up with something close to it, e.g. instead of **www.yourtown-accountant.com**, try **www.accountant-yourtown.com**; instead of **www.johnsmithcpa.com**, try **www.johnsmith-cpa.com**.

Don't be tempted into using an extension other than .com (or a .co.uk for British readers, a .ca for Canadian readers, etc.). You might be offered a domain name such as .biz or .info for your ideal choice of domain name. Resist the temptation of going for one of these though as they tend not to be taken as seriously by many people compared to the 'normal' domain names.

Once you have found your ideal name, where you register it depends on which method you are planning on using to create your website. In many of the options I gave above, you get a free domain name along with the paid version of the service. Even if it's not free, you will probably still find it easier to buy through the same company as the one which will be providing the tools.

If you plan on getting someone to create a unique site for you via Elance, however, then you will need to buy one independently. You can use **www. godaddy.com** for this or any other registrar that you find making a search. As well as a domain name, you will also need to choose a hosting company.

CHOOSING A HOSTING COMPANY

If you are using Central.ly, Weebly, Webs.com, WordPress.com or one of the specialist companies to create your site, then your hosting will be provided for you. If not, then you will need to choose one.

One option is to go with the same company who you chose to register your domain with. Although that's the simplest choice, it might not be the best one in the long run. While prices of hosting usually don't vary too much from one hosting company to another, the level of customer support which they offer can vary enormously. Whenever you run into a problem, fast and responsive customer support is going to be very important to you indeed. Changing hosting company once you have chosen one is a pain in the neck, so better to find a good one to start with.

To make sure that you're going to end up with a good hosting company, make a search under 'web hosting reviews' and take a look at which of the companies come out at the top. It's worth checking a few of the different review sites to make sure that the first one you looked at is unbiased and is offering genuine reviews. One company that gets consistently high reviews is **www.inmotionhosting.com**. I use them for my own sites.

Once you have chosen a hosting company, sign up with them. Although you should hopefully be getting quite a few visitors to your site as a result of the methods you learn in this book, you will be aiming for quality not quantity. A visitor from the other side of the world is worth nothing to you at all if there is no chance that they will ever become a client of yours. Because of this, and also because you don't need a particularly large site, you should find that the hosting company's most basic package serves your purposes just fine. Although prices vary a fair bit from one company to another, reckon on paying around $5-7 per month for the service. If you are paying more than $10 a month, then you have probably chosen a company that specializes in hosting for busier websites and so you should carry on searching.

As I warned you earlier when considering your different options, setting up your website yourself is not such a user-friendly process as the other options which I described. Your hosting company should have some 'How To' guides on the site in order to assist you, however, and they will have customer support available to help you if you encounter any major problems.

PLANNING YOUR SITE

Now comes the most important part of the exercise, which is designing your website. The principles are the same no matter which of the methods you are using to create your site (although, as I said, you don't have a huge amount of options with Central.ly).

Before you do anything to the design of your site, go back and read the information on copywriting in chapter 2, especially the piece about coming up with your 'Most Wanted Response'. Ask yourself the question:

"What action would I like the visitor to my website to take after viewing it?"

You know that each new client you get is likely to want some slightly different type of service. It's not going to be possible to set up an e-commerce site where they just choose a service, pop it in a shopping basket and 'proceed to checkout'. If only life was that simple!

No, chances are that potential clients are going to have several questions that they need answering and it will take a fair bit of communication between yourself and the client either by email, over the phone or in face-to-face meetings, before they are ready to make a commitment and go from being a potential customer to being an actual customer.

As a result, the action that you probably want the client to take after visiting your site is to get in touch with you to ask for more information. It doesn't really matter **how** they get in touch with you – by email, by phone, or even walking into your office – just as long as they get in touch. You also want to make sure that they don't think that you are going to surprise them with a big invoice if they ask a few questions, so ensure that you make it transparently obvious that you are offering a **Free Consultation**.

Once you have determined that this is what you want the visitors to do, you should always have this at the front of your mind while putting your website together.

If a potential client visits your website and doesn't get in contact with you after visiting it, then your website has failed.

Some books on website design will try and tell you that the more pages and content you have on your site, the better. While this might be the right strategy for a website that makes its money by selling advertising, it's completely the wrong strategy for a site likes yours. The **less** time the potential client spends on your site and the **quicker** they get in contact with you, the better.

Therefore, your aim with the site should be to give the visitor just enough information to let them know that you are a professional company that has the ability to solve all their problems, but not so much content that they get sidetracked, or that they can't find their way around your website and miss the most important parts of it.

So what pages do you really need?

Home Page

This is the one that really counts and the page that you need to spend most of your time working on. Get this page right and you hardly need worry about the effectiveness of the other pages of your site. Get it wrong and you'll have blown your chances; the clients will be clicking on the back button and will be checking out your competitors instead.

The information on your home page is by far the most important copy that you will be writing in your entire internet marketing campaign (although you're allowed to go back and tweak it at any time).

When it comes to writing copy for your home page, 'less is more'. No one has the time or patience to read an essay. Chances are that many of the prospects will have found your site from a search engine and will be comparing your services against those of your competitors. Use the tips in the section on copywriting to tell potential clients that you understand their problems and requirements and that you are the right person to help them. Your home page doesn't need to achieve any more than this.

You main copy should be in the most prominent position on the home page – dead centre of the screen when anyone opens up your site is the best location to aim for. Two or three short paragraphs should be all you need to attract a potential client's interest.

What else should you put on your home page? The trend these days is to try and cram as much information and as many options as possible on the home page. However, I think that this trend is counterproductive for most accounting firms. The more options you give visitors for links to follow other than the one you ideally want them to follow (i.e. to make contact with you), the more chance that they will wander off in the wrong direction.

So, other than your main copy telling visitors that you are able to solve their problems, the other feature that you want to highlight is your Free Consultation offer. Maybe this is a big enough offer that you want to put it in a big box all on its own. If your main navigation is at the top of your page (which is the most logical place for it) then consider putting a box detailing your Free Consultation on the left hand side of the page, which is where most people will look next because people read from left to right, exactly as they would when reading a book or a newspaper. Your Free Consultation offer is such an important one that you should consider keeping this box in the same position on all of your pages to give visitors plenty of other opportunities to see it if they decide to investigate other areas of your site before filling in their details.

If you prefer not to put your Free Consultation in a box, then put in a link at the bottom of your main copy telling them that this is where they should head next (there's no harm in asking them).

Another key item which you should include on your home page – and probably on every other page of your website too - is your phone number. If a potential client is serious about looking for someone to solve their problems, there's a good chance that he wants to do something about it **right now**, as in 'within the next 30 seconds'. Don't force the potential client to fill in a long form if they are the type of person who wants some immediate assistance, and don't force them to click on the link to your 'Contact Us' page. The navigation to your website might seem obvious to you, but you don't want to run the risk of losing the client because they missed it.

I've spent a large proportion of the book explaining to you the benefits of incorporating social media into your marketing campaign. You most definitely want to try and get any potential visitor to your site to join up with one or more of your social networks – Facebook, Twitter and/or LinkedIn. I would suggest putting links to all your social networks on the right hand side of the page. Again, it's where people will most expect to find them.

It's important when designing websites not too be **too** original. There are now certain conventions in place with regards to website design that web surfers have become used to over time. It makes their lives a lot easier when they can guess where to find most of the links that they are looking for. So, when designing your website, it's a good idea to look at a number of different sites from competitors of yours around the country. Follow the patterns that you see emerging and also feel free to add any information that you find on someone else's site that you would like to add to yours. Don't copy the actual text though – just the idea – or else that would be stealing!

The home page of your site is probably the only page you will need to change once you have the website set up, so any topical information that you intend to place on the site should probably also be given a home here. Are you planning on running some monthly promotions? If so, then allocate a place for them on the home page. If you aren't sure that you will come up with enough ideas though, don't bother with it as it will just end up as a waste of valuable on screen real estate which you can better use in other ways.

So putting all of these elements together, what have we got?

- At the top of the page, you should have your main navigation to the different pages on your site.

- Running right across the page and maybe taking up the top 20-30% of the screen space, you'll probably want a large banner featuring an eye-catching image, your logo and a 'tagline', explaining in one sentence exactly who you are and what you can do. This is sometimes known as an 'elevator pitch'.

- On the left hand side of the page, put in a box highlighting your Free Consultation offer, with both a link to your online contact form, plus your phone number.

- In the centre of the page is your main copy explaining what you can do for potential clients and why they should choose you. End this section with another link to the Free Consultation Form and give your phone number again.

- On the right hand side, put in the links to your social media networks and ask people to join them. Also consider placing a 'Twitter Widget' there which will automatically give your site constantly fresh content without your having to update your site manually.

- At the bottom of the page, repeat links to the different pages of your site that are included in the top navigation, put all of your contact information once more, your copyright notice and you can hide text that you want the search engines to read, but that is not so important for your potential customers.

About Us

In the copywriting section in chapter 2, I warned about talking too much about yourself rather than your clients' needs and how you can solve them. However, it is important that those clients who are interested in checking you out are able to do so in order that they feel confident in your abilities.

Your 'About Us' page is the place for all of this information. Feel free to sing your own praises loudly here – you can be sure that your competitors will be doing the same thing! Talk about your qualifications, the length of time your company has been in business, the number of staff you have, the number of satisfied clients you have assisted, speaking engagements, certifications and licenses you've been awarded, articles you have written, any awards or accolades you have received, etc. – anything which is going to impress a visitor reading it.

If you are not planning on making a separate page for testimonials, then you can consider running a few down the right hand side of this page if you have some. It is reassuring for potential clients to see positive feedback coming from existing clients.

If you run a small practice, then a one page will probably be enough here. If you have several partners in your practice though, consider writing a separate page on each of them, with links on the left hand side of the main 'About Us' page to a sub-page devoted to each person. If you and your partners all have detailed LinkedIn pages, it would also be a good idea to link them from here so that clients who are especially interested in knowing who they are dealing with can check you out in more detail.

Services

This page (or ideally, collection of pages) should contain the most information of all the pages on your site as it is where you will detail all of the services which you provide to your clients. Here you want to list as many services as you can in order to show your potential clients that, whatever service they need, you're able to provide it.

It's worth taking a look at websites belonging to a number of other accountants all over the country to see the services that they are listing on their websites. If you are able to offer the same services, then add them to your list.

Not only is this page going to be useful for your potential clients, but it is also going to be the one that Google and the other search engines find the most useful, as it should have lots of nice keywords incorporated in it.

If you really want to get the most from this section, then consider making a different sub-page for each of the services which you provide rather than listing them all on the same page. This is going to be essential if you are planning on optimizing your website so that it ranks highly for searches and also if you are planning on advertising using Google's AdWords. Again, be consistent when making sub-pages so that the navigation is in the same place each time.

Make sure that the subject of the page is in its title to have the best chance of ranking highly on the search engines, such as:

www.yourtown-accountant.com/tax-preparation.html

I will cover the subject of optimizing for search engines in more detail in chapter 11.

Contact Us

Although you should be putting your phone number and email address on every single page you have, you should also have a 'Contact Us' page putting all of your contact details in one place. Try and make this page as detailed as you can. As well as having your main office email address, if there is more than just you in your practice, list everyone's contact details separately – their email addresses, direct phonelines and, if everyone agrees, their cellphone/mobile numbers as well.

You should also include your fax number here, instant messaging systems that you use regularly such as Skype and also your office address.

Most of the website creation tools I listed earlier offer the ability to easily add an interactive map to a website using Google Maps. Definitely add one of these to your 'Contact Us' page to make it as easy as possible for visitors to find you.

Free Consultation

As I said earlier, the ultimate goal of your website will probably be to try and get visitors to contact you in order to receive a Free Consultation. As a result, this page is so important that it needs to be linked from your main menu rather than being hidden away as a sub-page. In fact, it is so important that you should finish every one of your pages with a link to it at the bottom with an invitation along the lines of, 'Click here now to arrange your Free Consultation'.

The page itself needs to be little more than a contact form, asking potential clients to fill in some of their personal details and a little information that will help you to be prepared when you get back in contact with them. The details of what they have filled in will then be sent through to you by email.

Don't go too overboard in asking potential clients too many questions at this stage. If they have to answer so many questions that it looks like they are having to take an exam, then they might just forget the whole thing. If they do, you've just lost yourself a promising lead. So just try to ask for the minimum amount of information that you need. If you do need to ask them questions, try to do so in a way that they can answer using 'tick boxes', 'pulldown menus' or 'radio buttons' rather than having to type in all of the answers.

Even if your contact form is concise, you should still list your email address and phone number clearly as alternative ways for potential clients to get in contact with you. Not everyone likes to fill in forms and you don't want to fall at the final hurdle by giving a visitor any reason not to get in contact – no matter how trivial it might seem to you.

What Else?

There are hundreds of other options for pages that you **could** add to your site. The question you need to ask yourself though is do you **need** to add more pages to your site?

If you follow my advice, then you should be creating a main menu at the top of your page with five different entries on them. Five main menu items is about the right amount – this number of options should fit easily onto any design of website. If you start adding more items, then it could be a problem to squeeze them all in. Also, as I said earlier, the more options you give visitors, the less likely it is that they will end up doing exactly what you want them to do.

If you read through other books on website design and website marketing, they will probably talk about adding pages for blogs, FAQs, testimonial pages, etc. While writing this book, I have checked out a **lot** of websites belonging to accountants and have seen that many of them are crammed full of links to tools and resources for potential clients; they're full of forms, calculators, etc. While it is charitable of these companies to provide all of this information, is it really going to lead to their gaining any more clients? I doubt it. If someone is looking for such tools, they are not going to stumble across your site when they are offered in so many other places online. And most of those people searching for them will be from outside your local area anyway.

If you see a section on some other site which you believe will increase the chances of someone getting in contact with you, by all means add it. Otherwise, remember K.I.S.S. – Keep It Simple (Stupid)!

CREATING YOUR SITE

By now, you should have decided which pages you are going to include on your site and what information you are going to put on each of them. Before you rush to whichever platform you are going to use though, slow down a little. A little planning now will save you a lot of time. Otherwise it's easy to start putting a website together only to find that it doesn't all fit nicely or that there are big empty areas that you don't know what to fill with.

As a result, I recommend planning your entire site out on pieces of paper before you try and put together your digital version. It doesn't need to be a work of art – it just needs to give you a guide as to what pieces of content need to go where. Use one full sheet of letter paper for each page of your website which you are going to create.

Start off by creating the header and footer for each of your pages. They should be the same for each page on your site so, once you have a design for one page, you have the design for all of your pages and you just have to change the 'body' in each one.

Your header should incorporate most, if not all, of the following elements:

(a) The navigation menu with links to all of the main pages on your site.

(b) The name of your company

(c) Your company's logo

(d) Your company's phone number (maybe prefixed by, 'Call us now on ...')

(e) Your company's 'tagline' or 'elevator pitch'

(f) Some kind of image

Probably the image is the one item that you'll struggle to make a decision on. Here are some suggestions:

- Use a professional picture of you or of your team, or maybe of your office, if it is attractive. Note the word 'professional'. Don't try and 'make do' with a quick snap which your spouse or friend took unless they are a pretty gifted photographer as it will make your site look less than professional. If you haven't already got professional photographs, then it's probably better to choose one of the other options as the cost of getting professional photographs taken could work out at being substantially more than the cost of the rest of your website put together.

- An accounting themed 'stock photo'. The majority of accountants' websites that I have looked at feature such stock photos – tax forms and pens, calculators, people in suits shaking hands, etc. The plus side to using these is that they do look quite professional and they immediately tell the visitor what they can expect from your site. The downside is that they look a little dull, clichéd, unimaginative and can make your company come over as looking rather impersonal. If you do decide to use a stock photo, I recommend using **www.stockfresh.com** which has a vast collection of photos available priced from just $4.99 per photo. Just make a search under 'accountant', 'cpa' or 'taxes' and see what comes up.

- Another option is to use an image of your local area – something that is immediately obvious as belonging to your town, whether it is a shot of a famous local landmark, the surrounding countryside, the beach, etc. The advantages here are that, firstly it will probably look more interesting than a pen and some tax forms, secondly the viewer (who should also be a local) will know that they have found a company which is in the same area and, thirdly, it shows that you are proud to be associated with your town (which ties in nicely with the social media campaigns I described earlier). Stockfresh should also have some local scenes to choose from, but there is also another (free) option available, which is to find photos on Flickr.

To find suitable images on Flickr that you can use, go to the 'Advanced Search' page at:

www.flickr.com/search/advanced/

Type the name of your town in the search box then select 'Only Photos'. Towards the bottom of the page, tick the box marked, 'Only search within Creative Commons-licensed content' and also tick the box marked, 'Find content to use commercially'.

If you don't tick the final two boxes, then you could end up breaching the photographer's copyright, which would not be good.

Unless your town is really obscure, you should come up with plenty of options for images to choose from. In return for using this photographer's photo, you need to give them a credit on your website. This can be done by adding a simple line to your footer along the lines of: Photo Credit: (user name on Flickr) linked through to their Flickr profile page.

Once you have come up with an attractive combination of all these elements for a header, then you can go on to the footer, which is a lot easier to design.

It's a good idea to repeat your navigation at the bottom of the page to save people having to scroll up to the top. It's also a good idea to repeat your main contact details here once again so that your potential clients don't have to hunt for it. You should also add a copyright notice along the lines of © (year). All Rights Reserved.

As mentioned earlier, your footer is also a good place to hide keyword rich information which is useful to search engines – something along the lines of:

John Smith CPA offers (list of services which you offer) in (list all of the areas within your catchment area).

Once you have your header and footer to your liking, you now have your own personalized template. Every page you now make will have the same header and footer, with just the 'body copy' changing on each page.

Now, on your pieces of paper, go through and put in boxes where the copy on each page will go. Most websites today organize their content in columns – the main content in the center and other narrower columns on the left (which is where any navigation to sub-pages should go) plus sometimes a column on the right as well. Try and keep all of your pages consistent in terms of the layout. If you have three columns on your home page, then use three columns on all of your other pages too. If you are struggling to fill the columns on some pages, consider making one column another advertisement for your Free Consultation page, or perhaps you could run testimonials in a column. On your 'Contact Us' page, you could run the map in one of the columns, etc.

Go through each of the pages in turn filling in the columns on each page. Also don't forget to make any sub-pages which you need if you are going to put each of the services that you offer on a separate page. Keep going with this exercise until you have designed every page of your site.

You're still not ready to get onto your platform yet and start building your site. Next, go through each of the boxes which you have positioned on your rough layout and write all of the text which you will need using Microsoft Word or some other word processing software. You should find it a lot quicker and easier to write all of the copy that you are going to need in one go, and the spellchecker in Word could help you to avoid making some embarrassing typos. Take as long as you need to come up with some really excellent text which follows all of the rules in chapter 2 on copywriting.

Although it might take you a while to come up with all of the text that you need and to get it to a state that you're happy with, I have some good news for you – you've done all of the hard work now – you're 90% of the way towards building your website.

Now that you have a good idea as to what your finished website will look like and you have all of the text that you are going to need ready to copy and paste into the relevant places, it shouldn't take you too long to piece everything together. It should be no more difficult than putting a jigsaw puzzle together. You have all of the elements now – you just need to put them in the right places.

If you are not going to create the site yourself – maybe you are going to use Elance to find someone to make it for you, or you have a competent friend who can do it – you are still going to have to go through most of this exercise. After all, even a web design genius isn't going to understand your business and what you want your website to achieve. So you are going to have to tell them exactly what you want.

If you are planning on using Elance, then post all of these materials you have created along with your Job Posting – scan your drawings and post them too. Don't be embarrassed if they look rough and amateurish – they will still do the job. Not only will it make it simple for those people or companies replying to your ad to understand exactly what it is that you want from your site, but it should bring their prices down considerably. It will be a quick and easy job for a qualified web designer to turn your sketches into a final design and then just copy and paste the text into the right places.

Once you have the first working version of your site, you will probably find that you need to do a little tweaking in order to make it look completely perfect. You'll probably end with a little too much copy in some places and too little in others. By adding or deleting a line or two in the right places though, it should be relatively simple to get it looking absolutely perfect.

ADDING SOCIAL MEDIA PLUGINS

Your website should nearly be finished now. Although it might have taken quite a while to get it set up, the good news is that, once it's finally up and running, you don't need to spend much time with it in future. Most of the content on it should be 'evergreen' – it should be as much of a useful marketing tool to you in five years' time as it is today.

However, one of the major downsides to having a site which you will probably very rarely need to update is that there will be little need for your potential customers to pay another visit to your site again once they have read all of the information.

This could be a major problem. After all, you know that not all of your potential customers are going to be ready to employ your services all of the time. A lot of your potential customers probably have an accounting company working for them already and so, today, they might not be interested in changing. Six months from now – a year – two years down the line, it might be a different matter though. Their current accounting company could get more complacent and provide them with a lower level of service, or else they increase their prices, etc. However, by this time they will have long forgotten all about you and your website and so all of the hard work which you put into creating your fabulous new website will have been in vain.

This is where social media comes into the equation. Whereas your website sits in its own little corner of the Internet waiting for someone to pay it a visit, your social media networks – Facebook, Twitter and LinkedIn, together with your email newsletters – should be actively getting in front of your prospects' eyeballs on a regular basis. So when your prospect decides that it is time to hire a new accountant, who are they going to get in contact with? The company whose website they visited a year ago, or the company whose content they've been reading daily, weekly or monthly over the last twelve months?

For this reason, it is vital to try and get as many of the visitors to your website to join one or more of your social networks and/or to give you their email address so that you can continue your marketing activities towards them.

Fortunately, each of the social networks is also keen on getting your prospects to join in as a way of growing their networks, because they are in competition with the others to get the most amount of interactivity. For this reason, each of them offers you a selection of 'Widgets' or 'Plugins' that you can quickly and easily add to your website to make it as easy as possible for visitors to join you there on your network.

Let's have a look at what each of the social networks can offer us:

Facebook

In order to access Facebook's collection of 'Plugins' as they are known on this site, go onto your Facebook business Page. Once you're on it, click on the 'Edit Page' button or 'Edit Info' link at the top in order to get into your control panel.

On the menu on the left hand side, click on 'Resource' first of all, and then select 'Use social plugins'. You will see that there are quite a number of different social plugins available. Most of them, however, are designed for more complicated sites than yours and so aren't going to be relevant.

One potentially useful tool is the 'Like Button'. This is the simplest tool on there. If someone with a Facebook account clicks on this button, then their 'vote' will be counted. Although this is useful as the visitor will have a reminder of your site whenever they look at the list of their 'Likes' on their Profiles, it will be a 'one off' piece of promotion for you as it does not sign them up as a Fan of your Facebook Page and so they will not receive any updates from you in the future.

More useful then, is the plugin called 'Like Box'. This gives you the opportunity of putting a button on your site which will allow your potential clients to become a Fan of your business Page with one click of the 'Like' button. Not only will a message appear in their News Stream, but they will also start receiving your regular updates, unless they choose to 'unlike' your Page at some point in the future. This is marketing gold dust as it will allow you to start a relationship with the prospect until hopefully, one day, they will be ready to become a paying customer.

Although this is the most useful function of the 'Like Box', there are a couple of other features to the box which you can choose to include or not. One of these is displaying your stream, i.e. the same content which is being displayed on your Facebook Page. See below for more information as to whether this is going to be a good feature to include in your box or not. The other optional feature is to show the pictures of some of those people who are already Fans of your business Page. To my mind, there are both advantages and disadvantages to using this feature. The advantage is that, if a prospect sees a friend of his of hers who is a Fan of your Page, then it is the same as their getting a personal recommendation that it's good to be a Fan and so it's more likely that your prospect will also join. The disadvantage though is that all those pictures can dominate the page of your own website, especially if it has quite a Spartan design. So think twice as to whether you want to keep this function or not.

Twitter

You can find the Twitter 'Resources' as they call them at the following link:

www.twitter.com/about/resources

The 'Follow button' is going to be the most useful one for most websites. It works the same way as Facebook's 'Like Box' in that anyone clicking on the button can immediately start Following your Twitter Feed and so will become part of your ongoing active marketing methods.

The other potentially useful Twitter addition to your site can be found in the 'Widgets' section of the 'Resources'. Once you've clicked on the 'See all widgets' link, click the link on the right hand side of the page for 'My Website'. Now click on the 'Profile Widget' at the top.

You will see that the 'Widget' is similar to Facebook's complete 'Like Box' in that it can display the most recent events in your Twitter stream. It doesn't have the facility to show all of your Followers here (whether you'd like to, or not) but it has a lot more options as to what colors and layouts you want to use than the Facebook equivalent.

LinkedIn

LinkedIn's plugins are a little bit hidden away on the site at the following link:

developer.linkedin.com/plugins

There are a couple of options here which might be of interest. 'Recommend with LinkedIn' works in a similar fashion to Facebook's 'Like button' – the fact that the person clicked the button will show on their News Stream. As most people don't tend to be as fanatical about checking their LinkedIn News Feeds as they are their Facebook and Twitter feeds though, this is probably going to have a limited effect.

More useful are the 'Member Profile' plugins which allow you to add the equivalent of a LinkedIn business card to your site, with the opportunity for the visitor to 'View Profile'. Hopefully, once they have viewed your profile, then they will add you as a contact – although it is not a 'one click' automatic action as it is with Facebook.

Adding the full 'business card' plugin to your site is fine if you are basically a 'one-man band', but if there are several partners in the practice, it would be too overbearing to put everyone's cards here. In this case, go with the other option in the 'Member Profile' section, which is to use just the LinkedIn icon plus a name. The full business card will open up when someone hovers their mouse over the link. As these icons are quite small, it will be possible to add several of them to your site without it becoming overbearing.

As well as, or instead of, adding these small icons together with your other social plugins, consider adding the full 'business card' in a relevant position on the 'About Us' page of your site so that visitors can check out your resume/CV in full detail.

Google+

As I described in chapter 6, Google+ is the latest addition to the social media scene and is still in its infancy. As a result, whether you include Google+ in your online marketing activities is a matter of personal choice.

To access Google's plugins, head to:

developers.google.com/+/plugins/

Because, at the time of writing this book, Google+ for Business is so new, Google's plugins are still a 'work in progress'. Currently Google offers two different plugins at the moment - both of which are useful while serving different purposes.

The first useful plugin is what Google calls its '+1 button' and is Google's equivalent of Facebook's 'Like button'. Already, next to every one of Google's search results is the option of '+1ing' the link and many of the largest sites on the Web have also added the button. By adding the +1 button to your site, visitors can achieve the same result of making what is the equivalent of a 'vote' for your site.

As well as the '+1 button', it's also possible to add a 'Google+ Badge' which acts as a link between your website and your Google+ business Page. Although the '+1 button' and the 'Google+ Badge' are separate at the moment, Google are already previewing examples of what they are calling a 'Google+ Badge Tag' which will combine the two separate plugins. Hopefully by the time you read this, the 'Tags' will be live and so you will only need to add the one plugin to your site in order to receive the benefits of both.

But is there any point in bothering with Google's plugins if hardly anyone is using the Google+ social network? Well, yes, actually there is - for two different reasons.

If you have clicked the +1 button to your site and a friend of yours on Google+, or someone Following you on Twitter, sees the link to that site when they make a search, then your name and profile picture will come up saying 'John Doe shared this', thus acting as a personal recommendation.

As for the 'Google+ Badge', this is not only a way of getting any visitor to your website to click through and join your Google+ network, but also proves to Google that your website is linked to a Google+ business Page. Although Google is not detailing exactly how businesses which have their own Google+ Pages are going to be rewarded, they are dropping hints that such businesses will benefit from increased visibility in their search engine results.

As being ranked well in Google's search results can bring huge amounts of additional visitors to a site, this exercise is well worth undertaking, even if linking your site to a Google+ business Page and having a few people click on your '+1 button' only makes just a small improvement to Google's perception of your site.

Newsletter Signup

As I will cover in detail in chapter 10, as good as the social networks are, a posting on them still doesn't carry the same impact as an email arriving in a potential client's email inbox. This means that the best possible way for customers to be reminded of you is by getting them to sign up for your regular newsletter.

This should definitely be included along with your other social network signups. So important is it that you might want to place a signup box elsewhere on your site as well.

Later on, I describe various options regarding online systems that you can use for maintaining a database of your contacts who have agreed to receive your regular newsletter and for making it simple to send out attractive looking mailers. Each of these systems comes with a simple way to collect the email addresses of those visitors interested in subscribing to your newsletter so that you, or whoever you choose to create your site for you, can add a signup box to your site in just a few minutes.

So above you have five different plugins from five different companies to think about adding to your site. With not every potential visitor to your site being on all the different social networks, it will be handy to have them all on there. The downside though is that it can make your site look like a bit of a mess if you put all of the options for all of the social networks on every page of your site.

Fortunately, most of the buttons come in different sizes and so you can scale them down if they look too overbearing.

A particularly difficult decision is whether to include your complete streams from Facebook and/or Twitter on your page. The advantage of having them there is that it means that you will automatically be getting fresh content on your home page constantly without having to keep going back and add it in manually. This is good as it shows anyone visiting your site that it's still alive and your company is being proactive. Having streams from **both** Facebook and Twitter together though is going to be complete information overload. Especially if you are using one of the social media dashboards, a lot of the content there will be repeated. So it is best if you choose to feature the full feed from just one of them here. But which one?

As I mentioned in chapter 4, Twitter users are used to receiving a much higher volume of Tweets coming through to their streams than Facebook Fans are used to getting updates. This is why I suggested sending four or more Tweets a day on Twitter, compared to just one every day or two on Facebook. This means that the last few Tweets in your stream are going to be more current than the last few Facebook postings you have. As a result, of the two options, I would suggest that it is better to start off putting your Twitter stream on your site rather than Facebook's.

As time goes on, however, you will probably find that one of your social networks starts to outperform the others. If this is the case, and you start getting a lot more interaction on your Facebook Page than on your Twitter stream, then consider swapping them over. If visitors can see that there's a constant party happening on your Facebook Page, then they're more likely to want to get in and join the fun!

MOBILE WEBSITE

As I have mentioned before, the incredible success of the iPhone and other smartphones are changing the way people access the Internet as people take advantage of the fact that smartphones allow people to walk around with the 'Internet in their pocket' 24 hours per day. If the rate of growth continues as its current pace (and there is no reason to expect that it won't) then more people will be accessing the Internet from cellphones than they will from desktops and laptops by 2014-15.

Even more surprising than this is that Microsoft research shows that, already in 2011, more local searches are performed on smartphones than they are on desktop computers – and local searches are exactly the ones that your prospects will be making in order to find your business.

This makes it vitally important that your website is usable not only just on desktop computers, but also from smartphones as well.

If you chose Weebly/Webs.com or WordPress (either created yourself or by getting someone off Elance to do it for you) for creating your website, then you are in luck, because these tools all come with options to generate dedicated mobile sites. The programs can automatically tell if a website is being viewed on a small smartphone screen and will display a totally different version of the site. The content is all the same, but the layout is completely different – all of the large images are taken out and the navigation is changed in order to make the text readable. As a result, there is no need to design a completely separate version of the site.

However, if you created your website in a different way, it could be worth your while to create a different version of it just for smartphones. If you own a smartphone yourself, you probably already know that viewing a full-sized website on a smartphone can be a frustrating experience. While you can zoom in and out to make the text larger, it's easy to lose your way on the screen and the little buttons are difficult to use in order to navigate around a site. If a prospect is searching for an accountant on their smartphone and finds it hard to find what they are looking for, there's a good chance that they will simply hit the 'Back' button and try a different site which is easier on the eye.

For a simple and free solution to this problem, head to **www.onbile.com**. Here you will find an easy to use system which will create a dedicated mobile site for you. Choose from over a dozen basic templates which you can then customize with your own color scheme, upload your company logo, choose your icons and write a sentence or two of copy for each page. Onbile.com gives you just three pages in addition to your home page – 'About Us', 'Services' and 'Contact Us', but this should be enough for the regular mobile user. If they are searching for you on a smartphone, chances are that they are just looking for some quick information in order to contact you rather than wanting to read the entire content of your site. So don't worry too much that the mini-site you have produced is too basic.

Once you are happy with the results, click on the 'Publish' button to download your site. You then need to upload the mini-site into its own folder so that it appears as something like **yoursite.com/m** (the easier that it is to type in, the better) and then post one line of code into the home page of your regular website. This line of code detects the size of the visitor's screen and, if it is too small to display the full version of your site properly, it will automatically forward the visitor to the mobile site instantly.

If you are not happy with the free template generator from Onbile and don't mind paying a little for something a little more unique, make a Google search under 'mobile template' and you will find many options available that you can choose from and then amend yourself.

If you choose to go with the Onbile option, it should take you only half an hour or so to create the mobile version of your site and it will be of great benefit to all your prospects browsing your site using a smartphone.

*   *   *

So the above was a general introduction and overview as to how to put a website together for your business. If it all seems rather complicated, I'm afraid that there is a pretty good reason why – it is! It can take web designers years to learn their craft and, even with plenty of study, it's as much an art as it is a science. It's not something that everyone is good at, no matter how hard they might try.

If this is the case with you, don't give up on all your marketing activities because your website is just one element of it. Just accept the fact that you'll be better off putting your hand in your pocket and getting someone to create the website for you. If you use Elance, then it shouldn't cost you too much. And, with the skills that you have learned here, even if you are unable to create it yourself, you will still have learned the elements as to what makes a useful and functional website. So now you know exactly what to ask for if you employ someone else to make it for you.

> Email us **now** at **accountant@informerbooks.com** to get our **free weekly updates** in case there have been any changes to any of the information contained in this chapter since publication.

TESTING AND ANALYZING YOUR SITE

HOPEFULLY, IF YOU followed all of the advice in the previous chapter, you now have a great-looking site that's going to be the workhorse of your online marketing strategy. However, so important is it going to be to all of your future activities that it would be a disaster if you made any mistakes during the creation process. You need to be 100% sure that everything is working correctly to start with and then to keep checking on its results to make sure that it is performing as well as it possibly can.

One of the great benefits of online marketing is that it is possible to measure and analyze the results of virtually all of the actions that you take, which removes a lot of the guesswork from your activities. Compare this with advertising using old media where you run an ad and have little way of telling what the results were and whether it could have been improved.

However, all these benefits are lost if you don't use the tools which are available to fine-tune your website and monitor the results of your attempts to get more people visiting it. Fortunately, Google provides a free suite of tools that, if used together, can alert you to any problematic areas and give you the opportunity to test different solutions without involving the need for any guesswork.

GOOGLE WEBMASTER TOOLS

Using Google's Webmaster Tools is the website equivalent of going to the doctor for a physical. Running through the tests will enable you to find out if your website has any problems that will stop it from working at 100% efficiency.

To access the tools, go to:

www.google.com/webmasters

Once you have logged in using your Google account, type in the URL of your site. You will then be asked to verify that your website really does belong to you, which can be done in a few different ways. The recommended way is to add a line of code just before the `</HEAD>` tag of your header. Alternatively, if you have set up your site to use Google Analytics, as per the next part of this chapter, Google can use the Analytics code for verification.

Once you have added the relevant code in one form or another, click the 'Verify' button and Google will check that the code has been entered correctly. If it has, then you will be inside the Webmaster Tools and looking at your dashboard.

If your site is new and you have not had Google Analytics set up, there probably won't be a massive amount of information showing on your dashboard yet. To get the most use from it, leave it for a month and then see what information you can gather from it then.

Much of the information here is going to be useful for your search engine optimization strategy, which I describe in detail in chapter 11. The first section is related to 'Search queries' and shows you how many times a page of your site has appeared in Google's search results, the average position in Google's rankings for each term and how many times people have clicked through. By clicking on the 'More' link, you can get detailed information on each of these queries and can click on the links in the header to sort the information by any column.

Underneath this is a list of all of the sites which have links to yours. This is another important factor for search engine optimization. By clicking on any of the links, you can 'drill down' to see the exact page of the link coming to your site and where exactly on your site the link went to.

On the right hand side of the dashboard, you can see the most significant keywords for your site listed in order of importance. As you will learn later in chapter 11, you should be seeing your main keywords such as 'accountant', 'cpa' and 'yourtown' ranking highly in this list; otherwise you have some tweaking of your copy to do.

The most important section at this point though is the information in the 'Crawl errors' section, particularly if anything is listed here as 'Not found'. If there are any links here that are listed as 'Not found', it probably means that you typed in a link incorrectly on one or more of your pages. To find out where the link came from, click on the list and you will see a column called 'Linked From'. Click on the links in this section to bring up the URL of the page and take a closer look at it. Then correct the mistake and re-upload it onto your site.

The dashboard gives you the opportunity to upload a sitemap onto your site. This is a useful addition to your site as Google's indexing 'spider' will look for this page whenever it checks your site.

There are several sites on the Web which will generate sitemaps automatically, such as:

www.xml-sitemaps.com

Just input the name of your site in the first box on this page, keep all of the other settings the same and then press 'Start'. The program will automatically crawl through your site and list all of the pages it finds linked there. Once it is finished, click the link called 'Download un-compressed XML Sitemap'. You then need to upload this file onto your server.

Returning now to Google Webmaster Tools, click on the 'Submit a Sitemap' link and input the name of the file, which should always be **sitemap.xml**

Now you've looked at all of the main sections on the dashboard, take a look at the links on the left hand side of the page. Most of them are for quite advanced functions which won't be necessary for a simple site likes yours. One section that is worth checking out, however, is 'Diagnostics > HTML suggestions'. The first section is about 'Meta descriptions' which I describe in more detail in chapter 11 about search engine optimization. Here you can check that you haven't accidentally given the same description to more than one page and also that they are neither too long nor too short.

'Title tags' are the name of each page which appears at the top of the browser window and in search engine listings. Here you can check to make sure that you didn't forget to add titles, that you didn't accidentally duplicate any of them and that, once again, they are neither too long nor too short.

Finally, take a look at 'Labs > Site performance' to check how fast the pages in your site are loading. If you get a message that your site is slow, then speak to the company which is hosting your website to ask them if there is anything that they can do to speed it up. You don't want all your hard work in creating your site to go to waste just because it took too long to load in impatient visitors' browsers, making them want to look elsewhere.

Once you have used the Webmaster Tools to fix any problems, you probably won't need to use them again too often. I would suggest, however, that you check on them once per month in case anything important changes.

The most important tool when it comes to monitoring the activity of your site on a regular basis is Google Analytics …

GOOGLE ANALYTICS

If you follow the advice in the rest of this book, your website should be getting a lot of visitors in the not so distant future as your website becomes the hub of your entire internet marketing campaign. The more that you can learn about the visitors to your site by analyzing how many people are visiting it, where they come from, how long they stay, what keywords they used to find you, what pages they visited, how long they stayed on your site and a whole host of other information, the more you will be able to fine-tune your marketing activities and fix any mistakes that you might inadvertently be making.

Until 2005, obtaining detailed information regarding who was visiting your website and what they were doing while they were on it was an expensive business. It could cost hundreds of dollars per year to get a full package of statistics. This changed forever though when Google launched Google Analytics – a powerful analytics tool which was both completely free for anyone to use and also simple for just about anyone to add to their website.

You should definitely add Google Analytics to your website – it takes just a few minutes to set up and it will then provide you with a lifetime of detailed information.

To get started, log into your account with Google and head over to:

www.google.com/analytics

Click on the 'Sign up now' link underneath the big blue 'Access Analytics' button, then press the silver 'Sign up' button.

Type in the name of your site and the website's URL, followed by your country and time zone. Make sure that the box is ticked for 'Share data with other Google products' – you will need this if you plan on running Google AdWords campaigns in the future. Once you have filled in all of the details, click the button marked 'Create Account'.

You should be directed to the page of the Google Analytics site which gives you the code which you will need to add to every page of your website. For a simple site like yours, you shouldn't need to change any of the settings – you just need to copy the dozen or so lines of code that are already shown on the page.

Google Analytics is such a commonly used program that most of the major site creation tools featured in this book make it very simple for you to add the code. So hunt around on your interface for an easy way of including it. WordPress, for example, have several plugins available that will take care of adding the code with just a few clicks. Otherwise, open up the HTML of your website and search for:

```
</HEAD>
```

You just need to copy and paste the code in its entirety **above** this tag.

Make sure that you copy and paste this code onto **every page** of your site – not just the home page. Otherwise you will be using only a fraction of Google Analytics' capabilities.

Once you have added the code to your site, it's best to wait a while until you have had a few visitors to the site that will show you some data. Otherwise it will be hard to understand the different elements which Google Analytics can track if there are zero results everywhere.

After a day or two, return to Google Analytics and click on 'View Reports' where you will start off with your dashboard which shows you the most basic data at a glance. Prepare to be assaulted by such a massive amount of information that it can be quite overwhelming at first! Don't worry – you're not going to need to monitor all of the data all of the time in order for Google Analytics to be a useful tool. Much of the functionality of Google Analytics is going to be only relevant for sites which are much larger than yours. Additionally, while a lot of data is quite interesting, it's not going to have any significant effect upon your business (e.g., it doesn't really make any difference to you if the majority of your visitors are viewing your site using Internet Explorer or the Firefox browser).

Starting at the top, the most useful feature, and the easiest to understand, is the number of visitors coming to your site. By default, the graph at the top shows how many visitors your site has received over the past month. You can use the calendar buttons on the top right hand side to set it for longer or shorter periods of time.

Underneath the main graph on the left, you see the most important information about the site usage during that period – the total number of visitors you received, how many of them were unique visitors, the total number of pages which the visitors saw in that time, the average number of pages each visitor read and the average amount of time each person spent on the site during their visit.

One of the more important statistics in this section is the percentage of new visitors, which is shown on the pie chart on the right hand side of the page. It's important to know what percentage of visitors have found your site for the first time and how many are returning to check it out again.

Another statistic you will see here is the 'Bounce Rate'. This is the percentage of visitors who left the site after just looking at one page of it (usually the home page). Having a high 'Bounce Rate' is generally not a good thing – it usually means that visitors didn't find what they were looking for when they arrived there and hit the 'Back' button to go someplace else. However, this is not always the case. If you feature your phone number on your home page (which you should do) and the visitor just came to your website in order to find it, then the job was done without their needing to explore your site in more detail. A more useful statistic than 'Bounce Rate' is, I believe, 'Engagement' which you can find at, 'Overview > Behavior > Engagement'.

This data divides up visitors according to how long they spent on the site. If they were on the site for less than 10 seconds, chances are that they weren't interested in your site at all. It's not long enough for them to read your copy and then click onto a second page and read that one too and it's not long enough for them to give you a call for more information either.

Beneath the main 'snapshots' about all of the visitors over the past month are three main sections which give you more general information about the visitors, starting with 'Demographics'. The 'Language' information is probably not going to be terribly useful for a local business sites like yours – hopefully the vast majority of users will be speaking English. Likewise, the 'Country/Territory' statistics should also hopefully show that most of your visitors are in the same country as you. Most useful in this section should be the 'City' report. Hopefully, this will show that the majority of visitors to your site are coming from your local area.

Underneath the 'Demographics' section is the information on 'System'. You're unlikely to learn any useful information that will help you with your internet marketing activities from this section.

The last section in the 'Overview' is dedicated to 'Mobile'. If you have not yet followed the advice in the previous chapter to set up a separate version of your site for people browsing on a smartphone, this data could be useful. If just a small percentage of visitors are coming to your site using smartphones, then there is no great rush to add this functionality to your site. If, however, a significant percentage of users are connecting to you this way, it will probably be worth your while adding a separate version of the site just for these users. This is especially true if you see that smartphone users are showing a higher than average 'Bounce Rate' versus the site as a whole, because this probably means that they are giving up in frustration at the difficulty of finding useful information on your site.

Now that you have looked at all of the main information coming from the 'Overview', take a look at the reports which are linked from the menu on the left hand side of the page. Most of the reports underneath 'Visitors' simply repeat those that were linked from the main 'Overview' screen.

The 'Advertising' section is concerned totally with results of any Google AdWords campaign you might be running. I describe AdWords in great detail in chapter 13.

One of the most useful sections in Google Analytics is the detailed information you can get on 'Traffic Sources'. Select this section from the left hand menu and take a look at 'Overview'. This shows where all of your visitors came from, and is broken down into three different groups:

Search Engines – most of the traffic here is likely to come from Google, but you will also probably find that some visitors came to you via Yahoo!, Bing and some other smaller search engines.

Referring Sites – this means that visitors have clicked on a link from somewhere other than a search engine. It could be from Facebook, or Yelp, or anywhere else you have a link going into your site.

Direct Traffic – this is where people have typed the URL of your website directly into their browser rather than coming from a link from a different site, or else they are returning to the site after bookmarking it.

Underneath the Pie Chart are sections which break down the traffic generated from each of the three different types of sources.

In the 'Search Engine' section, the first report tells you which keywords visitors used to find your site. Don't make the mistake when viewing this list of thinking that the top keywords listed are the 'best' ones for your business – they probably aren't. Instead, they are more likely to show those keywords where you are already ranking highly in the search engines. Compare this list with the most popular keywords that people are looking for (which I describe more in chapter 13 on Google AdWords) to see which ones you need to work harder on. The 'Source' section shows how many visitors each of the different search engines sent to you.

'Referral Traffic' shows you the 'Source' of all of the visitors which found your site through links on the Internet anywhere other than the search engines. If you take my advice in chapter 12 about paying for a premium listing in directories which rank well for your most important keywords, this data is like gold dust. The reason is that you can see exactly how many visitors you are attracting from the advertising. By dividing the cost of the advertising by the total number of visitors you receive from it, you can compare the cost per visitor against the price that you are paying for AdWords to see whether it is a good deal or not.

The final section, 'Direct Traffic', shows the page that those visitors arriving on your site through means other than clicking a link arrived on. Chances are that your home page shows most of the traffic here. If other pages are showing, then some of your visitors bookmarked it in all likelihood.

Next take a look at the 'Content' section from the main menu. Again start with the 'Overview' information. At the top of the 'Overview', you get some general information, this time concerning page views rather than the number of visitors.

The most useful information is on the submenus at the bottom of the page again. The link called 'Page' in the 'Site Content' section gives you a ranking of the most popular pages on your site. Chances are that, at the top of the list, is '/' – this means that it is your home page. Again there is some useful information to be learned here. If you made each of the services that you offer as a separate page – e.g. Bookkeeping Services, Payroll Services, Tax Preparation, etc. – then this list will tell you which of these services is getting the most interest from your prospects. This means that they are the ones which you should focus the majority of your promotional activities upon.

Returning to the left hand menu, at the bottom you will come to the last major section, which is 'Conversions'. One very useful facility in Google Analytics is the ability to set 'Goals'.

In the last chapter, I suggested that the primary goal of your site – your 'Most Wanted Response' – should be to try and get visitors to contact you for a Free Consultation and that you set up a form to make it as easy as possible for them to do so. By making the sending of this form a 'Goal', you will be able to receive a lot of useful information as to how successful you have been in achieving this objective and to find areas where the process could be improved.

To set up a 'Goal', from the 'Conversions' link, click on 'Goals' followed by 'Overview'. To get started, click on the 'Set up goals and funnels' button.

Click on the link below 'Goals (set 1)'. For your 'Goal Name', call it 'Free Consultation'. Keep it set as 'Active' and then, for a 'Goal Type', select 'URL Destination'.

Now, for the 'Goal URL', you need to select the name of the page which appears after the client has pressed the 'Send' button so that you know for sure that they have really completed the operation. Normally, upon hitting the 'Send' button, the visitor will be sent to a 'thank you' page. This is the page you want to track here. For the URL, you don't need to put the whole address here, just the page name which will look something like **/thankyou.html**

For 'Match Type', leave it at the default of 'Exact Match'. Ignore the box called 'Case Sensitive'.

'Goal Value' allows you to assign a particular cash amount to any visitor who completes this step. I describe a method for assigning a rough figure here in chapter 13 on AdWords that you can use here if you like, but the step is totally optional and so you can just leave it blank.

You can get even more information on the success of your site in achieving the goal of getting someone to complete the Free Consultation form by creating a 'Goal Funnel', so tick the box for 'Use funnel'.

For 'Step 1', first put in the URL of the page with the form on it (again there is no need to put your full site address here) so it will look something like **/form.html**. Give it a name such as 'View Form'.

If you only have one form on your site, tick the box for 'Required step'. If you perhaps put the same simple form at the bottom of several pages, then don't tick the box so that the 'Goal' will be counted no matter where on your site the visitor came from.

Click on 'Save' to complete the process.

Now you will be able to see how many people achieved your 'Goals' using any of the criteria anywhere else in the Analytics site. Want to see how many visitors from Google completed your Free Consultation form? From Facebook? From the premium listing you paid for in one of the directories? Now you will be able to tell for sure how many **quality** prospects you got from each source rather than just the raw numbers.

You can also get some useful information from the 'Funnel Visualization' link. This will show you in graphic form how many visitors arrive on your Free Consultation form page and go on to actually complete and send the form. Are you seeing that a lot of those people who arrive on the page aren't actually completing and sending the form? If this is the case, then maybe you are asking for too much information from them. If so, change the form by asking them just for their name, phone number and email address. Monitor the results for a while and see if more people make their way through the funnel successfully.

Another clever and useful function of Google Analytics can be found at 'Content > In-Page Analytics'. Click on this link and you will bring up a copy of your site underneath the main heading. This version of your site has little bubbles super-imposed over the site, showing exactly what percentage of the total number of viewers of the page clicked on each of the links leading off the page. This is a simple and graphic way of showing viewers' behavior when they read the page because it shows you, at a glance, where the majority of your visitors go after viewing the page. If your Most Wanted Response is for visitors to head straight to the Free Consultation page, these figures will show you if this is what they are really doing, or if they are checking out another page of your site instead.

Note that, if you have more than one link to the same page, it will show the same percentage for both links. For example, if you have a link to Free

Consultation as part of your main navigation and also as another link at the bottom of the page, they will both show the same amount. As a result, this does not tell you exactly **which** of the two links most of the people clicked on. This means that you are missing out on some important information as to the effectiveness of your bottom link or the lack of it.

There is a simple trick to get around this problem, however. In the previous chapter, I showed you how to make a simple JavaScript redirect in case you wanted to use a short address for your email and on your business cards, but a longer, keyword-rich address for your website.

You can use a similar trick to measure exactly how many clicks are coming from your bottom link. Rather than pointing the link directly at your 'Free Consultation' page, link it to a different page called something like **bottomlink.html**. This page should be empty apart from a redirect which instantly takes the visitor directly on to the Free Consultation page. The viewer will have no clue that they have gone via a different page, but the 'In-Page Analytics' breakdown will show this as a completely different link. This means that you will be able to determine exactly how many visitors are heading to your 'Free Consultation' page via the bottom link and how many are heading there through the regular navigation links.

In the first section of this chapter, I showed you how to set up an account using Google Webmaster Tools. Google Analytics gives you the opportunity to access your Webmaster Tools account via your Google Analytics Dashboard. This saves you having to bookmark it separately and log out of Google Analytics whenever you want to check the data there. Similarly, in chapter 13, I cover Google AdWords in depth. You can also access all of your AdWords data from the Google Analytics Dashboard as well, so that all of your main website data is all in the same place. This will save you a lot of time switching between interfaces.

If you work your way through all of the links from the left hand menu, you'll see that there is a lot of other information linked from here. Most of it though, for a small local site such as yours, is 'interesting' rather than 'useful'. Before fretting over a statistic that doesn't look good, ask yourself, "Can I do anything to change this?" For example, maybe you find that half of your traffic is coming from China. Can you stop it? No. Does it matter? Not really. Instead, in such an example, you would probably want to pay less attention to the statistics relating to the **overall** visitors to the site and concentrate instead on the statistics coming just from those visitors in your local area, which you can do by 'drilling down' to your city using the 'Geographic' data and analyzing just the data that you find there.

Rather than going through all of the links and trying to figure out what they all mean and whether or not they are relevant, I would suggest that you are better off approaching Google Analytics from the opposite direction. Rather than clicking on a link to a report and thinking, "What does this mean?" it is better off to start with a particular question and then use Google Analytics to try and find the answer, such as, "Is that listing I paid for in that directory sending me any useful visitors?" Analytics are also a vital tool whenever you decide to make some changes to your site to see if it improves the results you are looking to achieve or whether it makes the situation worse instead.

In this section, I have only given you an incredibly brief overview of the main data that it is possible to analyze using Google Analytics. I could easily spend the rest of the book describing all of the details about in-depth analysis of each of the features - but that wouldn't help you in generating more business.

If you would like to learn more about Google Analytics, Google has a lot of information on the subject, including many video presentations to help you understand each element of it. You can find this information at:

www.google.com/support/conversionuniversity

GOOGLE WEBSITE OPTIMIZER

I mentioned above that Google Analytics is a great tool for checking results if you decide to make some changes to your site. But actually Google has an even better tool in its collection for testing different pages side-by-side in the form of its Website Optimizer program.

Please note that this is a bit complicated compared to using Google Analytics and requires a little knowledge of HTML (either from you or someone else who you can ask to set it up for you). It is very much an advanced and optional feature and so don't worry if you leave it out.

If you would like to give it a try, then you can access the tool at:

www.google.com/websiteoptimizer

Once you have signed into the program using your Google account, click on the link called, 'Create a new experiment'. You will see that you have two options – either an 'A/B Experiment' or a 'Multivariate Experiment'. 'Multivariate Experiments' are more complicated and need a lot of visitors to test properly – more than a small website like yours is likely to receive. So just choose the 'A/B Experiment' option.

Now you need to decide which page of your website you are going to test against a new one. It should be a page that leads to a specific goal – otherwise it will be impossible to test whether changes are for the better or worse. Again, think about your Most Wanted Response that I mentioned in chapter 2, which will probably be connected with getting a prospect to apply for a Free Consultation. It could either be a new page which leads to the Free Consultation, or maybe the page with the Free Consultation form itself.

Create a new page to test against the old one – it could be completely different or it could contain just a minor change – the principle is exactly the same. It is possible to test more than one new page at a time. However, if you do this, it will take longer to see the results of the test. With a website like yours which probably does not receive so much traffic, it will probably be best to test just one new page at a time.

Once you have your new page ready, continue on to the next step of the operation.

Next, fill in all of the fields as shown in the examples. The name of the test is for your reference only, so you can call it, 'Test 1'.

Now you need to put in the full URL of the original page of your site (by full URL, I mean that it has to start off **http://www.**) Then put in the full URL of the new page you will be testing, and then finally the full URL of the conversion page, i.e. the page where you ideally hope that the visitor will end up if the test is successful.

Click on 'Continue' and select the option, 'You will install and validate the JavaScript tags'. If someone else is going to do it for you, you will still be able to send the information to them.

On the next page, you will get the code that you need to add to the three different pages of your site. You will need to copy and paste them right underneath the <HEAD> tag at the top of each page. Follow the instructions that you are given on the page to make sure that you have placed the correct code on the correct page. Once the tracking codes are added to the three pages and they are uploaded onto your website, click on the 'Validate pages' button and Google will test them to make sure that they are all working correctly.

You will then have a chance to check over all of your pages. If everything looks fine to you, then click on 'Launch Experiment'. The test will then be started immediately and, within 24 hours, you should start to see the results of the experiment come in. The results will show you how many times each of the two pages have been displayed, and how many times visitors have gone through to the conversion page from each one.

Google will continue with the experiment until one of the variations is sufficiently more successful than the other for it to be declared the winner. Exactly how many page views it takes to get to the stage depends on the results. If there is little to choose between the two pages in terms of results, the test will last longer than if one of them is an instant hit.

So that wasn't so difficult after all, was it? Now that you know how easy it is to set up a new test in just a few minutes, hopefully you will keep testing new ideas constantly. Keep an eye open for new ideas whenever you are browsing other companies' websites. What ideas are they using to achieve their Most Wanted Responses? Maybe you can try something similar to see if it performs better than what you are doing at the moment.

*   *   *

In summary, no matter how much effort you put into trying to make a 'perfect' site right from the start, there is always going to be room for improvement. So make regular use of Google Analytics and Google's other optimization tools to identify aspects of your site which may be underperforming and keep testing new ideas to try and improve upon them.

> Email us **now** at **accountant@informerbooks.com** to get our **free weekly updates** in case there have been any changes to any of the information contained in this chapter since publication.

NEWSLETTERS

POOR OLD EMAIL. Sometimes it seems as if she's a fading beauty queen, now middle-aged (email was actually invented way back in 1972). Once the Belle of the Ball, she now looks dowdy and outdated compared to sparkling young things such as Facebook and Twitter.

Appearances can be deceptive though – there's still **plenty** of life left in the old girl yet! Although Facebook's registered user base of 800 million is certainly impressive, it's still got a long way to go before it comes close to the number of regular email users, which is thought to be somewhere in region of 2 **billion**. Do you know anyone who doesn't have an email address? At least anyone who could be a potential client? I certainly don't.

As well as beating all of the social media networks in terms of pure numbers, email also beats them in terms of impact. Unless you change the default settings on your social media accounts, you get an email every time something important happens - a new Follower on Twitter, a new contact request on LinkedIn, etc. Even the social networks have to admit that emails beat their networks hands down when it comes to impact. The day we check our Twitter Feeds to see if there are any 'You've Got Mail' notifications is the day that email is finally superseded as the primary method of online communication between people. But that day looks to be still a long, long way off at this moment.

So, despite how sexy the new social networks appear to be, you should still consider email to be the primary and most effective way to grab a potential client's attention. Because of this, getting a potential client's email address, along **with their permission** to stay in contact with them in the future, should still be your primary objective today, just as it would have been a decade ago.

The **permission** aspect of the email marketing process is an important one. Without some kind of permission from the person who you intend to email, your newsletter would be just another piece of spam to them. So you should never buy lists of email addresses or obtain them in any way from a third party. You need to create your own mailing list comprising email addresses only from people with whom you have entered some kind of a relationship and who have indicated that they would like to receive emails from you.

Your database with each contact's email address is probably your greatest marketing asset, because it provides the best tool you have at your disposal for keeping in contact with potential clients and grabbing their attention.

CHOOSING YOUR LIST MANAGER

While your regular email account, whether it is Web based such as Gmail, Hotmail or Yahoo!, or it is operated from your desktop such as Outlook, is fine for sending emails to a few people at time, most of them have restrictions as to how many people you can email at once, particularly if you have them in the BCC section. This is to stop potential abuse of the systems by spammers. As a result, you will need to use a dedicated system if you want to send out a regular newsletter to all of your contacts (which you most definitely do).

There are many choices for online systems which will simply and painlessly take care of all your mail-outs as well as look after all your contacts – plus a whole lot more as well.

Some of the most popular mailing list programs are:

www.constantcontact.com
www.getresponse.com
www.icontact.com
www.verticalresponse.com
www.aweber.com
www.mailchimp.com

Feel free to check each of these options out, but you will find that they all offer similar functions at similar prices – except for MailChimp. At the time of writing at least, MailChimp is unique in that you can send emails to a group of up to 2000 addresses for free. After 2000 addresses, their pricing is similar to the other services, but it will probably be a while before you get to that level.

For the rest of this chapter, I'm going to be assuming you're using MailChimp. The principles are going to be similar if you are using any of the other systems anyway.

The first step is to sign up and activate your account. Once it is activated, you need to fill in details of your business, including your address. This is to comply with the CAN-SPAM Act, which was introduced in 2003 to try and stop spam. If you've looked in your junk folder recently, you will realize that it wasn't an unqualified success!

Once this is complete, you will be taken to your dashboard which will show you the steps you need to take in order to start creating email campaigns. Before you can do much though, you need to complete step one, which is to create your subscriber list.

The process starts off by asking you to create a list. Give it a name along the lines of '[your business name] Monthly Newsletter' both as the list name and the 'Default Subject' (don't worry if you change your mind later, you can change everything here or start a second list). Tick the boxes where it asks you if you want to be informed when people subscribe or unsubscribe and to give clients a choice as to the format of your emails.

Save your settings once you are done.

Next you will be asked to 'import contacts'. If you don't have permission from any of your contacts yet to send them regular mailings, you can skip this section. This next section assumes that you do have permission from your contact list to mail them.

There is currently no way to import contacts from your mail system directly. However, I have already made several mentions in the previous chapters regarding the use of CSV files for moving contact lists from one program to another. CSV files are also the easiest way to import information into MailChimp. Whichever program you are using to keep your contacts, use the 'export to CSV' function to save all of your contacts as a file.

If you have been following this book religiously, you may have all of your contacts in Nimble by now. If so, you should already have cleaned up your lists by merging duplicated entries, which will make your job in creating a 'clean list' on MailChimp that much easier.

To export your contacts from Nimble, go to the Contacts page of Nimble and tick the box above the first of your contacts. A link will come up just below it saying 'select all'. Then click on the link called 'Export' on the right hand side and select 'Export CSV'. Nimble will then compile a list of all your contacts which it will email to you as a zip file. Unzip the file and store it on your computer. You can view the contents of your CSV file by opening it up in Excel. In case you have any contacts listed for whom you don't have an email address, you can use Excel to quickly sort under the column which contains the email address for your contacts. This then makes it easy to delete all of the contacts without an email address at this stage. You can also delete all of the other columns on the CSV files which you won't need for your email list – leaving just their first name, last name and email address on the Excel sheet. Save a copy once you have done this.

Go back to MailChimp now. Browse for your CSV File on your computer and then upload it as per the instructions. If you cleaned up your list with Excel, then you should only see three columns now. If you uploaded a more 'raw' list, then you will need to delete any unwanted columns or describe what they are for.

Once this is done, click on the 'All done' button and MailChimp will begin importing all your contacts. This could take a fair while if you have quite a large list. You have the option of getting MailChimp to send you an email when it's finished processing. Now when you return to your dashboard and click on 'Lists' on the top menu, you will see the number of subscribers which you have added and can click on 'view list' to see the details of all of the subscribers there.

ADDING SUBSCRIPTION BOXES TO YOUR WEBSITE

The above is fine if you already have a list of contacts who have given permission for you to send them your newsletter, but what do you do if you don't have anyone who has given you permission yet? And what do you do about new contacts in the future who want to receive it (of which there will hopefully be a lot now that you are starting to get serious about your online marketing activities)? The answer to both questions is to add the facility for people to sign up to your newsletter to your website.

To do this, go back to your main dashboard. Right at the top, you will see that step two of 'Get Started With MailChimp in 3 Simple Steps' is called 'design signup forms'. Click on the button to access this menu.

If you know a little about web design, you can use all of the options to manually create a good looking form to add to your site. The basic form just asks for the visitors' email address, first name and last name. There are options available that you can use to ask for other information from visitors, but these three fields should be enough. The more information you ask from people, the more chance there is that they will think that it's too much trouble, or that they worry about giving too much confidential information about themselves, and so not fill it in. So before you ask them to give you more information, ask yourself whether you really need it.

If you really don't know anything about web design, don't worry because MailChimp makes it easy for you. If you click on the 'auto-design' button, MailChimp will check your website and create a form based upon the logo, colors and fonts that it finds there to make it consistent with the rest of your site. If you're not 100% happy with the results, click on the 'design it' tab where you can fine-tune the design to your satisfaction. As well as creating the main sign up page for your site, it will also generate the various different confirmation emails and 'thank you' pages that your visitors will see depending on what actions they take. You can check each of these individually but, once you are happy with the design on the main page, you will probably find that you don't need to make changes to any of the others. By using the HTML widget from Lujure or any of the other companies that offer you the facilities to create good looking Facebook Pages, you can also have your newsletter sign up form display on Facebook as well to get even more subscribers.

Once you're completely happy with the sign up form, click on the tab named 'share it'. Here you will see a box called 'HTML Link to Subscribe Form'. This contains the lines of code that you (or someone else who is building your site for you) will need to add to your website to make the newsletter sign up form appear on it.

This form is fine if you want to devote an entire page of your site to your newsletter sign up. In chapter 8, however, I spoke about adding a signup option together with the buttons for adding visitors to your social networks. To do this, click on the button called 'Create HTML code for a small subscribe form'.

Here you will see that you can add a much simpler sign up option which just asks for a visitor's email address, especially if you keep to the 'Super Slim Form'. Once you have changed any of the options, you then just need to copy and paste the code in the gray box into your site's HTML code.

CREATING EMAIL TEMPLATES

So now you should have a mailing list of some kind – maybe one with some contact addresses on there already – maybe one that's in the process of getting subscribers. But whether you have just one subscriber or 100,001, your mailing list is useless unless you send your subscribers something on a regular basis.

Before you start mailing out newsletters to your subscribers, take a while to create a good template for the email. If you're just going to send out a monthly email to all your subscribers, then you are only going to need to create one template. By keeping to a consistent design, it becomes your 'house style' and your readers will find it easier to read once they've seen the first couple. And why go to the trouble of reinventing the wheel every time you send a new one out?

To create a template, go to your main dashboard and select the third and final step of the 'Get Started' list by clicking on the 'create and send a campaign' button. You're probably not ready to send out a newsletter to your mailing list now but, don't worry, we're not going to mail anything to them just yet – you're just going to create a template. If you are of a nervous disposition, click on the 'set up a new list' and create a new list called 'Test Account' with just your own email address on it. Otherwise, you can click on the 'send to entire list' button – you'll get plenty of warnings before you accidentally send out a mailing to your entire list.

The next step is to give your campaign a name. You can just call it 'Template Setup' for now. You can leave all of the other fields alone for the moment.

Move on to Step 3, and now you are at the part of the process where you create your template. Click on the big button marked 'design genius' to make the process as simple as possible, then click on 'get started'.

The next step is to choose a 'header image'. MailChimp has quite a variety to choose from, so have a look through the categories to see if there is any that you like. Your newsletter will probably look more professional though if you can use your own logo as a header. If you have one, click on the 'upload your own image' button and then follow the instructions to upload one from your computer.

Once you have selected your header, move on to the next step. As was the case when you were setting up the template for your subscriber signup form, you can click on the 'get colors from my site' button to select colors and fonts that match your website.

Now move on to the third step, which is choosing your layout. Which of the layout options you choose is down to personal choice. Personally I like the 'right sidebar' option as it closely matches the design of most webpages, with links to social media already placed for you on the right hand side. If you do decide to use a template with links to your Facebook and Twitter profiles, you need to add the links to the relevant pages here because MailChimp won't automatically know them. Do this now so that they are part of the template and you won't have to remember to put them in each time.

Once you are happy with your template, click on 'save and then add content'. You will be asked to give a name to your template so that you can use it again.

Your template is now complete. It's best to keep it in its raw state like this so that you can use it for each of your future mailings. If you're not yet ready to send your first newsletter, click on the MailChimp logo in the top left corner of the page to head back to your dashboard.

CHOOSING YOUR CONTENT

You now have all of the raw elements of your email marketing campaign put together now – so what should you do with them? As I have already mentioned, the bedrock of an email marketing campaign is to send out a regular newsletter. How regular? I think that, for the average accounting firm, a monthly newsletter is going to be enough.

If you were running a nightclub with different events on each night, or a busy shop where you have new offers coming in every few days, then a monthly newsletter might not be regular enough to be of use to your clients. However, your existing clients and potential clients aren't going to change their accountants each month (hopefully!) so once a month should be sufficient. If you are absolutely bursting with things to tell people about – perhaps when you're in the middle of tax season - then it should be OK to email them every couple of weeks. But I would advise against emailing them more often than this. Most people are suffering from email overload these days and, if people think that you are emailing them too often to be useful, then they will be hitting the 'unsubscribe' link at the bottom of each email (which is mandatory under the CAN-SPAM legislation).

The ultimate goal of your newsletters should be to keep your company at the front of prospects' minds so that they remember you when they are next in the market for an accountant. It should also be another opportunity to remind potential clients about your Free Consultation offer.

So what should you include in your newsletter? If you have a special offer coming up, then this should definitely be your lead item on the newsletter. If you are going to come up with a special offer each month, then it's probably best to release the information on your newsletter first in order to give it added value, because emails have a greater impact than posting news to any of your social networks. You can post the same information to your social networks shortly after you have made your big announcement for the month in your newsletter. However, you don't want anyone who is subscribed to your newsletter and who is following you on your social networks as well to start ignoring your newsletters thinking that they have read all of your important information already.

As for the rest of the content for your newsletter, this should not be too difficult for you to come up with. If you have spent the previous month Tweeting on Twitter plus posting on Facebook and LinkedIn, you should have plenty of content to choose from by now. So it will just be a question of selecting your 'greatest hits' from the last four weeks to use as the content for your newsletter.

Go back over all of the content which you have generated since your last email to refresh your memory as to what created the biggest impact among your Friends and Followers. Now is probably a good time to check your Facebook Insights Analytics Dashboard as this will tell you, at a glance, which of your postings got the best reaction from your Fans in terms of the number of Likes and Comments. Make sure that the content is still relevant though – no matter how popular it might have been three weeks' ago, if it was something topical, then it might be old news by now.

Although I suggested that much of the news that you put out onto Twitter should be about local events, I would suggest that all of the content you put into your newsletters is either directly about your company and its activities or else professional news which would be of most use to potential clients so that it reinforces your position as being an expert on all accounting matters.

How much content should you put in your newsletter? As is the case with all online writing, less is always more. Think of your newsletter as the front page of your own newspaper. Make the first item on the newsletter your most important piece of news and then go down the page in descending order of importance. Probably four or five items are about as many as you are going to want to feature on the newsletter – any more than that and most people probably aren't going to get to the bottom of it. Probably even more so than while reading content on the Web, your readers are going to be scanning your emails rather than reading them word for word. Give your readers a descriptive headline for each news item so that they can quickly decide if they want to read more about it or not. Then just give them a couple of short paragraphs – just three or four short sentences in total – to give them a little more information so that they can understand the 'bare bones' of the piece, with a link to where they can read the full story. Wherever possible, make the links lead to one of your own pages, such as your Facebook business Page, if the full story is featured there rather than sending them to a site that you are not affiliated with. Long links can get broken on emails, so use a link shortener from your social dashboard like Seesmic Desktop 2 if you are using one, otherwise you can just go to **www.bitly.com** and get a shorter link from there.

It's probably best if you write your newsletter in Word first of all to check for spelling mistakes and to tweak it until you're happy with it before copying and pasting it straight into the template. This will mean that you then only need worry about the formatting.

With a little bit of attention in terms of deciding what to feature from all of the content you have generated across your social media campaigns over the last month, you should be able to come up with some highly useful and interesting information for each of your monthly newsletters. Your clients and potential new clients should come to value this, rather than simply hitting the 'delete' button or, worse still, unsubscribing.

SENDING YOUR NEWSLETTER

Now that you have your list, your template and your text all ready, it's time to actually send out your newsletter. Go back to your main dashboard and click on the big 'create campaign' button. You will have several options to choose from. Just select the 'regular ol' campaign' option.

Now you can continue with the exercise that you started when you created your template. Give your campaign a descriptive title such as 'January Newsletter'. The rest of the options you can probably leave as they are.

Click on 'next' and you should see the template which you designed earlier all ready and waiting for you. If you already created your content in Word, it should be a simple matter to now copy and paste the text inside your template. You should then spend a little time formatting it so that it's easy on the eye. You might find you also need to do a little editing to your text as well when you get to this stage, especially if you find that it's too long. Keep clicking on the 'popup preview' button to see how the finished email is going to look.

Once you are happy with the finished result, click the 'next' button once more.

So far you have just created the HTML version of your email. It should look professional and have a lot of impact. This should be the version that the majority of your recipients will see. However, not all email readers are able to display emails with a lot of formatting and graphics in them, especially if they are being read on a smartphone. For this reason, MailChimp also sends out a version of your email as Plain Text, which doesn't contain any of the pictures or formatting. The next step of the operation is to create this Plain Text version.

MailChimp will come up with some suggested text for the Plain Text version of your email but, if you have used one of the more advanced templates, chances are that the email copy will be filled with a load of junk. This is another reason why it is good to write your copy in Word first of all. Now you can just delete all of MailChimp's suggested text and simply replace it with the raw text which you paste in from Word. Click on the popup preview button and you'll see that it is now a lot cleaner and legible than the previous version. As you did with the HTML version, keep editing the text until you are completely happy with it and then click on 'next' again.

You will then be at the final stage of the operation, which will give you a summary of all of the options which you have chosen, with one last opportunity to make some changes before sending the email. Take advantage of this final chance to double check that you have everything right, as it really is your last chance now.

If you are absolutely sure that you don't want to make any more changes, you can go ahead and send out your first newsletter.

But wait a minute before you hit the big 'send now' button. Is now really the best time for you to send out your newsletter? Think about how you use email yourself. Do you come into work every Monday morning to find that your inbox is bursting with emails, some of them needing urgent answers? I certainly do, and so my solution to email overload is to immediately delete anything that is not absolutely vital so that I only have my important work emails to deal with. So, if you had sent me your newsletter at some time over the weekend, I would probably just delete it unread, even if the content would normally be of interest to me.

Compare this to if you had sent this to me, say, mid-afternoon on a Tuesday. By this time, I should have caught up with my weekend backlog and also everything that came in on Monday evening. I'll even have caught up on any emails that came in while I was away for lunch. Now emails are just trickling into my inbox and so I have time to read everything that comes through because I have less pressure on me for my time.

As a result, I recommend that you send your emails out on a midweek afternoon – a Tuesday, Wednesday or Thursday afternoon is ideal. Friday is not such a good day, because a lot of people will be trying to finish everything so that they have a clean inbox before the cycle starts all over again the following Monday.

So that you don't forget about sending your newsletter when it comes to the next available weekday afternoon, click on the blue 'schedule' button rather than the red 'send now' button. Now you can use the controls to set the exact time when the newsletter will be sent. Around 3.30pm would be an ideal time – just make sure that your time zone is correct, otherwise the time will be out. Click on 'schedule' and your campaign will be all ready to go as soon as it gets to the right time. You will receive an email from MailChimp summarizing the campaign once it has been sent.

MONITORING THE RESULTS

After you have sent out each newsletter, MailChimp monitors what your recipients do with it. The system checks exactly how many of your emails actually arrived in the recipients' inbox, how many of them actually opened it up to read it and how many just deleted it from their inboxes unopened.

MailChimp monitors the results of your email campaign in real time, so you will probably need to give it a day or two before you have meaningful results available, because not everyone checks their email accounts every five minutes. Once you have left it a while, go to the 'Reports' link at the top to bring up the relevant section and you should see the details of the campaign you recently sent out. Click on the 'view report' button to analyze the results of your campaign in detail.

You can now see a wealth of information about your campaign in front of you. The most important figure is the first one, which tells you how many recipients actually opened the email. As long as you specified which industry you are part of (Professional Services is probably the best choice) it will compare the results of your figures against other companies in your sector. At the time of writing, only around 18% of emails sent from companies in the Professional Services sector were opened and so, even if you think your open rates might look low, you could find that they are higher than can normally be expected.

The report also monitors how many people clicked on one or more of your links. Again, the industry average is only a little over 3%, so don't expect too many click-throughs from each email. You also get to see how many people unsubscribed from your list after receiving the email or, even worse, complained to MailChimp about the newsletter. 'Complaints' is an important figure to watch because, if you get too many of them, MailChimp could end up cancelling your account with them, which would be a major disaster. Providing that everyone on your list knew that they would be receiving your newsletter in advance though, there should be no reason for them to complain about it.

If you click on the 'view' button in the gray box called 'Recipients', you can bring up even more details. It tells you exactly who from your list did or did not open your email or clicked on a link, etc. Some important information here can be found under the 'Bounced' tab. This tells you if some of your emails didn't get through. 'Hard Bounces' mean that the email didn't get through at all; either the email address on your system was wrong to begin with or else the account has been closed. MailChimp automatically removes these addresses from future mailings. 'Soft Bounces' means that there was some problem in delivering the email – maybe their mailbox was full or their email service provider was down at the time.

MailChimp will continue to try and deliver the message over the next few days. After a while, it will mark the account as permanently dead and will remove the address as well.

You can't spot any trends emerging after sending just one newsletter but you should keep monitoring your reports after you have sent each one to check what is happening each time. By checking out the click-through rates and 'drilling down' to see which link was clicked each time, you should be able to determine what kind of articles are most interesting for your readers and which they have little interest in. If the percentage of people opening your emails tails off, then maybe you should think about changing the name of your email, or experiment with sending it on another day of the week.

In summary, MailChimp (or any other of the similar systems that I mentioned at the start of this chapter) is a powerfully effective tool for managing your newsletters. In this chapter, I have really only scratched the surface of what it is possible to do with the system – there's a huge amount of other possibilities and functionality that it offers. To some extent, using it just to send out your monthly newsletters is a little like using a sledgehammer to crack a nut.

If you are ever running any special promotions, then you can obviously use MailChimp to send out details to your subscribers in exactly the same way as you send out your newsletters. Make sure that you use a descriptive title for any special promotions that you run so that the recipients know that it is something different from your standard newsletters. Using the reports available to you, you can then see if it had a greater impact than your regular emails so that you can do something similar again after a suitable time period. Just be aware that, the more often you email your mailing list, the higher the chances that some of your subscribers will decide that they have had enough and unsubscribe.

Trying to explain all of the main functions of MailChimp in one short chapter was difficult because of all of the options available at each stage of the operation. Fortunately, however, MailChimp has a wealth of resources available on its site which will help you – both to better understand how to use the system and also how to get the most from your email campaign. You can find all of their resources at:

<u>**www.mailchimp.com/resources/**</u>

MailChimp also has its own 'Academy' where you can take part in online 'webinars' to learn how to get the most out of the system.

*   *   *

No matter which system you use for sending out your newsletters, it should definitely be an integral part of your marketing activity. It is a free, or low-cost, way of getting your most important messages in front of potential clients' eyeballs on a regular basis, even if they never return to your website again after their first visit.

> Email us **now** at <u>**accountant@informerbooks.com**</u> to get our **free weekly updates** in case there have been any changes to any of the information contained in this chapter since publication.

SEARCH ENGINE OPTIMIZATION

A s I will cover in more detail in the next chapter, Google sold more $20 billion worth of AdWords in 2011. Add some more for Bing (which sells ads for both Microsoft's Bing search engine and also Yahoo) and the other minor players and we can say that businesses spent around $25 billion buying advertising on search engines in 2011, with some Ad-Words costing over $50 per click.

However, Google says that only around 6% of visitors to its search engine click on the AdWords. The other 94% click on the normal (referred to as 'organic') results from Google, making these organic results 15 times more effective than AdWords.

Put all of this information together and what do we learn? We learn that top rankings for each business's top keywords are **insanely** valuable. It is probably the most useful promotion that it's possible to get from online marketing, because you know that a high proportion of the people making a search under these keywords are potential new clients. As a result, a top ranking on Google for the right keyword is probably the closest thing your business is ever going to get to a license to print money.

The problem though is that everyone who understands even the bare mini-mum about internet marketing knows this already and so nearly everyone is going to be fighting for that top spot – and there can be only one winner. As a result, the competition to get it is usually intense. Google and the other search engines are more aware than anyone as to how valuable these top spots are and the lengths that many people will go to in order to try and secure them for themselves. The search engine's ultimate goal though is to produce the best possible results for their users. If they don't, then their customers will start to use a competitor's search engine instead.

The result of this is similar to a constant game of chess going on. On one side you have website owners and agencies working for them who are trying to find ways of getting their sites to the top of the listings. On the other side, there are the search engines trying to stop people from unfairly manipulating the search results to get them. No sooner have website owners found a new way of exploiting the system than the search engines come up with a way of closing the loopholes by changing the algorithms which generate the rankings and the cycle starts all over again.

Because of the intense nature of this competition on an ever-moving playing field, a huge industry has grown up around Search Engine Optimization (SEO for short). Those people who understand how the system works and how to get sites to the top of the listings for their chosen keywords can almost name their price. They do earn their money though, as there is a huge amount to learn in order to master the system and they need to keep on learning new tricks all the time as the search engines keep changing their algorithms.

Before you get too depressed about the intense amount of competition and the difficulty of learning the fine art of SEO, I do have some good news for you. If your business was trying to get your customers to buy a system about how to 'MAKE MONEY ONLINE!' you would be out of luck. In this case, you would have literally hundreds of millions of competitors to fight against from all around the world and they would all be motivated to fight for the top spot because their entire business is based online.

With your business, however, as I mentioned in the introduction, 99.99% of the online population is of no interest to you whatsoever because you are only interested in those internet users who are in your local area. You don't need to try and become the top ranked site for searches on the keyword, 'accountant' where you are up against over 100 million competitors. Instead you only need to compete against other accountants in your area for the 'accountant yourtown' keyword. Whether you are in a large city like New York or London, or in a small town in the middle of nowhere, will have a major bearing on how much competition you will have for the top listing, but at least you should have whittled the competition down to a few million.

You're probably thinking that odds of several million to one are still not looking that great. But this is because Google is so brilliant at indexing sites. That 'several million' will include pretty much every site on the entire Internet which mentions both the words 'accountant' and 'your town'.

Have a look at the different pages on Google – by the time you're on page 10 or page 20, you'll see that most of the pages which are linked are not potential competitors of yours – they are mostly just obscure pages of obscure sites already. And you still haven't gotten out of the top 200 links from all of those millions yet.

Despite my reassurances, you might still be thinking, "It's just too hard and there's just too little chance of getting a good ranking". Well, guess what? That's probably what 90% of your competitors thought as well, and so they never did anything at all – not even the basics – to try and optimize their sites so as to appear high in the rankings. This means that, even if you just do the basic elements needed for SEO, you should still be ahead of your competitors – even if you only spend a couple of hours on the job.

Have I talked you into giving it a shot now? If so, here's how to do it.

ON-SITE OPTIMIZATION

There are two elements to any SEO campaign: 'On-site Optimization', which covers everything that you do on your own site to make it as attractive as possible to the search engines, and' Off-site Optimization', which covers links coming into your site which you can try and influence, but are not directly under your control.

On-site optimization is the easier of the two, and the best place to start.

As clever as Google's system is, it is only as good as the information that it finds the websites which it indexes. If you never mention the words 'accountant' and 'yourtown' on the same page, it's going to struggle to realize that this is what your site is all about, which means you need to make sure that it knows. There are several ways of doing this.

First of all, if you have not done so already, you need to choose the keywords you are going to optimize for. I covered the basics of this in chapter 2 and explain more advanced methods of learning them in chapter 13. For now, I'm assuming that you are going to optimize for 'accountant yourtown' and, if you are in the US, 'CPA yourtown' as well.

Domain Name

As I mentioned in chapter 8, one of the easiest and most effective ways of optimizing your site is by naming it after your main keyword phrase, preferably with a hyphen between the keywords so that the search engines are easily able to separate the words. A domain name such as **www.yourtown-accountant.com** or **www.accountant-yourtown.com** would be ideal. Chances are that someone has already grabbed these though, so you might need to get a little creative. Even better would be **www.cpa-accountant-yourtown.com** (although it's getting tricky to type now) or **www.yourtown-accountants.com** (plural) or you can try it without the hyphens. Google is clever enough to split the words up now – other search engines might not be though.

Web Page Title

The title of your webpage is what is shown at the top of your browser (if you are using Internet Explorer). More importantly, it is also the title of your listing on the search engine results page (or SERP for short). It is absolutely vital that this contains all of your keywords and as little else as possible. Something like this:

John Smith, CPA – Accountant Yourtown, TX, USA

It's important to get your main keywords as close to one another as possible; preferably adjacent. Try and vary the order on the different pages of your site so some say 'Accountant Yourtown' and others say 'Yourtown Accountant' in case the person searching uses the keywords the other way around.

Most of the website creation software packages will make it easy to choose the title of each webpage. If for some reason though it doesn't and you need to go into the HTML to change it, you will find it near the top of the code as follows:

```
<TITLE> Write the page's title here </TITLE>
```

Page Heading

This one is a bit technical and is also optional, so if you have no idea about the basics of HTML, then better just to skip this point.

HTML offers the facility to put in different categories of headings, in the same way that Microsoft Word does (although most people don't bother). H1 is the main heading and then there are lesser headings that go all the way down to H6. Because H1 should refer to the main subject of the webpage containing the header, it's one of the ways search engines categorize the content. As a result, it's a good idea to put your main keyword as the heading of the page. In your HTML code, it would look like this:

```
<H1> Yourtown Accountant </H1>
```

It sounds easy enough, but there are two problems with this. The first is that it could look out of context with the rest of your text and so might spoil the beautiful prose which you have written.

The second problem is that anything written as an H1 header comes out to be absolutely enormous on the page compared to all of your other text and so usually ends up looking both ridiculous and amateur. There is a way around this though. If your website uses CSS (Cascading Style Sheets), then you can set the font size of your H1 tags so that it is the same size as, or just slightly larger than, the rest of your text.

If you just read this section and have absolutely no clue what I was talking about, then don't worry. Either mention it when you are asking someone to build a website for you, or simply ignore it altogether. Most sites don't bother with this step at all – it's just a little more icing on the cake.

Body Copy

What **is** important though is to make sure that your keywords are included in the main copy of your page – and preferably more than once. Ever since the first search engines were introduced, there has been great debate amongst SEO professionals as to exactly how many times you should repeat your keywords and where they are placed, but no one has ever cracked Google's formula exactly (and if they did, it wouldn't take long before Google changed it again anyway). As a result, it's not worth fretting over the details too much as long as you take the big picture into account.

Most important is to get your keywords as early as possible in your copy and it doesn't get much better than being in the first sentence of your text, e.g.

Looking for an accountant in yourtown? John Smith CPA has been providing accounting services to yourtown since 199X …

It's not so difficult but, if you cast your mind back to my introduction to copywriting, you'll see that it goes contrary to my advice for writing good copy, which is to focus on the potential client (you) rather than yourself (I or we). It is a bit of a trade off to start out with a 'me'-focused statement on your home page but at least it's just the first line. Once you have your keywords out of the way here, you can follow the good copywriting rules by making the rest of your copy mostly 'you' focused.

It's also a good idea to make your main keyword bold the first time you use it, as in, "Looking for an **accountant in yourtown**?" Don't worry about the 'in' that separates the two words in your keyphrase – the search engines ignore most prepositions and conjunctions. You only need to bold the first instance of your keywords – there isn't much benefit in bolding all of the others.

If you followed my advice in chapter 8, your home page should only contain perhaps three or four short paragraphs of copy to introduce your company to anyone visiting your site. In this case, I would recommend your mentioning your key phrase just once more during the copy – somewhere near the end of it, in order that the search engines know that the page is definitely all about your keyword. If your copy is a bit longer, mention it a third time as well – but that should be enough.

When it comes to optimizing for search engines, the expression 'everything in moderation' is a good one to follow. If you mentioned your keyword in every single sentence, then not only would your text be horrible for anyone to read, but the search engines will also spot that you are using the expression in an unnatural way. As a punishment for trying to cheat them, they will mark your site down. They might even delist your site completely from their pages, which would be a disaster. So don't think that you've come up with any clever tricks that the search engines won't have thought of – they will have done.

Finally, it's good to mention your keyword one last time on your home page – ideally in the footer (which hardly anyone is going to read anyway). You can finish off the footer for each of your pages with a sentence along the lines of 'John Smith CPA – yourtown accountant'. You can also include your address and phone number there so there is some use to it as well.

Image Tags

Another way of letting the search engines know that they have found what they are looking for is through the names that you give to the images on your page. As pictures don't 'sell' as well as words do, you probably won't be using a lot of them. But you should try and get your best keywords into those images that you do use, even if it is just to put in a name to the main image that you have on every page of your site (whether it's the tax form and calculator image or the nice local landscape image that I suggested in chapter 8).

There are two ways to do this, and you should do both.

The first is that you should name the image after your keyword rather than keep it as whatever file name it came as. So instead of the picture staying as something like **main-image.jpg**, change it to **accountant-yourtown.jpg** before you even upload it onto your site.

In addition, it is recommended that every image has an 'ALT-tag'. This is a description of the picture that every website should contain. Probably the only time you will have seen this is if a picture didn't load properly while you were browsing. There are some browsers, however, that don't display pictures at all and they are used by the blind in special browsers that speak the content of websites. Again, whenever you are asked to give an 'ALT-tag' for an image, use your keyword as the description.

The finished result should look like this in your HTML:

```
<img src="images/yourtown-accountant.jpg"
width="100" height="100"
alt="Yourtown Accountant" />
```

This is another optional one which is not going to add a huge amount to the page's attractiveness to search engines, but it takes only seconds to implement if you know what you're doing. If not, it's another step you can ignore without losing any sleep over. One additional tiny benefit of including your keyword here is that if, for some strange reason, someone is searching for an accountant in your town using Google Image Search, you should be at the top of the pile!

Meta Tags

Meta Tags is another optional extra area – in fact it's such an optional extra that it definitely **won't** increase your rankings on Google. So why bother? The main advantage of using Meta Tags is that many search engines (including Google) uses the text they find in Meta Tags as the description of your site underneath the link on the SERP. This is useful because you get to write exactly the copy that visitors to Google will read about your company before they (hopefully) click on the link. If you don't write it, Google will take the copy from your website and it might not be exactly how you would like it to be because it could be... broken up ... like this.

Google displays 20-25 words here so it's best to aim for around 20 to make sure that the sentence isn't cut off. Perhaps you can write something along the lines of:

John Smith, CPA is a full-service accountant offering tax advice to businesses in yourtown and the surrounding area of yourstate.

As well as the description, the Meta Tags also gives you the chance of listing your keywords. Google doesn't use these at all, but there might be some small search engines that do, so there's no harm in putting them in. List around a dozen or so and separate them with commas, e.g.:

cpa, accountant, yourtown, yourstate, ny, usa, tax, payroll, accounting, services, business, irs, taxes, rebate, refund

There is also an 'Author' tag which you can use as well although, again, there is not so much benefit.

A relative newcomer on the Tag scene is the Geo-Tag, which tells search engines exactly where your business is located. Although Google doesn't use this Tag, it has been said that Bing does and, with the rapid increase in people using smartphones to access the Internet, it could increase in importance over time. As a result, I think that it is well worth spending the couple of minutes it will take you to add this data to your header.

To create your Geo-Tag, head over to **www.geo-tag.de**. Write your full address in the box at the top of the page and click on the 'Address Search' button. Your location should now come up as a pin on a Google Map. Zoom in on the map to check that the pin is positioned exactly where it should be.

Your code has now been generated in the blue box below. You just need to copy the code into your header after the others.

If you put all of the above together, then you should end up with HTML code which looks like the following:

```
<meta name="description" content=" John Smith,
CPA is a full-service accountant offering tax
advice to businesses in yourtown and the sur-
rounding area of yourstate.">

<meta name="keywords" content=" cpa, accountant,
yourtown, yourstate, ny, usa, tax, payroll, ac-
counting, services, business, irs, taxes, re-
bate, refund">

<meta name="author" content="John Smith, CPA">

<meta name="geo.region" content="US-DC" />

<meta name="geo.placename" content="Washington"
/>

<meta name="geo.position" con-
tent="38.897678;-77.036517" />

<meta name="ICBM" content="38.897678, -77.036517"
/>
```

Other Pages

Google and other search engines love home pages. If you look through the list of webpages that come up in your local search for your best keyword, chances are that the first few results are only going to consist of home pages. This is because the search engines know that, although sites can have an infinite number of other pages, they can only have one home page and so the site owners can only optimize them for one major keyword.

But this doesn't mean that you should completely forget about all of the other pages on your site. Google looks at the other pages on your site to check the theme. If your home page was perfectly optimized for 'accountant yourtown' but the rest of your site was about selling Viagra, you would definitely be penalized in a big way.

Your other pages are also great ways to optimize individual pages for keywords of lesser importance. It is really easy to do this if, rather than having one page listing all of your services, you make a short page for each. The process is exactly the same as the one that you went through to optimize your home page. Just remember to add the name of yourtown to every page.

Let's take the example of 'payroll services'. Here are the actions that you would need to take:

(a) Make the name of the page **payroll-services.html** so that its full web address would be something like:

> **www.accountant-yourtown/payroll-services.html**

(b) Add the keyword to your page title, e.g.:

> John Smith, CPA – Accounting & Payroll Services in Yourtown

(c) (Optional) Use the H1 tags to make Payroll Services the Heading of the page (which is actually a perfectly logical heading to have on a page that's all about Payroll Services.

(d) Start off your copy by mentioning Payroll Services again (preferably bolded) and close to the name of yourtown, e.g.:

***Payroll services** provided by John Smith CPA allow businesses in yourtown to forget about the time and effort needed to prepare their employees' monthly payroll.*

Are you spending hours at the end of each month working out your company's payroll when your time could be better spend providing services to your clients?

Notice how I slipped in another 'payroll' and 'services' into the second sentence and also went back to concentrating on the client and how your practice can solve their problems? By optimizing this page for 'Payroll Services', anyone who has made a search under 'payroll services yourtown' will be arriving on your site at this page rather than your home page. As a result, this page needs to sell the visitor on your payroll services as much as your home page needs to sell them on your general services. Your client has targeted needs to be making such a narrow search and so is an excellent prospect. Don't make them have to visit the rest of your site to get all the information they need. Remember AIDA from the copywriting course in chapter 2? You got the prospect's **Attention** from the search engine listing; you got their **Interest** from your headline that tells them that Payroll Services are one of your specialties. If your copy is well written, then they should now **Desire** your services to take away the frustrations they feel at trying to find time for take care of the Payroll Services. So all that's needed now is some Action:

Fill in our Contact Form now for your Free Consultation and let us take care of your Payroll headaches from now on.

Done right, and it could be the quickest sale you've ever made!

Once again, keep the keyword density in mind when you are writing the copy – one mention every four sentences is about right. On your footer, you can mention it one last time – "John Smith, CPA – accounting and payroll services in yourtown, yourstate."

> (e) If you have any images on this page apart from your main header, give it the name **payroll-services-yourtown.jpg** and an ALT-tag of "Payroll Services in Yourtown"

> (f) In the description Meta-Tag, make sure that the words 'Payroll Services' and yourtown are included

Go through the same exercise for every single one of the services that your company offers. Yes, it's quite a lot of work to do if you offer twenty different services, but you only ever need do it once. And, **because** it's such a lot of work, very few of your competitors are going to be bothered to go through the exercise. This means that you have a good chance of ending up on the first page of Google for your other keywords, even if the competition is simply too great for your home page to rank in the top spot for your main keyword.

OK, so the amount of searches that people make for 'payroll services yourtown' may not be anywhere near the amount of people searching for 'accountant yourtown' but, if you have twenty different pages all high up the rankings for twenty different keywords, taken together they should be bringing you a lot of potential new clients. And they will be good prospects as well, because they have a specific problem that they need solving.

Maybe you have read through all of the above and your head is hurting. If it all sounds horribly complicated then, don't worry – it's not just you – it **is** pretty complicated. Otherwise the experts wouldn't be charging thousands of dollars to do it for you.

Maybe it would make more sense with a few examples. To check out examples of those people who are doing it right, make a search under the keywords you are optimizing for – 'accountant yourtown'. The first three to five sites you see listed are your competitors – the companies that you are going to have to beat if you are going to gain the top spot. As you check each of your high ranking competitors' sites, you should see that they follow most of the rules that I have outlined in this section. Take a look at their titles, the amount of times they mention the keywords in their body copy and their Meta-Tags (which you can find by using the 'View Source' option on your browser. They might also use H1 tags and ALT tags but, as I said, this was far from being essential and only has the most minor impact on the rankings.

You'll see that a lot, if not all, of the top ranked sites get all the above right and their optimization methods might give you some hints as to how you can better tweak your own page. Don't make the mistake of thinking the top ranking site is 'perfect', however, and try to copy it slavishly.

While going through some of these sites though, you might find that one or more of the top ranking sites seems to follow absolutely none of these rules. So how on earth did they get to be there if they haven't even done the basics of search engine optimization?

Unfortunately, you still have quite a bit of work left to do if you want a crack at the top spot on the search engines - I did warn you that this wasn't going to be easy! Despite your hard work to date on making sure that the search engines know that your home page (and the other pages on your site) contains exactly the sort of content that people searching for that particular keyword are looking for, the search engines have other criteria that they base their rankings upon. And these criteria are a lot harder to manipulate than tweaking a few words on your website.

Which leads us to the second stage of the operation …

OFF-SITE OPTIMIZATION

Were you online in 1998? If so, you were probably finding content using Yahoo! (which was mainly a human-moderated directory back in those days) or maybe Excite, Infoseek, Lycos or AltaVista. Maybe you've forgotten over the mists of time, but those search engines really weren't very good at finding exactly what you were looking for. This was because they used simple algorithms that were fairly easy for the first generation of search engine optimizers to break down. This resulted in the SEO experts being able to manipulate the results fairly easily, using methods only slightly more advanced than those I have gone through in the first half of this chapter.

Google changed everything when they launched their search engine in 1999 though. Their new search engine was so successful – so incredibly good at finding what people were looking for – that apart from Yahoo!, all of the other search engines I mentioned above were tossed onto the garbage heap within a couple of years.

So how did Google get to dominate the search engine market so quickly? By offering a vastly superior product. But why was it so vastly superior to all of the other search engines around at that time?

The complete answer to this question would take the rest of the book to answer and would still contain holes that Google want to hide from the public. The basic answer to the question, however, is that their site contains an algorithm which assigns each page on the Internet with a score, which it calls a 'PageRank'.

When a site is first launched, it has a PageRank of 0 because it has zero influence on the rest of the Internet. At the opposite end of the scale, Google itself and Facebook have the maximum scores of 10. Everything else on the Internet is somewhere in-between. The main influencers on PageRank are the amount of visitors a page is already getting, the amount of links going to that site and, more importantly, the quality of the links going to that site.

Let me give you an example. Let's assume that our old friend John Smith, CPA has launched a new website. The pages are completely optimized as per the first half of this chapter. Unless his competitors' sites were really bad or he was the only accountant in his town, it's unlikely that his site would get inside the top 30. Then he gets ten links to his site, but they are from only minor sources – his daughter's blog, the local church, his own Twitter and LinkedIn accounts – none of which many people see. Maybe by now, he's getting in the Top 20. But then John Smith is involved in a major scandal – one of his clients is a Presidential candidate who was found to have embezzled millions of dollars of party funds and the Presidential candidate blames John Smith for it. Suddenly, John's website is linked to by every major news website in the world – the BBC, CNN, New York Times, Wall Street Journal, Der Spiegel – they all put in a link to the website of "John Smith, CPA – the yourtown accountant under investigation". With dozens of huge PageRank 8 or 9 websites linking to John Smith's site, his own website's PageRank would increase rapidly and his site would almost certainly be number one shortly afterwards for his keyword (although for all the wrong reasons, obviously!)

So this is why "off-site optimization" is so important in order to rank at the top of the SERPs. Each link to your site can be looked upon as a vote for its value – but not in a 'one man; one vote' completely democratic fashion. For Google, the Internet is an oligarchy where the most popular sites' votes are worth much more than those of your daughter's blog.

What this means is that, chances are that your competitors' sites which are occupying the top spots of the SERPs for your best keywords have a lot of links going into them. No matter how well your own website is optimized, if you can't match or beat them on incoming links, then you're not going to beat them to the top of the search engines.

I can understand now if you are ready to give up the whole search engine optimization plan in frustration. But wait a moment – you **can** beat your competitors with a little time and application – together with a certain amount of industrial espionage!

But how exactly? Some 'internet marketing gurus' will try and charge you $50 for the answer to that question - but it's actually quite simple. You just need to find out what links your competitors at the top of the SERPs have pointing to their sites and get the same links pointing to yours.

Here are the steps you need to take in order to do it:

Identify where your competitors links' are coming from

The first step of the exercise is to get a list of all of the sites which link to the one that you want to check up on. The best free place to find this information is at the following link:

www.backlinkwatch.com

Type in the address of the website you want to check out and then click on the 'Check Backlinks' button. If the website that you are checking out has a lot of incoming links, it might take a while to generate the full list. Once it has finished, however, you should see a list of the most important websites which contain links to the site which you are checking upon.

Try and get your links on that page too

Click on each of the links listed on the page which Backlink Watch is showing to bring up each page linking to your competitor's site. You should find the link somewhere on this page. Ask yourself what type of page this is. What did your competitor have to do in order to get a link onto this page?

Sometimes the link will be from some kind of directory which anyone can sign up to for free. You should definitely sign up to those as well. Sometimes it will be links from the owner's LinkedIn account or Twitter page – you can do that as well (from your account at least – not your competitors'!)

Sometimes you might see links coming in from pages that don't have some sort of automated sign up form attached. Ask yourself why that site would link to your competitor. What other links are contained on that page? Would your site fit in there as well? If so, find the contact information for the site owner and ask them if they wouldn't mind adding your site details as well.

Sometimes people will be happy to provide you with a free link back to your site. On other occasions though, site owners will be trying to increase their own visibility on the search engines and so will want you to link back to them in return. Check to see if your competitors have a page on their sites for 'Links' or 'Recommended Sites', etc. If they do, then you are going to need one as well.

If you do decide that you need a Links page, then you don't need to heavily promote it on your site. Don't make the link to the page part of your main navigation tabs. It's not that important and you really don't particularly want your potential clients to head over to check the list out. As a result, you need just put in a small link on the footer of your website along with the links to your Privacy Policy and Terms & Conditions if you have them (hardly anyone bothers to click on these either). On this new Links page, you should place links to the sites you want to trade with. In case you end up making a lot of trades, divide the page up into several sub-pages, none of which has more than 25 links on them as otherwise the search engines can penalize these pages for being 'link farms'.

You should always put a link to the site you want to trade with on your site **before** you ask them to return the favor and put in a link to yours. Once the link is live, write them a polite email saying that you found their site to be useful (or some other comment that flatters them a little) and that you have added a link to their site from yours. Give them the address of the webpage where it can be found. Ask them if they are happy with the link you gave to them or if they would like to make some changes. Finally, ask them if they would be prepared to return the favor by linking back to you from their Links page. Include the copy and link which you would like them to use.

As you will have chosen the website carefully – and they are already show-ing your competitor's link - the majority of site owners should be happy to oblige. Some of them might not do it, however. Wait around a month to see if they get around to it. If they don't, then delete the link which you gave them – why should you continue to help their marketing activities if they aren't prepared to reciprocate!?

With some websites, you might find that they don't want reciprocal links back to them in return for giving you a link – they want cold, hard cash. Don't dismiss this totally out of hand – after all, your competitor obviously thought it was worth it or else their link wouldn't be there. Before you part with any cash though, check how important the page that you are offered a link from is going to be.

Remember Google's PageRank which I mentioned earlier – the 0-10 rank-ing as to how important they consider a webpage to be? It's possible to check on the PageRank of any webpage on. You can do this if you have the Google Toolbar installed on Internet Explorer, or plugins for the Chrome or Firefox browsers. Alternatively you can check the ranking of any site from sites such as **www.checkpagerank.net**.

Use one of these tools to find out the PageRank of any site that wants some money off you. If the PageRank is just 1 or 2, then it's probably not worth bothering with. If it's 3 or 4, then it might be worth a token amount like $5-10. If it's 5 or more, then it will bring you some real benefit and so it could be worth your paying $20, $30 or more for a link like this. Only you can decide if you can afford this kind of investment though. If you have no budget at the moment to buy links like this, just concentrate on the free ones.

Sometimes you will realize, however, that you are not going to be able to get a link with a particular website, even for money. But it can give you ideas as to where you can find other useful sites to link to you. Maybe your competitor has links from several of the sites belonging to clients of theirs? You won't be able to get a link from these particular sites, but you could look through sites belonging to your own clients to see if it looks likely that some of them might agree to trade links with you.

Maybe your competitors are members of some local organizations that you are not a member of. Are you a member of some different organizations though? Maybe you could swap links with them instead.

Sometimes though, you are just going to have to accept the fact that you are not going to be able to get a link from the same site as your competitor. Maybe your competitor who occupies the top spot is a massive company with hundreds of employees covering a huge area. Maybe they have a massive marketing budget which is more than your entire turnover for the year, which means they were able to afford to pay good money to advertise on these sites. In this case, you are just going to have to accept that you are not going to be able to get the top spot.

However, you still shouldn't give up faced with such huge competition. Big companies usually charge high prices and a lot of people see them as being faceless, so quite a few potential clients are going to carry on searching past the big company onto the second listing, which could well be yours.

Once you have performed this exercise on your competitor who is at the top of the SERPs, go through the entire process once more for your competitor who comes second on the list, then the third, then the fourth, etc. Chances are that the different high ranking sites will be getting their links from completely different sources. This gives you a chance to beat the top ranking site even if you are unable to get links from all of the same sources as them. Maybe the top ranking site has 500 incoming links going into their site, but you're only able to copy 200 of them. If you were able to copy another 200 links from the second ranked site and another 200 links from the third ranking site though – all different – then you should eventually get to the top spot (assuming all of the links are from sites with similar PageRanks).

Write your links correctly

As well as the PageRank of the site which is linking to you, Google also pays close attention to the words used for the link to your site. The power of this can be seen from the fact that, from 2003 to 2007, the keyword 'miserable failure' on Google led to George Bush's profile at the **www.whitehouse.gov** website. How did this happen? Thousands of pranksters littered the Internet with links for 'miserable failure' pointing to this page, which resulted in the page bubbling to the top of the rankings for that keyword.

Although Google put a stop to this practice (known as Google Bombing) in 2007, the importance of the words used in the link can be seen if you make a search under 'click here'. This phrase links to the download page for Adobe's Reader even though the words 'click here' don't appear on that page at all. This is purely because there are so many websites containing PDF files that invite their users to '**click here** to download Adobe Reader to read PDF files'.

What this means is that, the most effective link back to your website is going to be one that has your keyword as being clickable.

To give a couple of examples:

John Smith, CPA – **Yourtown Accountant**

John Smith, CPA, is an accountant who covers Yourtown and the surrounding areas.

In the above examples, the first one where the keyword is clickable is going to be a lot more use than the second one where John Smith's name contained the link, even if that version seems to be more logical.

In many cases, you won't have as much flexibility for choosing exactly how the link appears. All links are valuable – but this is the optimum way of making the links if you have the option.

Learn to be a little patient!

As the saying goes, Rome wasn't built in a day – and nor is a site that appears at the top (or very near the top) of the search engine rankings. It is going to take time before you see the results of your hard work – the exact amount of time will depend on how good your competitors are. If you have a fairly well optimized site, it should appear in the search engine rankings after just a few days or weeks. You can find out where you rank on Google's SERPs through checking your Google Webmaster Tools results, which I mentioned in chapter 9.

Although it's nice to now see that you rank fiftieth on the results, being fiftieth is not much different from being the millionth – you aren't going to see much, if any, traffic coming from the listing. Unless you're on the first page of Google, you're unlikely to see much of a result at all.

A top ten listing should not be too hard to get if you follow the advice above, but it will not happen overnight. Google only makes a major reshuffle of its listings once every month in any case.

Another reason for being patient is that you could end up getting penalized or blacklisted if you obtain too many links too quickly. Normally a new site would go live with no links for a while and then slowly start to attract a few. Your competitors' sites have probably built their links up over a period of a decade or more. Google is going to get suspicious if it lists your site one day and, in less than a week, you have 100 links going to it.

So rather than spending one weekend analyzing hundreds of your competitors' links and trying to copy them all, just do it a little at a time – 5 links per day is a reasonable target to go for. The other advantage of taking it slowly but surely is that you'll know when to stop. If that wonderful day comes when you open up Google and find that your site is number one, you'll know that you've done enough (I think that you'll deserve to throw a party if that day ever arrives!).

Automating the Process

If you are serious about trying to get to the top of the search engine rankings and want to employ the methods that I have described above, but you're worried that it's just going to take more time than you will have available, it is possible to automate part of the process in order to save time – by using some of the software that the professionals use.

There are many different options available, which all follow the same broad methods that I described above for checking your competitors' links and copying the process. Here are four which receive good reviews from users:

Traffic Travis – www.traffictravis.com – The basic version of this software is free and so it is a good starting point. The Pro version currently costs $97.

SEO Elite – www.seoelite.com – Currently selling for $197, with several different bonuses thrown in.

SEO Power Suite Professional – www.link-assistant.com - $249 currently. Used by several Fortune 500 companies and guarantees Top 10 positions.

Internet Business Promoter – www.ibusinesspromoter.com - Also $249. Also offers a Top 10 guarantee and is used by many blue chips.

Only you can decide whether it is worth investing in such expensive software. If you're in a relatively small town where your top ranking competitors have just a few hundred links, you probably don't need such 'industrial strength' tools to get high up on the rankings. If you are handling the marketing for a large practice in a major city though with some organized and well-entrenched competitors, then it could be well worth the investment. Even $249 is a small price to pay to ensure that your site ranks highly on the search engines.

DOMINATING THE RESULTS PAGES

So far in this chapter, I've probably given you the impression that search engine optimization is a pure battle between you and every other accounting company in your town for complete dominance – the Olympic Games of internet marketing where the gold medal winner gets the front covers, the multi-million dollar advertising contract with Nike, meets the President and becomes an instant celebrity; the silver and bronze winners get some congratulatory pats on the back and their pictures in the local paper, while all of the other participants just get commiserations and hopes that they have 'better luck next time'.

Fortunately, search engine optimization is not quite as black and white as that. There are other ways that you can get some good business from the search engines, even if you follow none of the advice above for optimizing your pages or seeking out all your competitors' links and copying them.

Take a look at the first page of Google for your keywords. It is not just a list of ten of your biggest competitors listed – there's a lot more on that page than that.

First of all there are the Google AdWords. This is a big subject and a big opportunity for any business that wants fast results (and is prepared to pay handsomely for them). I cover AdWords in depth in chapter 13.

Also at, or near, the top of the results there is probably a map of your town and links to 'Places for accountants near Yourtown'. Although this map does not always appear in searches for smaller towns, again this is a massive opportunity for you (a free one as well) which I cover in detail in the next chapter.

Then there are what are known as the ten 'organic results'. If your search engine optimization activities are successful, this is where your listing will appear along with the other accounting companies which you are competing against.

However, when you go through all ten listings one by one, you will probably find that not every single one of these listings are for accounting companies like yours. Some of the listings – maybe even **most** of the listings – will be for directories and not competing businesses. While these sites are your competitors when it comes to topping the rankings, they can also be your allies in terms of sending you through some good prospects.

Take a look at all of these listings that make the first page of Google. They will probably just consist of links to other accounting companies similar to yours. Many of them will probably list you for free if you ask. If this is the case, you most definitely want to get yourself listed on there. I explain the process in the following chapter.

As well as the regular listings, they are almost certainly likely to have 'Premium Listings', 'Featured Listings' or 'Sponsored Listings'. Although the names might be different, the principle will be identical. If you want to appear at the top of their page, then you are going to have to pay for the privilege.

It's worth finding out how much it would cost you to advertise your business in one of these top spots because it could be a relatively low-cost method of finding potential new clients. If you have not used AdWords before, then it may come as a shock to you to learn how much it is going to cost you for each person coming through to your site from one of your AdWords. Although advertising on these listing sites gives you no guarantees as to how many visitors you will be getting from such sources, usually you don't need to get many to make the advertising pay for itself.

There are other advantages of being here as well. If these directory pages are ranking so highly, it will mean that they have high PageRanks (it is a good idea to check exactly what their PageRank is using the method I described earlier). This means that a listing here is going to help your own ranking as it's another valuable 'vote' for your site.

The second advantage is that advertising in these directories can get you some quick results. Pay for an ad and you should be getting visitors in a day or two, as opposed to the long wait that you will probably have before your search engine optimization strategy starts to pay off with a top three listing.

The final advantage is that it increases the frequency of your message. As you know, employing a new accounting firm is not an impulse decision – it's a big step for a client to take and clients are likely to conduct a lot of research before they even make the initial contact to set up a first meeting. Even if you get the top ranking on Google, chances are that potential clients are not going to simply decide that they've found who they're looking for and give you a call without checking out any of your competitors. Advertising simply doesn't work like that – customers need to be exposed to an advertising message several times before they start to gain confidence in a company (some marketing gurus say that three is the magic number; others say that it's seven). If the potential client goes through all of the top ten listings on the search page, finds half of them are directories with your company's name at the top, plus your own company's listing, by the end of the customer's research, you will have made a much greater impact than even the company which has the top listing.

I have used this 'results page dominance' strategy to great effect with several local businesses. In one case, I could only get up to the #3 position for my main keyword as the business was quite new and there were a couple of directories taking the top two positions which had a lot of links coming into them. My solution was to buy the best advertising position available on both of them. I was also running AdWords which, even if clients didn't click on them, introduced them to the name of my business. Potential clients working their way down the organic search results saw my company's name a couple of times as featured advertiser on the two listing sites so that, by the time they got to my own listing in the #3 position, it was already the fourth time they had come across my company and my advertising message. In total, the two ads on the directory cost me less than $500 for a year. It turned out to be a small price to pay for the huge amount of business I was able to bring in via the search engines.

So it is definitely worth checking out every single link on the first page of Google to see if it is going to be possible for you to dominate the page as well through advertising on all of the directories linked from there. It could end up being a much better investment for you than buying Ad-Words.

You are only going to be able to find out the value of these directory listings by closely monitoring their effectiveness though, and this is why it is important to have Google Analytics running on your site, as I described in chapter 9. If you are running Google Analytics, you will be able to see exactly how many visitors to your site you received by advertising in these directories. By dividing the monthly cost of the advertising by the amount of visitors during that period, you can work out the average cost of acquiring each one. Compare this price to the amount that you are spending per visitor with Google AdWords to see how good or bad a deal it is.

For this reason, it is better not to sign up for too long a period with these directories if possible (although many of them will only sell an advertising position for a minimum twelve months). If you get the option though, take a three month trial first of all. One month is going to be too short a period for a consistent pattern to emerge.

OTHER SEARCH ENGINES

In this chapter, I have used the words 'Google' and 'search engine' to mean pretty much the same thing. With hindsight though, this is probably rather 'brandist' of me to totally ignore the other search engines. My only defense is that most people in the tech business are just as guilty as I am!

However, although Google is undoubtedly the most important search engine by a long way, it does not have the entire search engine market to itself. According to Experian Hitwise, the most respected monitor of searches, Google accounted for 66% of all US searches in October 2011. Google's only serious competitor is Microsoft's Bing, which also provides the listings for all Yahoo! searches. Together, Bing and Yahoo! account for

29% of all US searches. Although this is still a long way behind Google, 29% of all of the searches being made still amounts to a lot of potential traffic. As a result, although I definitely recommend concentrating on Google, you should not completely discount Bing. The strategy that I have outlined above should work equally well for both search engines.

Outside the US, Google is even more dominant. In Canada, Google is slightly more important and Bing slightly less important. In the rest of the English-speaking world though, Google really does have an almost total monopoly, taking 90% in the UK and a whopping 94% of the Australian market, leaving only 6% and 5% for Bing respectively in the two markets. In these other countries, there is probably little point in spending too long trying to optimize for Bing unless you can easily spot some 'low-hanging fruit' that's quick and free to grab.

> Email us **now** at **accountant@informerbooks.com** to get our **free weekly updates** in case there have been any changes to any of the information contained in this chapter since publication.

DIRECTORIES AND REVIEWS

A FEW PAGES BACK, I mentioned that, when you search Google using one of your main keywords such as 'yourtown accountant', chances are that the majority of the top listings that you see will also have a red marker with a letter on it which refers to the business's location on the map next to it. In addition to the regular information that you would expect to get back from a Google Search (i.e. the title, the URL and a summary), you will also see the business's address, telephone number and a second link to 'Place page'.

So what's the difference between these listings and the regular 'organic' ones?

The difference is that all these businesses are also listed with Google Places. As you can see from the search results, the businesses that have this information are a lot more visible than regular listings. They even stand out above the listings which rank higher than them because of the red indicator and the additional information. As a result, you most definitely want to get your business listed here.

As usual, Google are pretty secretive about what difference to their rankings having a Google Places entry makes. But, from the evidence you can see with your own eyes every time you make a search, Google seems to like businesses listed with Google Places a lot. For local businesses, this is logical from Google's point of view. After all, the fact that you are able to prove that you have a local address and phone number is proof to Google that you really are a 'yourtown accountant'. Logic says that this proof will lead to more accurate listings than even Google's standard PageRank system of checking pages for relevancy plus counting up the number of links and their importance, as described in the previous chapter.

CREATING YOUR GOOGLE PLACES LISTING

To get started on creating your listing, head to:

www.google.com/places

Then click on the 'Get started' button underneath, 'Get your business found on Google'.

Sign in with your Google account. To start the operation, check that your country is correct and then input your phone number.

Although Google Places has only been integrated into Google searches since 2007, it has been around since 2004. It was previously known as 'Google Local' up until 2010. As it has been around for so long, it has already amassed an impressive database of local businesses. Most of which were taken from other listing sites. As a result, your business might be listed on the Google Places database already, albeit in a rather 'bare bones' form.

To check whether your business is already listed on Google Places, you are asked to input your phone number as a way of checking. If Google has got your phone number on file, you will be asked to amend your current listing. If Google Places has no record of your business though, it will invite you to create a listing from scratch.

You will now be presented with a form to fill in giving a lot of information about your business. If Google already has your business on Google Places, some of the information could be filled in already. Either way, you should fill in every field on the form. Not only is it useful information for your prospects, but Google seems to reward those businesses with fully completed Google Places information over those without it.

As you type in your full address, a pointer will appear on the map showing your business's location. In the unlikely event that it's wrong, click the link marked 'Fix incorrect marker location' to move it.

Once you've put in your basic information, you have 200 characters to come up with a description. This is an important part of the listing – think keywords, keywords, keywords! If you are reading this book in order and came up with the text for your Description Meta Tag already, you can use this for your description here as they will be roughly the same length.

'Category' underneath it is also a vital part of this exercise – even more important than the description in fact, because it will be the determining factor as to which search terms your listing appears under. Google Places allows you to list your business under five different categories. Make sure you use all of them to appear in as many searches as possible.

I cover the way to scientifically choose your best keywords extensively in the next chapter on AdWords. If you've already gone through the exercise, then you'll know which the best five categories to choose are. If not, I would suggest you use the following five categories based on my own research:

- Accountant
- CPA
- Accounting Firm
- Tax Preparation
- Bookkeeping

Now you have finished the basics, move down to 'Service Areas and Location Settings' and select 'Yes, this business serves customers at their locations'. Select this option even if you don't normally go out to visit clients because it will make your listing appear across a wider area.

Next choose which area you want to put down as covering. 'Distance from one location' allows you to input a radius around your zip or post code, while 'List of areas served' allows you to list individual areas. Select the largest area that you can realistically cover. Are you really prepared to travel 100 miles plus to meet potential clients? There is a law of diminishing returns on these areas because Google generally ranks businesses according to proximity. So, if there are 1,000 other accountants nearer to the prospect than you are, you won't get a lot of business from that far away.

Next fill in your 'Hours of operations' and 'Payment' options. Fill in all those that apply. You also have the opportunity to add pictures and videos. If you have some photos to hand as I suggested in chapter 2, upload them now. Not many businesses take the trouble to add photos to their listing and so it can really help yours to stand out from the crowd if your listing has some. Photos don't have to be just of the outside of your office – you can also add your logo there or your own personal photo.

At the bottom of the form, you have the opportunity to add 'Additional Details'. Here I would suggest that you set up a new field called 'Other Services' and then list all of the main services that you offer other than those that you have mentioned in your original list of keywords, so that it comes up as 'Other Services : Payroll Services, Small Business Accounting, etc.

The complete information that will appear on your listing will now be showing in the panel of the right hand side. Check it over to make sure that you are happy with it. If not, edit the information; if you are, then click 'Submit'.

As long as you have made no mistakes, you should now see a page telling you to verify your listing. Depending on your location, you may or may not have the option of confirming your listing by phone. If you have, then take the option as it will speed the process of getting your listing live dramatically. If you don't get the option to verify by phone, you'll need to wait for Google to send you a postcard, which will take a while longer. The postcard will give instructions as to how to verify that you are the owner or representative of the business. Once you have done this, your listing will appear on Google Places and other people won't be able to change it.

That was all pretty simple and painless compared to all of the other marketing activities I've described to date, wasn't it? In fact, if you took my suggestion in the Introduction about scanning through the entire book before you start to implement the activities, I wouldn't blame you at all if you put the book down for half an hour and filled in your Google Places information right now. Depending on your location and the amount of competition you have, you could be on the first page of Google for free in a matter of days or weeks, which would be an excellent start to your internet marketing campaign.

OTHER LISTING SITES

Because adding your business's information to Google Places was so easy, it's not so much harder to add your business to all of the other major listing sites as well. Your #2 priority should be to list it on Yahoo! Although Yahoo! Search has lost a lot of ground to Google over the years, people still spend more time on the Yahoo! collection of sites than anywhere else other than Facebook or Google.

To sign up for Yahoo! Local Listings, go to:

listings.local.yahoo.com

You will see that Yahoo! offers both Basic and Enhanced Listings. Enhanced Listings cost $9.95 per month and that can add up over the years, so I suggest that you start off with just a Basic Listing. It's then just a question of filling in the form exactly as you did with the Google Places Listing.

Although Yahoo! and Bing share the same database for search results, Yahoo! Local Listings appear only on Yahoo! Search – they don't appear as part of Bing's search results. Yahoo's non-US sites use listings from other sources, however – see below for information on Yahoo! in the UK when it comes to local listings.

Bing is the last of the three large search engines. It's playing catch up with Google and Yahoo! on the local front, but it's still well worth spending half an hour to get your business listed. To do so, head to:

www.bingbusinessportal.com

Once again, the process is a similar one to that of creating your listing on Google Places.

Then there are a host of review and listing sites that you can (and probably should) list your business on. This list is roughly in descending order of importance:

Yelp.com
Yellowpages.com
Whitepages.com
Merchantcircle.com
Citysearch.com
Superpages.com
Local.com
Yellowbook.com
Angieslist.com
Insiderpages.com
Yellowbot.com
Judysbook.com
Magicyellow.com
Mojopages.com
Infousa.com
Localeze.com
iBegin.com
Citysquares.com

I say 'roughly' in descending order of importance because there are likely to be huge differences in the popularity of the sites in different parts of the country. In addition, these sites are quite an incestuous bunch, connected in a complicated web of shared data and reviews. Although the traffic to the bottom few sites on this list is not so high, their databases are used by a large number of smaller sites, so their reach can be huge.

Because of this, don't be surprised if you find that all your data on sites at the bottom of the list already exists. It just means that they are sharing data with some of those websites further up it.

Angieslist.com is a subscription site, although the cost is only a dollar a month. The site is becoming increasingly more important and so that's probably a small price to pay to find out what users of the site might be saying about you. Chances are that there will be less competitors' reviews on there as well, so you should really stand out. Users are likely to trust this site more than the free ones because Angieslist.com prides itself on how hard it is to manipulate the reviews.

Most of the pages above are for the US only (some of them cover Canada as well; some don't).

Here are some of the top listings sites for the UK:

Yell.com
Freeindex.co.uk
Qype.co.uk
Yelp.co.uk
Hotfrog.co.uk
Thomsonlocal.com
City-visitor.com
Touchlocal.com
Uksmallbusinessdirectory.co.uk
Brownbook.net
Business-directory-uk.co.uk
Bizwiki.co.uk
Welovelocal.com
Tipped.co.uk

The **City-visitor.com** site provides data for the UK version of Yahoo! Local and so is well worth signing up for. They only list addresses and a phone number unless you pay them a not inconsiderable sum for a premium listing. This is probably not worth it considering how Google has wiped the floor with Yahoo! in the UK over the past decade. Touchlocal.com provides search results for Ask.com and some of the national newspapers, including The Sun, and so they are also worth listing with.

It is a repetitive exercise to complete form after form for all of these listing sites. There are various browser extensions – for Internet Explorer, Chrome and Firefox – which can auto-complete such fields as your address, phone number, address, etc. This can save a lot of time while filling in these forms. It's also good to have the information such as description and keywords on a Word document so that you can copy and paste the text into the appropriate fields.

Even semi-automated though, it can get pretty dull to fill in all those forms, so pace yourself. Just complete a handful each day rather than giving up. Alternatively, you can sign up for a service which will take care of listing your business on all of these sites (plus quite a few more as well) in the form of Universal Business Listings at **www.ubl.org**. The price of UBL's basic service is $39, which is probably all you need. They do hide the link to their basic service quite cunningly, however, so you need to hunt around their site a little in order to find it. UBL also offers a similar service in both Canada and the UK as well.

Not only are these directory listings all good advertising in order to reach the users of each site but, as you will have learned in the previous chapter on Search Engine Optimization, all of these free one-way links are going to help your site's own 'organic' ranking in the search engine a huge amount. So keep on going as long as you can. Make a Google search for 'local business directory' to search for more directories to add until Google is only producing junk results.

FOURSQUARE AND OTHER CHECK IN SITES

Local businesses have generally been latecomers to the internet revolution. In many ways, this is understandable because it was the international nature of the Internet and the fact that people with niche interests could find what they were looking for that initially was part of the great attraction. By the start of the 21st Century, however, more than half of the population were active internet users and the Web became an integral part of virtually everyone's lives. This meant that local started to become an integral part of it. Who these days can be bothered to go and locate a copy of the Yellow

Pages before guessing what category they should be looking in when they can just search for a phone number online and get the answers in less than a second?

This revolution entered a second stage in 2007 following the release of Apple's iPhone. Although it was not the first smartphone to be released (the first BlackBerry appeared in 2003), it was the first time that smartphones were promoted to the mass-market – and such is the cachet of the Apple brand that they were phenomenally successful with the launch. The rapid adoption of smartphones also increased as a result of the introduction of Google's rival Android operating system in 2008, which today has a significant edge over the iPhone in terms of sales.

One of the reasons for the success of both the iPhone and Android handsets is the fact that, as was featured heavily in the iPhone's advertising, "There's an app for that". Apps are individual programs (short for applications), available for download via online app stores, which enable the user to perform a vast variety of tasks.

Many of the most popular apps took advantage of the fact that all smartphones contain a tracking device which can pinpoint the user's location to within a few feet, anywhere in the world. This functionality was a natural fit for these local business directories. The major players in the world of local business directories, like Yelp, were quick to take advantage of the new opportunities offered by smartphones, releasing apps allowing users to quickly locate the type of businesses that they were looking for in their immediate vicinity. These Apps would show reviews and other important information such as price and opening hours to give users an informed decision as to whether the location was a good choice for them.

The social networks including Facebook, Twitter and now Google+ were also quick to make use of this technology as well, allowing users to 'tag' their location along with their updates.

In addition to existing sites upgrading their functionality in order to provide a better experience for the user, a whole new breed of service has emerged with this location technology at the core of the experience. Several of these services launched around the same time offering a variation on a similar theme and, for a while, the area was very competitive. Now, however, a winner has emerged from this group, and that is Foursquare.

Foursquare can be thought of as a cross between a social network and a local directory. As of September 2011, Foursquare had just passed the 10 million user mark who, between them, had managed to rack up a billion 'check-ins'. A 'check in' is where a user logs into the Foursquare app on their smartphone and announces to all of their friends who are also part of the network that this is where they are. Unlike most of the local directories, Foursquare is not so focused on reviews – instead users are asked to give 'tips' to other users.

Business owners are invited to claim their locations in much the same way as they do for Google Places. Once you are verified as the owner, you will get access to a dashboard which makes it easy to run promotions and offers for any visitors who check in to your office. While this facility is probably of more use to restaurants and retail outlets which are dependent upon trying to get clients into their premises as often as possible, there is the opportunity here for a little extra promotion. This is because, if you have a promotion running, it will be marked on the apps of all Foursquare users in the vicinity of your office. Therefore, consider offering an inexpensive promotional item (as I mentioned in chapter 2) to anyone who comes into your office. Every person who checks in to your office will be announcing the fact to all of the users in their Foursquare network, thus exposing your business to an audience who might not otherwise have heard of you.

If any of the users comes into your office one day and says that they are 'The Mayor', it doesn't mean that they have gone completely mad! On Foursquare, the user who has checked into a particular location the most times is referred to as 'The Mayor'. These 'Mayors' are important to businesses like restaurants and coffee shops as it means that they are some of the business's best customers and so they are often rewarded. In your case, however, there's probably little benefit in having Foursquare users making regular appearances in your offices, so no need to make any special offers.

Facebook and Google+ also allow users check in facilities and so it's a good idea to incentivize users of these services to check in as well, although they don't offer the same easy tools for offering promotions as Foursquare does. It's all extra exposure though and gives you something new to add to your promotional postings on your social networks.

THE IMPORTANCE OF REVIEWS

Around 2002, people started talking for the first time about 'Web 2.0' or, more descriptively, the 'Read/Write Web'. Prior to this time, internet users were only able to read content written by site owners. As this was before the introduction of easy-to-use blogging platforms, anyone wishing to publish their thoughts on the Internet had to be reasonably proficient with HTML. After this time, however, the leading websites started adding more and more interactivity, giving users the ability to not only consume content, but also to create it themselves.

This gave consumers a voice for the first time and, due to the viral nature of Internet, this voice can be amplified – greatly amplified in some cases. Back in the Nineties, if you had a major problem with a company, what could you do about it? You could tell your friends about it, but how many friends does the average person have? The answer to this question is apparently around 150 according to sociologists. Except in extreme circumstances, the media is generally uninterested in the problems of one individual.

Today though, everything is different. Now, with the rise of blogs and such social media tools as Twitter, consumers' complaints can circulate around the Internet at lightning speed. One of the first examples of this was when a blogger posted a video showing that it was possible to open a 'Kryptonite Evolution' bicycle lock, one of the most expensive and supposedly 'toughest' locks on the market, using just a Bic ballpoint pen. The video went viral and ended up costing the company $15 million in recalls and immeasurable damage to their brand.

In 2009, United Airlines broke a guitar belonging to singer/songwriter, Dave Carroll. After failing to get any compensation from the airline, he uploaded a song and video onto YouTube which also went viral with over 10 million views. It is estimated that this debacle ended up costing United perhaps over $180 million in lost business.

As a result, most major corporations now employ PR companies to monitor mentions of their brands online so they can react quickly to the first signs of any problems from disgruntled customers.

Although these two cases were pretty extreme examples, there are now so many review sites on the Web which makes it simple for any customer to give feedback – both positive and negative – on their experience with different products and businesses that no company can afford to ignore them. Compared to the situation 15 years ago, it's a great time to have a business which really looks after its customers, and a bad time to have a business which doesn't. On the Internet it is said that, "Information wants to be free".

According to a survey from **www.e-marketer.com** in 2010, a massive 92% of internet users check reviews online before making a purchasing decision. There's a good chance that you bought this book online from Amazon and that you checked the reviews before buying it. I certainly never fail to check reviews before I buy a book, or reserve a hotel, or buy a new phone, etc.

If these days, customers are checking out reviews on a $20 book, or a new restaurant in town, on a regular basis before making a buying decision, you can bet your bottom dollar that they are definitely going to be checking their options carefully before they make such a hugely important decision as hiring a new accountant. After all, the ramifications for making a mistake and ending up with a bad one could be disastrous. Nearly all of the directories mentioned in this chapter offer customers the chance to review businesses and, collectively, such is their reach that you can expect that a large number of your prospects will read them.

As a result, these review sites offer your business a tremendous opportunity for gaining new customers … as long as you really **do** offer an excellent level of service. At the start of this book, I mentioned that, before you begin to aggressively market your business, you really need to ensure that you are providing your clients with an excellent service. If not then, at best, much of your marketing efforts will be wasted. At worst, your business could actually suffer as a result of your online activities.

Phineas T. Barnum may (or may not) have said, "There's no such thing as bad publicity" but he was promoting circuses and wasn't living in the internet age. Personally I would have to disagree (and I'm pretty sure that shareholders of BP and Toyota would agree with me here!) Today, in an age where scales of one to five stars are ubiquitous, it's much better to have no reviews at all than to have lots of one-star reviews.

Not only will seeing several five star reviews in a directory give potential customers an enormous amount of reassurance that they would be making the right decision in giving you their business, but a lot of these directories rank their listings in each category according to the results of the reviews. Some of these listings work in the same way as Amazon's, where the business with the highest average rankings will be at the top. Others, such as Google Places, rank the number of reviews in total without taking the number of stars into account. Although, as with all other details of their algorithms, Google's formula is a secret, it looks as if a business which has several low review scores will still appear higher than a business with just one good review. In all cases, businesses with no reviews at all are always ranked after those which have at least some reviews, no matter how good or bad they might be (so maybe Phineas T. Barnum did have a point after all!)

So how do you get people to review your business? The answer to that question is quite a simple one – you just ask them to!

Every time a client thanks you for a job well done, get into the habit of asking them if they could do you a favor by writing a review of your business and make it as easy as possible for them to do so. If it's going to take too much effort on their part to do so, then few of them will. As a result, I suggest that you put together a Word document containing links to all of the directories where you have listings. List them in order of importance. Your clients aren't going to write reviews in twenty places and they probably aren't going to register with a site just for the purposes of giving you a review either. So it will be good to give them a list of different options to choose from. Chances are that they are registered with one or more of the larger ones already.

If you don't have so many clients yet, consider 'incentivizing' your contacts to write reviews for you. Through mentions in your newsletters or across your social networks, either offer a small gift to everyone who writes a published review for you or else enter them into a sweepstakes to win one of the low-cost 'prizes' that I described in chapter 2. Notice that I said 'write a review' and not 'write a **good** review'. If you only gave incentives away for people giving you good reviews, it would be blatant bribery. However, it is unlikely that those people who are part of your network are going to give you a bad review, so you are on fairly safe ground here.

If your number of newsletter subscribers and those on your social networks are still quite small at the moment, you shouldn't have too much to worry about. However, if you have large networks and offer a desirable reward, then there is a slight chance that you will get too many reviews too quickly. If this happens, there is a danger that the directories will think that the reviews are fake, which could end up in your listing being taken down. This would be bad news for you indeed. Fortunately, if you give your contacts quite a large number of directories to choose from, then the reviews should be spread thinly between them rather than your ending up with a deluge of reviews on just one or two sites.

Trying to obtain reviews from satisfied clients should be an ongoing process. Over time, you will probably find that you end up with a lot of reviews in some of the directories and none at all in some of the others. If this happens, then try and steer potential reviewers into reviewing you in those directories where you still don't have a review yet. Your first review on one of the relatively smaller directories is still going to be more useful than your sixth review on one of the larger ones such as Google Places.

In some cases, you won't need to push people to write a review of your business – they will write one unprompted. Unfortunately though, there is a good chance that these reviews will be negative.

As the saying goes, you can please some of the people all of the time, all of the people some of the time, but you can't please all of the people all of the time.

In all walks of life, accidents happen from time to time. In addition, there are some people who have unrealistic expectations and are simply never going to be satisfied no matter how hard you might try. As a result, it is inevitable that, sooner or later, you will end up with a disgruntled client.

As I mentioned earlier, in the Information Age, one dissatisfied client has the potential to cause an enormous amount of damage to any size of business. For this reason, you should do whatever you can in order to try and resolve any grievance that the client might have. If you really did make a mistake, don't try and cover it up – admit it, apologize and try to resolve the problem. The magic phrase when it comes to conflict resolution is, "So what would you like me to do about it?" Quite often, the unhappy client won't know how to answer this question and, by simply admitting guilt and apologizing, you will have nipped any more potential problems from the client in the bud.

Sometimes, however, the situation won't be so easy to diffuse – there will be occasions when the problem is actually completely down to mistakes made by the client, which they will not admit to making. Alternatively, the client might ask for a totally unreasonable amount of compensation from you which you simply could not afford to give. In these cases, there is a chance that the client could take 'revenge' by giving you a bad review in one of the directories.

I have noticed that many people act abominably online. The fact that they can make comments anonymously, plus the fact that they don't need to look their 'victim' in the eye when they are saying terrible things, leads them to write things that they wouldn't dream of saying, or dare to say, if they were standing face-to-face with the subject of their wrath. In addition, these people (sometimes known on the Internet as 'trolls') love to get into arguments. The longer and nastier they get, the more of a kick they get out of them.

Because of this fact, there is no easy solution when you find yourself as the target of one of these types of people and they can be highly damaging for your business. If you simply ignore their comments, other readers could think that the person making the complaint is right and that you have nothing to say in your defense. If you keep responding to them, however, the argument will simply continue *ad infinitum* getting more and more nasty with every exchange as the complainant will not be satisfied until they have the last word and, to their mind, 'wins' the argument.

As a result, my recommendation if you end up in such a situation is to reply just once to the complaint. If you really did make a mistake, then admit it, apologize for it and state what you will do, or have already done, in order to rectify the problem. If, however, you are totally blameless for the situation, then state the facts clearly and professionally without showing your emotions. Tell the complainant that you will be happy to continue the discussion by email if they would like to discuss the matter further.

Chances are that the complainant will immediately respond with an even more unreasonable argument than the original one. I know that it's difficult to resist the urge to respond to these new criticisms that they have made, but resist them you must. The longer the argument goes on, the more attention it will get and it will start to overshadow all of the other positive reviews on the directory. By acknowledging the complaint and showing that you have done all that can reasonably be expected of you, you will show readers that you really do care about your clients. The fact that you have one bad review will give credibility to the positive ones, at least, and show that they aren't all faked.

If the complaint is totally unreasonable, then you can try and contact the directory's customer support and ask if they will remove it. Don't raise your expectations too highly that they will, however, as it is not really their job to censor bad reviews on their site. After all, the reason why these sites exist is to provide a forum for unbiased reviews – not to act as a promotional vehicle for those businesses listed in them.

You can lessen the impact of bad reviews on a directory by asking for more reviews from your loyal and satisfied clients. If you have nine good reviews and one bad one, you should still be near the top of the rankings. Try and avoid the temptation to ask your loyal supporters to join in with an argument with a disgruntled client, however; if they feel as if people are ganging up on them, then they will simply become more and more unreasonable.

*   *   *

Don't let the fact that this is one of the shorter chapters in the book lead you into thinking that directory and review sites are not important – nothing could be further from the truth. The only reason why this is a short chapter is that it is such a simple exercise to get your business listed on a variety of sites that detailed instructions as to how to achieve it simply weren't necessary.

As a result, listing your business with all of these directories should be one of the first stages in your internet marketing campaign. A few hours spent on the task now can bring in a stream of new prospects for many years to come.

> Email us **now** at <u>accountant@informerbooks.com</u> to get our **free weekly updates** in case there have been any changes to any of the information contained in this chapter since publication.

GOOGLE ADWORDS

As I mentioned briefly at the start of the chapter 11, Google Ad-Words have been a phenomenal success – transforming the fortunes of Google from being just the provider of a useful free resource for internet users to becoming one of the biggest and most profitable corporations in the world.

In some ways, Google AdWords can be considered as the 21st Century equivalent of classified advertising in local newspapers – they're short, text-only ads that are relatively cheap because they are well-targeted, e.g. if someone is looking to buy a pet, then they are going to be paying close interest to the 'Pets for Sale' section of the classifieds, not the real estate section.

One of the major differences between AdWords and newspaper classifieds, however, is that with the newspaper classifieds, you pay a one-off flat fee for the ad. Whether no one, just one person or a thousand people see the ad and call you wanting to buy a kitten, you end up paying the same price for the ad. With AdWords, however, you only pay for results. If a thousand people see your ad but no one responds to it by clicking on the link to your website, it doesn't cost you a dime. So there is no risk of spending a lot of money on an advertising campaign that results in no response from visitors. It's this 'no risk' element to Google AdWords, plus the fact that you have an incredible amount of control as to who does or doesn't see your advertising, that has led to the phenomenal success of AdWords.

Not surprisingly, there are so many businesses wanting to take advantage of this great new advertising medium. So how does Google decide which advertiser gets which advertising spot? Actually Google doesn't decide – the advertisers decide for themselves upon the value of each spot because

Google basically holds an auction for the best positions. The advertiser who bids the most gets the best position. Those who bid a little less get less well-positioned advertising spots and those that don't bid enough don't get their ads shown at all.

This has led to massive competition for some of the most popular keywords. The insurance business is currently the area which sees the highest bids on keywords, which can often reach as much as $50 per click. Remember as well that all you are getting from AdWords is one person clicking from the ad to your website. It doesn't necessarily mean that they are going to buy something once they get there. They can (and in most cases, will) click through to your site, glance at it for less than a second before hitting the 'Back' button of their browsers to return to Google – and 'poof!' – you're $50 poorer for absolutely no benefit whatsoever.

As a result, anyone intending to use AdWords needs to be very careful with them. Used carefully, they can be a license to print money. Used incorrectly though and they can quickly become a practically bottomless money pit that will max out your credit card while giving you absolutely nothing in return. Hopefully, after reading this chapter, you will know how to make it the former and not the latter.

SETTING UP YOUR ADWORDS ACCOUNT

Start off by heading to:

adwords.google.com

Once you are inside, you will be asked to confirm the country you're in and the currency you want to use. You should then receive an email confirming that you are signed up and will go through to the main AdWords dashboard. There are a vast number of options and information sources on your dashboard which can be quite intimidating to start with, so it's best to start off by following the steps which Google suggests to take you through the process, although personally I think they make you go through them in almost completely the wrong order.

Click on the 'create your first campaign' button to get started.

First of all, come up with a name for your Campaign – it won't appear anywhere – it's just for your own personal reference in case you decide to run several different ones.

Now comes 'Location and Languages'. This is an absolutely vital step for any local business. Get this wrong and your advertising efforts are definitely going to be doomed.

For the 'Locations' section, click on the radio button for just your country and then click the link called, 'Select one or more other locations'.

Once you are inside, you will see that the whole of your country is listed in the box called 'Selected locations'. You definitely don't want the whole country viewing your ads, so remove that straight away so that the box is now completely empty.

Look at the tabs at the top of the box and click on the one marked 'Custom'. Now, in the field marked location, type in your office address. Next, click on the box which says, 'Allow address to show in my ads'. This is going to give you an additional selling point if your ads are competing with a national advertiser, as it will show immediately to everyone seeing your ad that you really are a local business located close to them.

Finally, select the radius from your office that will be covered by the advertising. Think carefully about this – make the radius too small and you will be missing out on some additional potential business; make it too wide and you could end up wasting quite a bit of your advertising budget on people who will probably want to use a company located closer to them. Check the map that comes up after you have selected it to make sure that all of the areas covered are likely to deliver some potential business for you.

Once you are happy that the location is exactly right to cover all of your potential clients – but no more than is necessary – click on the 'Add' button and you will see the location appear in the 'Selected locations'. Unless you have offices in locations other than your main one, you only need this first location. Click the 'Save' button now that you have selected your 'Location'.

Next there is an option for languages other than English. If you are targeting certain ethnic groups, then add another language. But, for most businesses, this will not be necessary.

You can ignore the 'Advanced location options' link – the default settings will be the best ones for your needs.

Moving down the page, next we come to, 'Networks and devices'. There are three possible places where your AdWords could appear. The first option is to have your ads just appearing on the regular Google Search (which is where the vast majority of the ads will be served anyway). The second option is also to include Google's Search partners – this includes such websites as AOL's search plus a few other rather minor search engines. The final option is to show ads on the Google Display Network. If you've ever been to a website and they have boxes showing 'ads by Google', then they are a member of the Google Display Network.

Advertising on the Google Display Network is not generated by someone making a specific search, but is displayed when content similar to the keywords you have used is on the same page. This means that, if a page is about a movie called 'The Accountant', your ads could well display along with it and there's a chance that someone could click on it purely out of curiosity without having any intention of buying from you, wasting your money in the process. As a result, set up your Network to display ads only on the Search Network – not on the Content Network as well.

Under 'Devices' you should leave that as the default 'All' setting.

In the 'Bidding and budget' section, you should set the 'Bidding option' on the 'manual maximum CPC bidding'. Although this will require a bit more work than keeping it on 'Automatic', it means you have more control over exactly how much you are prepared to spend to get each click through to your site.

The most important section on here though is the field for 'Budget'. Here you need to set a maximum budget that you can afford to spend each day. It's probably easiest to think in terms of what is the maximum amount you can afford to spend each month and then divide the figure by 30 (e.g. if you can afford a maximum of $600 per month, then you would set your daily budget at $20). Note that this really is the **maximum** that you will be billed for each day – Google will stop running your ads if or when the daily spend reaches this amount and will restart the next day. If you aren't spending too much for each ad and/or there aren't many searches performed in your area, you could end up spending a lot less than your maximum.

The 'Ad extensions' section can help your ads stand out from those of other advertisers. It takes a little more effort to set them up, but it's well worth the time investment to get the most from your AdWords campaign.

Select the tick box for 'Location'. Here you will see the options for Google Places. You definitely do want to link your AdWords with your Google Places account as it will enhance both your Google Places listing and also your AdWords listing. So go through the process of setting it up here.

Ignore the 'Sitelinks' options. It's useful for lazy advertisers who just set up one ad to go to one page for all of the keywords which they bid on, but I'm going to show you a much better way of getting the best value for your investment than leaving it up to Google's algorithms to decide which link should be shown when.

The 'Call' option is well worth ticking. It only works if someone sees your ad while using a smartphone and so you probably won't get too many potential clients taking advantage of it. If they do though, it's good news for you. You will pay your standard bid price for the call as it is monitored by Google. However, a call is much more valuable to you than a click. A lot of people will click through to your ads without taking other action, meaning that the money you spent on the ad was wasted. But if the potential client called you instead, you are assured that the ad really has delivered a serious client to you.

It's best to leave the 'Call-only format' box unticked though so that it displays your regular link as well in case a client simply is not ready to call you yet – otherwise you might lose some potential leads. 'Call metrics' is optional – if you want to be able to track exactly how many calls you got via AdWords, this facility will be useful. However, it means that you will get a new number assigned to you by Google which forwards to your regular number. As a result, if you are not intending to devote a great deal of time to analyzing the results of your AdWords activities and fine-tuning them constantly, it might be better just to have your regular number advertised here.

The links to the 'Advanced Settings' really aren't worth bothering with for a small and geographically well-targeted advertising campaign, so you can finish off now by clicking on the 'Save and continue' button.

SELECTING KEYWORDS

I quickly touched on the subject of choosing keywords in chapter 2 and mentioned it again in chapter 11. At that point though, we were only looking at the most popular and relevant keywords such as 'yourtown accountant'. Although these main, coverall keywords are probably going to bring the most traffic, with AdWords it's better to try and come up with as long a list as possible so as to get your ads displayed as often as possible and also because you're more likely to find some bargains with the less popular phrases than the most obvious ones.

Instead of continuing to follow Google's step-by-step guide, skip over writing your ad for the moment and jump straight to keywords now. Click on the dark green tab at the top of the page called 'Reporting and Tools' and select the option for 'Keyword Tool'.

First of all, under the keyword box, click on the link called 'Advanced Options and Filters' and select just your country rather than leaving it as 'All Countries' to get a more accurate idea of what people will be searching for in your country.

Now, in the main box at the top of the page, type in your best keyword, which you have been using so far in this book, namely 'yourtown accountant', and then click on the 'Search' button. Google will now come back with several pages of suggestions based upon your search term. Next, click on the header of the last column, 'Local Monthly Searches', to sort the suggestions by the number of clicks each search term gets each month in your country.

At this stage of the exercise, you are brainstorming – looking to find as many different keywords as you can think of that people might use in order to find an accountant. If a suggestion is relevant, click on the star next to the word to save it.

Going down the list, you should be clicking on 'cpa', cpa in', 'accountant' and 'accountant in'. Google is clever enough to realize that a CPA and an accountant is the same thing in the US, which is why they are coming out as the same number of Local Monthly Searches.

After this, you will probably be getting plurals of the words. You definitely want to include those too. As you get lower down, you will probably start to see some other associated words that are not either 'accountant' or 'cpa', such as 'accounting', 'tax services' and 'bookkeeping'. If you offer tax and bookkeeping services, then you should add these as well.

Jot down all these new suggestions of keywords that you might not originally have thought of like these three – 'accounting', 'tax services' and' bookkeeping'. There are obviously a lot of people searching for these terms and so they are worthy of further investigation. Click the star next to them all.

Next you could be seeing the word 'firm' next to your main keywords – you definitely want those as well, so star them.

Sooner or later, you will start getting results that are not going to be relevant as a keyword that your prospects will use to find you, such as 'cpa exam'. You don't want to waste advertising money on someone who is more interested in being a future competitor of yours, so you don't star that one. The same thing goes for any keywords with 'jobs' in them. As well as making a list of all the 'good' keywords that Google is telling you are often searched for along with your main keywords of 'cpa', 'accountant' and 'accounting', make a second list of the 'bad' keywords which would not be used by potential clients. You will use this list of 'bad' keywords later to ensure that your ads don't run against searches for these.

Once you get to the bottom of the first page of results, you'll probably find that most of the keywords on the page are starred. As you go through the other pages, however, Google's thinking gets more and more lateral and a lot of the keywords will have nothing to do with your business, such as 'yourtown lawyer' or 'yourtown doctor'.

As you continue with the exercise, you'll see how useful this tool is. Would you call yourself a 'tax firm'? Well according to Google, a lot of your clients are using this expression and so you should definitely include it in your keywords.

Continue onwards and you will probably start to pick up the names of your main competitors. Add them too – the keywords will be cheap to bid on and you could get a few gifts from your competitors that way!

Go all the way through all of the pages starring every search term that anyone might be using to find you.

Once you have finished that exercise, start the whole exercise again under 'cpa yourtown'. You will find that the majority of the good keywords you will want to use are repeated because they were found during the last search. But it's worth scanning through all of the pages again in case it brings up a handful of new ones that are useful too.

Once you have gone through your most obvious two keywords, 'cpa' and 'accountant', start to search using some new keywords that you came across regularly while going through this exercise, starting with 'accounting your-town'. As you get further from your main keywords, there are going to be more completely irrelevant terms coming up, but this lateral thinking can take us off into different directions. For example, you might now start to pick up a lot of searches for 'payroll' which you can also analyze. Jot down all these new terms that come up so you can analyze them later.

Next take a look and see what comes up for 'tax yourtown' as this word (not surprisingly) will probably come up a lot. Don't get too carried away when you are searching through these less relevant keywords as you don't want your ads to come up every time someone looks for the IRS/Inland Revenue site. But you should find some useful new keywords coming up which are getting a lot of searches, such as 'tax preparation' and 'tax service'.

After 'tax', try 'bookkeeping yourtown'. That could bring you in a lot more keywords than you expected. Continuing in the same vein, now add 'pay-roll yourtown'. Another word that you might find cropping up often with your main keywords is 'small business'.

Probably by now, you've exhausted the main keywords using this method, but Google has another useful function. Above the listings, you will find a button called 'More like these'. Click on it and select 'Starred' to come up with even more suggestions. Once you have gone through all of those suggestions as well, you're probably done. You should have a list of several hundred great keywords now which should be plenty to provide you with a lot of traffic if you have a large budget, or to find a few hidden gems if you only have a tiny budget and want to take things conservatively.

However, if you offer some additional services that weren't suggested with the Google search, then add them as well. Maybe you offer lessons in the main computer software programs, assistance with mergers and acquisi-tions, forensic accounting, financial advisory services, etc. If so, then make some searches for these services as well. Although they might not get as many searches as the major terms, there will be less competition for them and so you should be able to buy them quite cheaply.

You now have your 'keyword master list' and this is going to provide the bricks which you build your AdWords campaign from. Before you do that though, you need to analyze the keywords which you have.

Now click on the 'Download' button above the listings and select 'Starred'. Select the format that you would like to use – 'CSV for Excel' is probably going to be the best. Next, download the file onto your computer. It might take a little time to crunch all that data if you have a lot of keywords.

The next step of the operation is to divide up your keywords into different groups. The majority of your keywords are going to contain one or more of the following words in them:

- accountant
- cpa
- accounting
- tax
- bookkeeping
- payroll
- small business

Rather than running just one ad for all of your keywords, you will have more success if you have a slightly different ad running for each of your major groups. If someone is searching for a 'tax service', they might not think you can help them if all you talk about is the fact that you are a CPA.

The quickest way to divide the keywords into groups is to create a new worksheet in Excel for each of your groups and then copy your entire list of keywords onto each sheet. Then, go through each sheet deleting the keywords which are not relevant so it leaves just those that are. Sometimes you will find words that don't fit exactly into one category while on other occasions you will have keywords which fit into two or more. Try and decide which group is likely to be a better fit for the keyword than the others. If the keyword really does seem to fit equally as well in two or more groups, place it in all of the relevant groups for a while to see if one does much better than the other. Alternatively, if it is one of the keywords which are likely to receive a lot of traffic, you could put it in group of its own with its own ad.

Now, on the seven spreadsheets you have created, one for each category, copy the list of keywords two more times, with a couple of columns between each one.

Leave the first column as is but, to the left hand side on the next column put in an angled bracket like '['. To the right of the second column, put in the other angled bracket, like ']' so that you end up with a keyword like [**accountant**]. Copy the brackets all the way down the keywords to leave all of the words in brackets.

Now repeat the exercise with your last column of keywords except that, instead of putting a [bracket] on each side, you should put a "quotation mark". Once you have done this, you will end up with all of your keyword phrases in three different formats:

keyword phrase

[keyword phrase]

"keyword phrase"

"What on earth is the point of all this?" I hear you cry!

Let me explain. Google offers three different types of what they call 'Match Types' – instructions as to how precise, or how vague, a user's search term will need to be in order to trigger the display of your AdWords. To give an example, let's assume that we are targeting the keyword, 'yourtown accountant'.

The keyword without any brackets or quotation marks is known as a 'Broad Match' and is the widest of the three options. This means that your ad will display whenever both of the words are displayed anywhere in the user's search, no matter what order they are in or what other words are in the search. As a result, your AdWords will display even for the following search:

Where can I find a good accountant in yourtown?

Keywords in [brackets] are known as an 'Exact Match'. In order to display, your keyword has to contain the right words in the right order. So these examples would trigger the ad:

affordable **yourtown accountant**

yourtown accountant and bookkeeper

However, they would not display if someone was searching for:

accountant in **yourtown**

The final option, with the keyword in "quotation marks", is the most precise of all – it's called a 'Phrase Match'. Your Adwords will only display with that **exact phrase** in that **exact order**. If there is anything else other than this exact search, your ad will not be displayed. In this case, your AdWords will not display for any of the searches in the above examples. It will only display if someone is searching for:

yourtown accountant

But if the keyword without either brackets or quotation marks will bring up your AdWords for any search, why bother with either of the more precise options? It's a way of getting your AdWords to display for the lowest possible prices. Most of your competitors will probably be too lazy to bid on each keyword in each of the three formats and so there will be less competition for the Phrase Matches, which means that they should cost you less. Google will only display one of your ads at a time and will always display the cheapest option.

We're nearly finished with keywords now, but I have one more trick up my sleeve. Leave the 'Keyword Tool' section of the dashboard and click on the 'Campaigns' tab.

In the main window, you will see some more tabs, one of which is 'Keywords'. Click on that tab.

At the bottom of this page now, you will see a link called, 'Negative keywords'. Click on that link. Now click on the 'Add' button.

Remember that, while you were looking through the list of suggested keywords, you probably came across several words which would be searched for by people who would have no interest in paying for your services? Here is where you use that information to stop your AdWords from displaying (and thus costing you money if anyone clicks on them) when they make a search including any of these terms. Perhaps you came up with a list of the following words:

- job
- jobs
- exam

- exams
- career
- careers
- free
- what
- who

Click 'Save' once you have input all of these, plus any other words which came up when you made the search which you are sure will not be used by anyone who might potentially become a paying customer.

CREATING GROUPS AND WRITING ADS

Now that you have chosen all of your keywords, you can move on to the second half of the operation. This is to set up different groups for your key-words containing your long lists of relevant keywords and to write the ads which are going to be displayed when someone searches for those terms.

If you are not already on the right page, click on the 'Campaign' tab at the top of your dashboard. Click on the name of your Campaign on the left hand menu and then click on 'Ad groups' in the main window.

Click on the button at the bottom of the page called, 'New ad group'.

At this point, let me clarify the difference between a 'Campaign' and a 'Group'. You will probably only ever need to start the one Campaign unless you plan on launching one local Campaign and one national Campaign, as I will explain towards the end of this chapter. You should, and probably will, have several Groups beneath each campaign. Each Group will consist of a number of different keywords, each of which triggers the same ad.

You have already grouped your keywords into seven different groups on your spreadsheet, and so now you just need to input each of the keywords into a different Group on the AdWords dashboard. Start off with the 'ac-countant' Group.

In the field underneath 'Name this ad group', call it 'Accountant'. Skip over the writing of the ad part for the moment to input all of your keywords in the box at the bottom.

Copy and paste each of the three different columns which you should now have on each page of the spreadsheet. Make sure you include the [brackets] on either side of the bracketed keywords and the "quotation marks" on either side of the keywords in quotation marks. Don't worry about the white spaces between the keywords and the brackets/quotation marks – these gaps will disappear after you have saved the ads.

Now it's time to get creative and start writing the ads, so scroll back up the page to the 'Create an ad' section.

You now have a tiny amount of space to get your entire advertising message across. Every character counts, so use each of them wisely.

The headline is the most important line of the ad. If you can't attract their attention with the headline, they probably aren't going to read the lines underneath. You know that everyone who sees this ad is going to have used the word 'accountant' and you know that they are located in your catchment area, because this is how you set up the campaign right from the start. You need to show the prospects that the ad is completely relevant to their needs by including both the word 'accountant' and 'yourtown' in the headline. Also, these terms will appear in bold if the client has used those terms, which will help your ad to stand out from the other AdWords on the page. You have a maximum of 25 characters here only and so you're not going to have a lot of additional characters to get creative with.

The following headline would just fit inside the 25 character limit:

Accountant in Yourtown TX

If the name of Yourtown is longer than 8 characters, then you can forget about the state. If it's still coming out too long, then you can change it to:

Yourtown Accountant

The next line is the one that needs the greatest creativity. Remember AIDA from the crash course in copywriting in chapter 2? You've caught their **Attention** in the Headline. 'Description line 1' now needs to both **Interest** them and arouse **Desire** all in just 35 characters.

Remember also the WIIFM part? What's In It For Me? Try and get yourself inside the mind of the prospect which is making the search. Why would they be making such a search? Write the ad from their perspective as a potential buyer rather than from your perspective as a seller.

How about:

Accounting Headaches? Need Help?

Asking questions is always a great tactic when writing copy. If the prospect is saying 'Yes' inside their head, then you're heading in the right direction. Even though the word 'You' is not actually included in the line because you have cut the line down to its bare essentials, it's still there – the more grammatically correct version of the line would be:

Are you suffering from accounting headaches? Do you need some help?

Again, you are showing the potential client that you have their needs in mind, rather than simply talking about 'We' or 'Us' all the time.

Now for 'Description line 2'. You have already taken the prospect through Attention, Interest and Desire, so now you need to seal the deal with the last one – **Action**. You need to ask the prospect to do something and to create some urgency. Remember in chapter 8 on website building, I described your Most Wanted Response, which was to ask the client to make contact for a 'Free Consultation'? You can start offering this to them now rather than 'surprising' them when you make your offer on the website.

So one idea would be the following for the 'Description line 2':

Call Us Now for a Free Consultation

'Call Us' is a strong call to action; 'Now' gives the ad a sense of urgency, and 'Free' is a 'magic marketing word' that gets everyone's attention. Who in the world doesn't want to get something for free?

Next you have the Display URL. Although most people will just put their regular website address here, there are advantages in displaying something different here. If your website is something like **www.YourtownAccountant.com** then there is probably no advantage. However, if your URL is **www.johnsmithcpa.com** then there is. Again, as was the case with the header, there are advantages to including your keywords in your URL as well. So if your website address is just your company name, consider making your display URL along the lines of:

www.JohnSmithCPA.com/YourtownAccountant

Once again, the Yourtown and Accountant in the URL will be in bold if they appear in the user's search.

Finally, you have to put in the **real** Destination URL. I will talk about that shortly.

So now you have your completed ad, which looks like:

Accountant in Yourtown TX
Accounting Headaches? Need Help?
Call Us Now for a Free Consultation
www.JohnSmithCPA.com/YourtownAccountant

Notice how I have capitalized the first letter of each word? This is allowed in AdWords and has more impact than if it was all written in lower case. Don't write the ad in ALL CAPS though as this is not allowed. If you had one more character for Description line 2, you could have added an exclamation mark to it. You are allowed just one per ad and it can attract a bit more attention.

So that's your first Ad Group set up. You have another six Groups to set up before you are finished, but the principles are identical to the first one. You just need to tweak your ads a little to make them more relevant to the search terms which users are searching for. As you set up each new Group, you will find that Google gives you the text from the last ad that you wrote as a starting point.

Go through each of them in turn. CPA is a pretty easy one as you can simply replace the word 'accountant' in your first ad Group for 'CPA' which would give you:

CPA in Yourtown TX
Accounting Headaches? Need Help?
Call Us Now for a Free Consultation
www.JohnSmithCPA.com/YourtownCPA

'Accounting' is not too different either. Here, to make the headline read correctly, I would suggest:

Yourtown Accounting Firm
Accounting Headaches? Need Help?
Call Us Now for a Free Consultation
www.JohnSmithCPA.com/YourtownAccounting

You might find that 25 characters are not enough to include the name of your town plus 'Accounting Firm'. Change 'Firm' to 'Co' if you need another couple of characters. If your need more than that, then leave it just as Yourtown Accounting.

When a client is searching for 'accountant', 'CPA' or 'accounting firm', they are not giving you a huge amount of information as to exactly what their problem might be, so all you can do is to talk generally about 'Accounting Headaches?' Your other four keywords are more precise in terms of what the potential client is looking for though, so you can target your ads more precisely to them.

'Tax' is a nice short word, but it's quite vague. Looking back at your keyword research, you will probably see that searches were split fairly evenly between 'tax preparation' and 'tax service'. Try and get both words in the same ad so that one of them will be in bold no matter which one the client searches for.

Tax Service in Yourtown
Need Help with Tax Preparation?
Call Us Now for a Free Consultation
www.JohnSmithCPA.com/TaxPreparation

Here it is particularly important to put the keywords once again in the 'Display URL' to make it clear to the potential client that the page they will be clicking through to is going to be about Tax Preparation and so will be completely relevant to their requirements.

'Payroll' can be handled in a similar way. In this case, 'Payroll Services' seems to get the lion's share of the searches, so you can optimize for just that phrase:

Yourtown Payroll Service
Payroll Headaches? Need Some Help?
Call Us Now for a Free Consultation
www.JohnSmithCPA.com/PayrollServices

Next you have Bookkeeping. This can be nearly identical to the ad for Payroll Services, although you will need to cut down a few words in order to squeeze the longer words in.

Bookkeeping in Yourtown
Bookkeeping Headaches? Need Help?
Call Us Now for a Free Consultation
www.JohnSmithCPA.com/BookkeepingServices

'Small Business' is slightly trickier as you're not a Small Business – but you can help them. In this case, even though you're not talking about yourself in the headline, it's still most important to attract the potential client's interest by showing them that they have found what they are looking for. 'Small Business Accounting' is the most popular keyword in this group. It's exactly 25 characters long as well, so it's the only choice for our headline.

This means that the Description line 1 needs to tell the potential client exactly who you are as well. So here's my suggestion:

Small Business Accounting
Need Help from a Yourtown CPA?
Call Us Now for a Free Consultation
www.JohnSmithCPA.com/SmallBusiness

Maybe the person who made the search doesn't, "Need help from a Yourtown CPA". Maybe they are just looking for a software package like QuickBooks. Well that's fine too. If you had been vague about whom you are and what you are offering, then you would have just wasted the price of a click for someone with no intention of buying from you.

Once you have all seven groups finished, you can click on the 'Save and continue to billing' button. You will now be asked to complete your business details and also to select a billing option. The 'Automatic payments' which is recommended by Google is the best option.

So now we have all of our elements on the AdWords platform ready to get started. But is your site ready to receive these new visitors for whom you will have paid good money?

LANDING PAGES

Writing compelling ads that result in lots of potential clients clicking on them doesn't just benefit you by getting more visitors to your site. You'll also benefit from having to pay less for each one, because Google rewards good ads and punishes bad ones in the form of the prices that the advertiser pays.

For example, let's say that you have a competitor with a very average ad which only one visitor in a hundred clicks on, and the advertiser is paying $3 for each of those clicks. Your ad, however, is much better at attracting people's attention and so three visitors in a hundred end up clicking on it.

In this example, Google should only charge you $1 per click if your ad was in the same position.

Why does Google do this? One reason is that it is in Google's interest to give their users the best possible results with their AdWords. If they do, more people click on them in future rather than clicking on the organic results (from which Google doesn't earn a cent). More importantly, Google is earning the same amount of revenue from each 100 visitors in each case. They can either sell one click at $3 or three clicks at $1.

Google's system is so sophisticated, that it not only tracks how many people click on your ad, but also how long they stay on your site for once they are on it and whether the content of the page that your ad leads to matches the content of your ad. In the highly unlikely event that you gave up your practice tomorrow and decided to sell Viagra from your website instead, Google would find out and stop your ads from running unless you either changed the text of your ad to be more relevant again or else you pay them an insane amount of money (well actually, in that extreme example, they'd probably just give you an outright ban).

This means that there are two good reasons for making sure your landing page (i.e. the page that the visitor arrives at immediately upon clicking your ad) is as relevant to the potential client's needs as possible. In your ads, you promised to solve the potential clients' headaches. If they get there and the text on your website doesn't give them more reassurance that you are the solution to all their problems, then they will be gone – and you've just wasted the cost of a click.

For potential clients searching under the more general keywords – 'accountant', 'cpa' and 'accounting', it is OK to send them to your home page providing that it is optimized as much as possible. Reread chapter 8 on designing your website if you haven't gotten around to optimizing the text on your home page yet. Don't think that you can cut corners by buying AdWords to get some quick traffic before your website is as good as you can possible make it. The only result will be throwing your money down the drain.

Most amateurs or lazy marketers will send everyone who clicks on their AdWords through to their home page. While this is fine for the more generic searches, they will almost certainly be missing out if they send all of their visitors there.

Let's say that you got a client to click on your ad for 'Bookkeeping Services'. Chances are that you didn't mention the specific fact that you offer bookkeeping services on your home page. There probably isn't space there to list every single service you offer – that's why you have a specific page, or collection of pages, for 'Services'. Don't make the prospect go to the trouble of hunting around your site to find the right page. It might be obvious to you that, because you've stated on your home page that you offer a full range of services, all the prospect needs to do is to click on the link for 'Services' and then select 'Bookkeeping'. But it might not be so obvious for the prospect. So instead, you should direct the link from your ad directly to your page for 'Bookkeeping Services' so that the prospect finds exactly the information that they were looking for immediately that they hit your site.

If you gave up on chapter 11 on Search Engine Optimization (it's OK, I know it was hard!) go back and read at least the first section about 'On-site Optimization', particularly where I describe using the tactics on pages other than just your home page. What you should be doing, in effect, is creating several different home pages – all of which provide a different 'doorway' by which visitors can enter your site. You should also be sure to include the link to your 'Free Consultation' page or, better still, put the form actually at the bottom of the pages themselves. Every time you make a prospect click to another page of your site, you run the risk of losing them. After all, it's just as easy for the prospect to click on the 'Back' button as it is for them to click through to another page of your site.

By the time the client has clicked on your ad and arrived on your site, you will have already spent money to get them to that stage. You should do everything that you possibly can to make sure that the prospect goes ahead and completes your Most Wanted Response now so that your money is not wasted.

BUDGETING AND OPTIMIZING

If you have followed all of the advice above, your ads and site should now be as good as they can possibly be and should be able to turn as many people searching for the keywords into new, paying customers as possible.

But now comes the (potentially) $64,000 question – how much can you afford to pay for your AdWords?

You will notice that every other way of marketing your business on the Internet that I have described in this book apart from ads on Facebook and

LinkedIn is either free or costs a relatively token amount - $10 a month here; $20 a month there, etc. With such a low level of expenditure, all it's going to take is for your internet marketing to bring in one or two new clients **per year** and you will be in profit. Because of this, having accurate data as to exactly which of your online promotional methods brought in what clients who produced how much revenue for your company is a 'nice to have', not a 'need to have'.

With AdWords though, it's a whole different ball game. You could easily burn through $10-20 in just a few hours, let alone a whole month and so, unless you can figure out how much a visitor to your website is actually worth, you will have no idea as to how much you can afford to pay per click in order to attract them.

Let's work backwards in order to come up with a figure as to what a click could be worth to you.

For companies selling something tangible, this is not such a difficult exercise, but for professionals like accountants, it's not such an easy exercise. The lifetime value of a new client could be huge if you end up working with them for the next decade. Realistically though, who can afford the cash-flow implications of waiting five years to get their advertising investment back? A better figure to use here is how much you could realistically afford to make in profit from a client over the first couple of months you work for them. Maybe you charge your clients a set up fee or a monthly retainer? Make sure that you base the figure on the **profit** that you earn from them over that period – not just their turnover. Although there is no such thing as an 'average' client, it should allow you to come up with a rough idea – always err on the side of pessimism if you are unsure.

Throughout this book, I've been recommending that your Most Wanted Response is to get the client to contact you for a Free Consultation. What percentage of those Free Consultations end in your getting business from the client (not necessarily after just one meeting)?

How many inquiries are you getting each month which may or may not lead to your meeting with a potential client for a Free Consultation? This is probably the most difficult question to answer accurately. It is possible (with a bit of effort) to find out exactly how many clients came from Ad-Words and filled in your online form requesting the consultation. However, you should also be putting your phone number as an alternative way for prospects to contact you – and the hottest prospects will probably want to call you immediately rather than filling in the form and waiting for you to get back to them. It might help to ask each prospect that contacts where they found out about you but, even then, they are likely just to answer 'Google' at best, which still doesn't tell you whether the prospect found your site through AdWords or through the organic listings.

Although it still doesn't enable you to determine which calls come into your office via AdWords and which come in through other visitors to your website, there is a way to determine how many calls your website is generating in total, and this is by signing up for a free account with Google Voice. You can sign up for this service at:

www.google.com/voice

Currently it is only available in the US and Canada at the time of writing, but hopefully they will roll out the service to other countries over time.

Google Voice gives you the opportunity to obtain a new number, which you can then forward through to any or all of your other phones. There are a variety of other advantages to the feature, but the way in which it can be of great help to you in analyzing the effectiveness of your internet marketing activities is by featuring this contact number on your website instead of your regular one. You will then be able to see from the call log how many inquiries were generated from your website each month.

Whether or not you decide to analyze the number of inquiries your website is generating by using Google Voice, you can come up with a 'best case scenario' by monitoring how many new inquiries you are getting each day and comparing them with the amount of clicks-throughs you are getting to your AdWords. If your stats showed that you received 10 clicks yesterday and you ended up with one form filled in, one phone call and one email, then you know that the response rate is no more than 30%. If, up until you started the AdWords campaign, you were receiving an average of one new inquiry per day anyway, then you can probably say that 20% of the click-throughs ended up with an interested prospect who wants a Free Consultation.

Let me give an example to show how these figures might work in practice.

Assume that the average profit from a new client in the first month or two you decide is $100.

Assume that, from all the Free Consultation meetings, one third of the prospects become paying customers. That means a Free Consultation to you is worth $33.

Assume that you decide that one in ten clicks from AdWords results in the prospect making contact with you in one form or another to request a Free Consultation. This means that the click through is worth to you, on average, $3.30.

So, you would now have a maximum budget for each click of $3.30. If all of your clicks end up costing $3.30, then you will at least have covered your advertising costs for acquiring the clients after a month or two, with the remainder of the net profits from client's lifetime spend with you going to the bottom line.

Although $3.30 would be the maximum that a click would be worth, hopefully they will end up costing less. Unfortunately though, AdWords are now so popular that your competitors will probably have been making similar calculations and have come up with similar numbers.

I would definitely recommend a cautious approach to AdWords in the early stages, particularly as it will take a while for patterns to emerge where you get a better idea as to how many click-throughs it takes to get each Free Consultation. If you are **too** cautious though, so few of your ads will be running that you will never get the chance to test the effectiveness of AdWords thoroughly. As long as the Daily Budget is set at a low enough amount that it won't cripple you if it all goes horribly wrong, at least there is a limit to the downside. This is certainly the case when compared to 'old media' advertising where you take an ad in the local newspaper and cross your fingers that anyone responds to it at all.

To get an idea as to what your competition is paying for keywords at the moment, go to your dashboard, click on the 'Reporting and Tools' tab and select the 'Traffic Estimator'. If you go to the 'Locations and languages' section, it will default to showing you results for the entire country. Click on 'Edit' and then select your exact location in the same way that you did when you set up your account so that it will only be judging you against your local competitors.

In the 'Word or phrase' box, copy in all of your keywords from the spreadsheets you made earlier, including all of the versions in [brackets] and all of those in "quotation marks".

Now, where it says 'Max CPC' put in some crazy figure like $20. Click on the column called 'Estimated Avg. CPC' to sort everything in this order. Even from this totally hypothetical example, you can learn a lot. The first thing you will probably learn is that, even with an infinite budget, you're still not going to bring hundreds of people to your site every day through AdWords. Not every person in your town is looking for an accountant 365 days per year! You will also see that, from the hundreds of keywords that you entered, all but a handful of them are getting no traffic at all. Does this mean that it was a complete waste of time entering them then? No – it just means that there is going to be so little traffic coming from them in your area on a daily basis that they hardly register. Still, if they just gain you a handful of additional cheap clicks during a month, the exercise will still have been worthwhile.

Look at the 'Estimated Ad Position'. You should almost certainly be at #1 if you were crazy enough to bid such a high amount.

Most importantly, look at the 'Estimated Avg. CPC' column in detail as this is where you will learn the most. One thing you should learn is that, when you set a 'Maximum CPC' it really does mean 'Maximum' and you will usually be paying a lot less than that. You will really only ever be paying $20 per click if a competitor sets their maximum CPC at $19.99 (assuming that your ads are getting similar click through rates as theirs).

You should also learn a lot about which keywords are going to be the most expensive and which are relative bargains. In an example which I made for an average-sized city in the US, I see that 'payroll services', 'tax preparation' and 'book keeping services' (all without brackets or quotation marks) are expensive – around $10 per click for the number one spot. The main keyword of 'yourtown accountant' though is coming out at a pretty reasonable $1.36 and there are some surprising bargains as well. Although 'tax preparation' is nearly $10, 'tax service' is coming out as a steal at just $0.57. This just goes to show that it was worthwhile adding all of the little keywords along with the main ones.

On the left hand side of the page, take a look at the summary. In the example that I just made for myself, it's giving me an 'Average Estimated CPC' of $3.02-$3.69, a 'Total Estimated Clicks' of 7.45-9.11 and a 'Total Estimated

Cost' of $25.01-$30.57 – coincidentally not a million miles away from the $3.30 valuation that I put in the earlier example of pricing a click.

Next I changed the Maximum CPC from a crazy $20 down to a more reasonable $3.30 to see what happened to the results. One major change was that I was not #1 everywhere any more. In fact, on my example, 'book keeping services' and 'tax preparation' the ads were down to around #11 – that means that they wouldn't be showing at all on the first page any more. A few others are a little further down the page, but most of them are still #1. In the summary, the 'Average Estimated CPC' is down to $1.60-$1.95, the 'Total Estimated Clicks' at 5.99-7.32 and the 'Total Estimated Cost' at $10.64-$13.00. So I would lose maybe 30% of my clicks, but the cost has gone down by 60%. That would work for me.

Fiddling around with it a little more and I find that $2 Max CPC would generate around 4.63-5.66 clicks at an average price of around $1.24-$1.52. Reducing it still further to $1.50 would only bring in 2.53 to 3.09 clicks at an average of $0.94-$1.14. It's getting to the point now where the exercise would hardly be worth bothering with at all for so few clicks. So, for this sample campaign, I would start off with a maximum of $2 per click, which should generate around 150 clicks per month, as long as a monthly cost of $200 was within my budget. You wouldn't get much advertising in a local newspaper for this price, after all.

Again though, this is only a rough estimate as to how many clicks you're likely to get. For one thing, the area of the survey is so small that there will be big differences between one day and the next. As you know, there is likely to be a huge difference in the amount of people looking for an accountant during tax season compared with the number who will be searching during the quieter periods. In addition, these figures don't take the content of your ad into account. If you have an above-average ad (which you should have if you followed my advice earlier) you should get an above-average number of clicks for below-average prices. You can really only use it as a starting point which you can then tweak once you have some real numbers coming in.

Once you have decided on a price, click the 'Campaigns' tab and then click on the name of your campaign on the left hand side. All of your Ad Groups will be listed on the main window. The default bid will probably be set at $5.00. Click on each number and change it to $2.00 if this is the figure you are happy to start off at. All of the keywords in the group will now be set at $2.00.

Once your ads are finally running, you will need to go into each group individually to amend your 'Max. CPC price' for each particular keyword if you decide you would like to raise or lower them.

So what should you do with your bid prices once you have some real results coming in? Firstly, avoid the temptation to do anything to them too quickly. As your catchment area is so small (most AdWords campaigns will be running across the country or across the world) it will be a while before any patterns start to emerge. Depending on a lot of factors, including the size of your area, the time of the year and the amount of competition you have, it could take several weeks before you start to see some trends emerge. On the day that your campaign goes live, Google has no idea how well (or how badly) your ads are going to perform. It's only after the ads have been displayed a significant number of times that a realistic click through rate will emerge so Google knows whether you should be rewarded or penalized for them.

Another reason why you don't want to rush into making too many changes is that it will take a fair amount of time before you know the full results of your click-throughs. If the first person who clicks through to your site requests a Free Consultation and goes on to become a customer, it would be dangerous to assume that everyone else who clicks is going to do the same! Conversely, don't get too discouraged if you've had some clicks in the first few days and no one has made contact with you yet – Rome wasn't built in a day, after all.

At some point, however, you will want to make some changes. Unfortunately it is beyond the scope of this book (or any other book that I am aware of) to give you a complete set of instructions along the lines of 'if x happens, you should try and do y' that would cover every eventuality. There are just too many variables at play. My only advice is to try a few minor experiments to see what happens. If you are at #1 in your area for a certain search term, can you pay less and go down to #3 or #4 without losing a lot of potential clients? If you are at #3, is it worth increasing your 'Max. CPC' to go up to the #1 position? Is it worth paying a lot more for the more expensive keywords to get on page one, or should you just bow out of the fight gracefully and leave your competitors to bankrupt themselves? There are no right or wrong answers to these questions – they just depend on too many factors.

In general though, Google has been fine-tuning their system for over a decade and so it works pretty well now, which means that there is only so much you are going to be able to do to 'game' the system. In general, it's simply going to be a case of, the more you spend, the more prospects you get and vice versa. Just keep an eye on your conversion rates – and customer values – so that you never get into a situation where AdWords are costing you more than you're making from your income from new clients.

ADVANCED TECHNIQUES

Although I just said that it's difficult to 'game' Google, this certainly doesn't mean that there is nothing that you can do in order to improve your click through rates once your campaign has started.   There are several techniques which you can use to keep tweaking your initial campaign in order to keep improving the results.

Split Testing of Ads

As time goes on, you'll learn more about which keywords are drawing in the traffic, and which aren't working for you at all. It would also be highly unlikely that the first ad that you come up with is going to be the best possible one. Look at other people's ads whenever you are Googling for any search term – not necessarily just those in your field and in your local area. Always be on the lookout for ideas as to how your ads might be improved. If someone else's AdWords caught your attention, chances are that they will catch your prospects' attention as well. Look to see if the ads can go through the entire AIDA process inside 95 characters.

Also, maybe you want to run some kind of a promotion from time to time – a special offer – rather than simply promoting the 'Free Consultation' offer indefinitely?

There is always the worry when you change an ad though that it will actually perform worse than the old one. Fortunately, Google has a system in place where you can avoid that danger by allowing you to test two (or more) ads against one another in the form of 'split testing', similar to the system which I described in chapter 9 for testing two different webpages against one another.

To create a new ad, go to the menu of the Group for the ad you wish to change and click on the 'Ads' tab at the top, followed by the 'New ad' button at the bottom. Now write a new ad. You don't need to completely rewrite every single word of the ad – in fact it's better to tweak the odd word or phrase rather than starting completely from scratch. If you change everything all at once, you won't know what it is about the new ad that did or didn't do better than the old one.

Once you have written your new ad or ads for each Group, click on the link to your main Campaign and then click on the 'Settings' tab. Scroll down to the bottom of the page to the 'Advanced Settings' link and then click on the first one called, 'Ad delivery: Ad rotation, frequency capping'.

Click the 'Edit' button against 'Ad rotation' and change it to, 'Rotate: Show ads more evenly'. Without this, Google will guess which ad is performing the best and they could be wrong. Click on 'Save' and your test should now be set up. The two different variations of the ads should roughly be shown evenly now. Now it's just a question of waiting and watching the results of the test to see which of them has the highest click through rate. You will need to get a fair few clicks through before you can say with certainty which is better than the other. The first ad to reach 30 clicks is a good starting point unless one of them is obviously performing a lot better than the other before it gets to this level. Conversely, if one ad has reached 30 clicks and the other is on 29, then you'll need to leave it to run longer still, because there's obviously little to choose between the two.

Once you have a winner, scrap the loser. Even better than that though would be to replace the losing ad with yet another new ad which is a slightly tweaked version of the winner. Keep on doing this for as long as you can because you will never have a completely perfect ad – there will always be room for improvement.

Optimizing Best and Worst Performers

As your catchment area is so small, you will probably find that most of your keywords get little regular traffic. Look out though for those keywords which are getting a lot of searches and put some energy into trying to improve on your results for these best performers.

Take your best performers out of the Group that they are in at the moment and start off another Group just for that keyword. Although you will have gone further than most of your competitors by dividing your keywords into maybe seven Groups, you could still have around 100 different keywords in each of them. By taking out the most popular keywords from the Group and putting them into a Group of their own, you get the chance to write an even more specific ad for them. Try and include the exact keyword phrase in the exact same order on your headline for the keyword. Also, think about giving the keyword its own landing page as well. Chances are that your competitors will also have noticed that this keyword has the potential to bring in a lot of new business and so the price per click could be quite high in comparison to the prices you are paying for less popular keywords. Remember that Google checks the landing page for each of your ads. If the content of the page matches the keyword you are bidding for closely, you will be rewarded by lower prices for your ad.

Sometimes you might find that some of your ads are not showing at all for searches and Google suggested that you increase the bid price. You then increased the bid price a little but it still didn't show up, however – not even in 10th or 20th place. If this is the case, check whether that particular keyword is quite different from all of the others in the Group. If so, Google could be penalizing you for having a relatively irrelevant ad and landing page. The solution to this is to use exactly the same strategy as for your best performing keywords – take them out of their Group, write an ad which specifically mentions the exact keywords and create a new landing page just for that particular keyword.

If you find that, in order to create landing pages for your best and worst performing keywords, you're coming up with relatively slight variations on a theme, don't worry about having to add links to all of these pages from your 'Services' menu. It's OK if these landing pages are 'orphans' that don't have links back to them from the rest of your site.

Track Your Conversions

This technique involves a little tinkering around inside your website. If this is beyond your technical abilities and you don't have anyone to ask for help, move along to the next section. After all, we are on the 'advanced techniques' now – not the essentials.

A few pages back, I said that it's not going to be possible to track all of the Free Consultations which are generated by your AdWords campaign. Unfortunately, this is still true as there's no precise way of knowing which of the prospects called or emailed you after finding you via AdWords. However, due to a clever gizmo from Google, it is possible to find out how many people who found you through your AdWords completed the form on your website. The process is similar to setting up the 'Goals' and 'Funnels' which I described in chapter 9.

To set this up for AdWords, click on the 'Reporting and Tools' tab at the top of your dashboard and select the option called 'Conversions'. Then click on the button called 'New conversion'. For 'Conversion name', call it 'Free Consultation'.

For 'Conversion category', choose 'Lead'. Leave the 'Page security level' as 'HTTP'. For 'Conversion value', you can either leave that blank or, if you performed the exercise I suggested earlier in working out how much, on average, a Free Consultation is worth to you, then you can put in this amount here.

For 'Tracking indicator' it's probably safer to leave that as it is for legal reasons. There is also no need to bother with the 'Advanced options' either. Click on 'Save and continue'.

For the final step, choose, 'I make the changes to the code'. If you don't make changes to the code yourself, you can still send it to the person who does.

This will generate some HTML code to add to the relevant page of your website. The best place for it is at the bottom of the page, just before the </BODY> tag.

It is vitally important that you place this code on the correct page. If you put it on the page of your site which has the 'Free Consultation' form on it, then it could tell you that 100% of the people who clicked through to your site ended up filling in the form. Instead, you should place it on the page that the visitor to your site sees **after** they have clicked 'Send' on the form. This will usually say something along the lines of, "Thank you for requesting a free consultation. A member of our team will be contacting you shortly."

Now go back to your Groups and have a look at all your keywords. You will see that there are four new columns added to each keyword on your dashboard:

- Conversions
- Cost per Conversion
- Conversion Rate (percentage)

- View-through conversion (this is not relevant if you are just using the regular form of AdWords coming from Google's search results)

As I said earlier, these figures won't be 100% accurate because they can't monitor any prospect contacting you in ways other than sending you the form. But at least it will be accurate in showing you the **minimum** amount of business you got from each ad. With the low level of clicks you are likely to be getting on a daily basis, it will probably take a while to get some meaningful information back from this, but it could be a real eye-opener. Maybe you will find that you're spending a lot of money each month under your 'payroll services' ads and getting quite a lot of clicks, but they rarely request the Free Consultation, whereas you might be getting a great number of inquiries from your 'bookkeeping services' ads. In this case, you would either need to try and improve your 'payroll services' landing page or just stop the group of ads altogether if they are costing you more than you're getting back from them.

It's times like this when you can really benefit from a little industrial espionage. Are there one or two companies whose AdWords always appear in the #1 spot for these keywords that you are struggling with and which are really expensive to buy? Those advertisers must be doing something right if they can afford to pay those kinds of prices. Study the text of their ads and also their landing pages carefully to see if you can figure out how they are managing to make money this way whereas you're not. While it would be wrong for you to copy their text exactly, you should still be able to get some good ideas from their ads and landing page which you can use to enhance your own offerings.

Advertise Nationally

Currently your advertising is only showing in your own catchment area. After all, what value is there to you if someone from the other side of the country is viewing your ads? In most cases the answer to this will be 'none'. However, occasionally, you might be missing out on a few potential clients. Perhaps some potential clients commute a long way to work each day but their offices are still in your local area. Perhaps someone is doing a little research while on vacation. Perhaps someone is planning on moving to your area. There are several reasons as to why they might be searching for you from outside your area.

To reach these clients as well, you would need to set up an entirely new Campaign. Repeat exactly the same process you went through in order to set up your first Campaign – with one major exception. Instead of selecting an area which just covers your own town and everywhere else within a small radius, set your Location for being the entire country.

The next step is to take all of your keywords and add 'yourtown' to them, otherwise you will get a massive number of clicks from totally irrelevant prospects. There is a quick and easy way to do this providing you still have your spreadsheet with all of your keywords listed. Just create a new column next to your column of keywords and then copy and paste both columns into your list of keywords on your dashboard. The end result will be that you have a list of keywords that now read 'yourtown accounting firm', 'yourtown cpa', 'yourtown payroll services', etc.

For this campaign, just use the Broad Match keywords (that's the keywords listed without either [brackets] or "quotation marks"). As Broad Match covers every permutation using those keywords, you will catch everyone searching for those keywords no matter what order they are in.

Changing the Location plus adding the name of your town are the only changes you need to make from the process of creating your first Campaign – the rest of the process is exactly how I outlined earlier.

Once your new Campaign has been running for a while, take a look to see how the keywords are performing. If you see that one or a few of your keywords are performing exceptionally well compared to the others, then you can optimize for those keywords. As well as the Broad Match, yourtown accountant, you can also add [yourtown accountant], [accountant yourtown], "yourtown accountant" and "accountant yourtown". This should bring down the price of any clicks or increase their rankings for the same price because your AdWords will be better targeted.

YAHOO! AND BING

If, after a while, you realize that you are getting a lot of business from your AdWords campaigns and would like to expand your activities in Pay-Per-Click search advertising, then consider also advertising on both Yahoo! and Bing's search engines too. Fortunately, an account with either Yahoo! or Microsoft (the owner of Bing) will allow you to advertise on both networks without having to go through the hassle of signing up and creating your campaigns on each of them separately. This was a smart move on behalf of Yahoo! and Bing. If you had to go through the process of setting up accounts with both of them separately, then it probably wouldn't be worth doing because each of the networks on their own gets only a small percentage of the traffic of Google. Together, however, they currently account for a little under a half of the volume of searches which Google gets.

The above only applies to the US and Canada. For the UK or Australia, even Yahoo! and Bing together is like a drop in the ocean compared to the amount of traffic that Google brings. So it is really not worth bothering with for the average local business.

One advantage of advertising on Yahoo! and Bing is that, because it gets a lot less traffic than Google, a lot of your competitors probably won't bother with it. This means less competition, which means higher visibility for your ads and lower prices. As a result, although the numbers finding your business might be low, there's a good chance that advertising on this network could actually be more profitable for you than advertising on Google.

If you would like to give advertising on this network a try, then head to:

advertising.yahoo.com/search/

You might find some minor differences in the process of setting up your Campaign on Yahoo!/Bing compared to Google, but the principles will be pretty much identical. As a result, I am not going to write another dozen pages giving you a click-by-click guide to setting up your Campaign here. If you are already seeing some decent results from your AdWords campaign, you've proven the fact that you're already pretty good at this. The hardest part about Pay-Per-Click advertising is choosing effective keywords and writing compelling ads. You've already done that for Google and so you've done most of the hard work already. Replicating your AdWords campaign should be little more difficult than simply copying and pasting your data over.

In fact, you can even automate the whole process to make it even easier. To do this, you will need to download the Google AdWords Editor, which you can find by clicking on the 'Reporting and Tools' tab of your AdWords dashboard and clicking the link for 'More Tools'. Here you will find a download link for the AdWords Editor listed under 'Manage Your Account'.

Once you have downloaded the Editor and uploaded your campaign to it, click on 'File' and then 'Export Spreadsheet (CSV)' followed by 'Export Whole Account'.

Now, once your account with Yahoo! is set up, click on 'Import campaigns' on your Yahoo! dashboard in order to have all of your Google AdWords Groups, keywords and ads there to start working with. Please note, however, that Yahoo! doesn't work in exactly the same way as Google and so you will need to check everything to make sure nothing got changed during the importing. Make doubly sure that you are going to be showing the ads only in your local catchment area. It could be an expensive mistake to make if you accidentally set your campaign to national and didn't have a maximum daily budget!

Although this is a brief guide to setting up a Yahoo! Account, Yahoo's Advertising Center is very comprehensive and so you should be able to easily find answers there for any questions that you might have.

*   *   *

In summary, although AdWords is one of the few online activities I have described in this book that costs real money on a regular basis, their ability to deliver excellently targeted prospects which you can 'buy' for set prices still makes it an excellent form of promotion. This is particularly the case when you compare it with 'old media' where you pay a fixed price for advertising with no guarantees that you'll get any interest in it whatsoever.

Another great advantage of AdWords is that you will obtain fast results. Most of the other activities I describe in this book might be free, but don't achieve results overnight. If you are looking for quick results, and don't mind paying a little for them, AdWords campaigns can be an excellent way of bringing in new prospects to 'fill the gap' while waiting for your other methods to take off.

Email us **now** at **accountant@informerbooks.com** to get our **free weekly updates** in case there have been any changes to any of the information contained in this chapter since publication.

DAILY DEALS SITES

T HIS CHAPTER PRESENTS an opportunity to gain a large amount of new clients quickly, but it only works for acquiring personal clients – especially female clients. If your practice deals only with business clients, then it is not going to work for you and you can skip it in its entirety.

The first major company to launch the concept of Daily Deals was Groupon, which launched in November 2008 in Chicago and is still the largest company in the sector, although its success has led to many competitors using the same business model, the largest of which are starting to catch up with them.

Groupon's name – derived from the words 'group' and 'coupon', gives a rough idea as to how the system works. The core product of Groupon (or any of the other Daily Deal sites) is a simple one. They are just selling vouchers which offer potential clients large discounts on a variety of products and services – a new one every day. That's the 'coupon' part of the equation. The 'group' part is what made Groupon such an innovative service, and led to the company's phenomenal success over such a short period of time.

Groupon harnesses the viral power of the Internet in order to spread the message about the offers which it is promoting. With each Groupon deal, they set a figure for the minimum number of people needed to sign up for the offer before it becomes activated, For example, if the number of deals is set at 100 , it means that, if only 99 were sold, no one can claim the deal. Because of this threshold, buyers are motivated to spread the word of the offers to all of their friends and contacts via such means as their social networks in order to ensure that enough are sold so that they are able to take advantage of the offer. Those subscribed to Groupon receive a new email each morning targeted to their local area, which makes it easy for people to share the deals with their friends. Offers only run for 24 hours, which gives buyers a tremendous sense of urgency about the whole process. They don't have time to procrastinate – they need to take urgent action if they wish to take advantage of the deals.

As a result, Groupon, plus the local business making the offers, both benefit by having interested customers acting as sales people for the service. The viral nature of the system has led to explosive growth for the company, which has gone from zero to 85 million customers in just three years, not to mention the enormous number of clones which were quick to set up in order to exploit the same business model. Forbes Magazine actually claimed that Groupon was the fastest growing company of all time, such was its staggering rate of growth.

Another reason for Groupon's stellar success is that there is no upfront payment or risk to the businesses wanting to work with the company in offering a Daily Deal. For this reason, Groupon claims that around 90% of businesses offering a Daily Deal with them are pleased with the results and are interested in offering more deals in the future. Unlike 'self serve' promotional methods such as Google AdWords, Groupon handles just about everything businesses need in order to run a promotion – they even write the copy for you.

If this all sounds too good to be true, there are a few negatives about Groupon's offer that you need to be aware of before leaping in to it. First of all, in order to be eligible for a promotion, businesses need to offer a fixed service with a discount of at least 50%. If that's not enough of a turnoff already, Groupon then takes around half of the revenue that's left and pockets it for their troubles. As a result, you are only going to keep around 25% of the revenue which you would normally charge for such a service. This means that, if you are interested in running a Groupon promotion, you have to be careful as to exactly what service you are going to offer and the maximum number of offers you are going to make. Some businesses have made the mistake of using a Groupon promotion as a loss-leader and not putting a cap on the number of people who could take advantage of the offer – nearly bankrupting themselves in the process. As a result, you really need to calculate in advance the maximum number of redemptions you are able to handle. Get it wrong and you could spend the next six months working for next to nothing!

Groupon's clients are predominantly female – 77% are women, and they are also young – 68% are under 34. They have above average education and levels of income. For this reason, the majority of promotions run by Groupon are either for restaurants or are in the health and beauty category, with spas and hairdressing salons using them extensively. Groupon is not used so much by regular retailers because few retailers are able to offer 75% discounts on many products unless they are prepared to take a major loss in the hope that they will make it up from repeat business coming from these clients.

Currently only a few CPAs have taken advantage of a Groupon Daily Deal to date. I spoke to one of the Groupon pioneers – Kedra A. Williams, CPA of Dallas/Ft. Worth - about her experience of running a Groupon promotion in July 2010. She was pleased with the results of her promotion, which was to offer a Federal Tax Return Preparation for $29 instead of her regular price of $150.

She sold more than 33 Groupons as part of the promotion. More importantly though, she received many more responses from clients who required more complex services which she was able to sell to them at full price. Most of these new clients who found her as a result of the promotion are still with her today. The promotion therefore led to a long-term increase in her business, which more than offset the cost of the promotion. As a result, she says that she would definitely run another promotion with Groupon again at some point in the future, if she has the opportunity.

As you can see, with half of the discounted amount going to Groupon, no one is going to get rich from the revenues that they bring in from the offers alone. The benefits from the Daily Deals come either from selling additional services to those responding to the offer, plus the massive exposure that your business gets from having your details emailed to every person in the local area who is on Groupon's database.

Because there is only one Daily Deal per area each day, demand for them exceeds supply by a wide margin. Apparently Groupon turns down 90% of all of the businesses asking to work with them. Groupon obviously values its reputation highly and so checks each business carefully before agreeing to work with them. In their inquiry form, they ask for links to where your business has been reviewed online. So if you don't have any reviews up on the major directories yet, you would be advised to leave this opportunity until you have some. They also check to see how your website looks, so make sure that it looks professional and answers any questions that Groupon, or their clients, might have about your business.

For more information on Groupon and to make contact with the company, go to **www.grouponworks.com** (**www.grouponworks.co.uk** for the UK).

If Groupon deems your business to be of interest to them for a possible Daily Deal, they will get in contact with you. In most cases, one of their representatives will come to visit you in order to give you more information on their service and to find out more about your business before discussing a deal that you can offer their clients. Prior to the meeting, you need to work out the maximum number of deals that you can afford to offer. Groupon will want you to agree to as many deals as possible because the more they sell, the more money they make. For you, however, who is going to be more interested in the promotional opportunities from having your business advertised to Groupon's local database, the less Daily Deals you can get away with offering, the better it is going to be for you. So get ready for a little horse trading to come up with a figure that works for both parties!

Once the deals have been thrashed out, Groupon will create the page for you and ask you to approve it. The page will have a link to your website (which is from a PageRank 7 page and so it will do wonders for your Google rankings) and will also give potential clients the opportunity to ask you some questions.

The day that your Daily Deal is promoted by Groupon is likely to be a busy one, so be prepared for it. Expect to receive a lot of visitors to your site that day, plus emails and phone calls from potential clients who want to ask you questions as to exactly what your offer does or does not include.

As for the promotion itself, you will be able to monitor the results in real time as people sign up for it. Groupon takes clients' details as they sign up, including their credit card information. Once enough Daily Deals have been sold to trigger the promotion, their credit cards are charged and they are issued with vouchers which are individually numbered. In order to claim the deal, buyers will either give you a printout of the voucher or else they can show it to you on their smartphones. You will get a list of all of the buyers' names once the promotion is finished so that you know exactly who to expect.

Each deal will have an expiration date, which is usually set from three to six months following the date of the promotion. It would be totally up to you as to what period you would like this to be. One advantage of making the expiration quite far into the future is that you shouldn't get swamped by too many clients all wanting to redeem the offer at the same time. The disadvantage of spreading the business out over a long time is that you get paid by Groupon with checks in installments over the period so, it can take a long time to get paid if you stretch it out too long.

Despite the amount of competitors which entered the market following Groupon's spectacular growth, Groupon still dominates the sector, with a share of around 50%. In fact, Groupon's market share was increasing in the latter half of 2011 as some competitors fell by the wayside. Even Facebook tried and failed with its Facebook Deals project, killing it in August 2011 after a mere four months on the market. As a result, for any business wanting to try a Daily Deals offer and who is looking to get the maximum exposure for their business, Groupon is the obvious choice.

If, however, Groupon turns down your request, there is one alternative in the form of LivingSocial.com, the second biggest Daily Deals site. LivingSocial is backed by Amazon.com and has a market share in the region of 20%. LivingSocial works in exactly the same way as Groupon. More information on how their system works can be found at the following URL (it's the same address for all English-speaking countries):

www.livingsocial.com/getstarted

This duopoly could be in for a shakeup though in 2012 as the mighty Google entered the market in May 2011. Initially Google Offers was just available in Portland but then they quickly expanded to a handful of other US cities over the summer. With Google already having a local infrastructure in place throughout the US, they should be able to roll out their service a lot faster and more economically than smaller companies and so there is a high likelihood that they should be a major player in the market by the end of 2012.

*   *   *

In summary, Groupon and the other Daily Deals services are definitely not core elements of any accountant's internet marketing campaign. However, for those businesses which are able to qualify for a scheme and offer services to individuals, participating in one of them can lead to some quick additional exposure to the local market at no cost and no risk and so is it well worth doing if you have the opportunity. Just make sure that you don't end up selling a larger quantity of heavily discounted Deals than you are able to handle comfortably or else you could actually end up losing money from it.

> Email us **now** at <u>accountant@informerbooks.com</u> to get our **free weekly updates** in case there have been any changes to any of the information contained in this chapter since publication.

PUTTING IT ALL TOGETHER

WELL THAT'S NEARLY it now as far as this book goes. Over the previous chapters, I have presented you with a wide variety of tools which, when used together, comprise a full toolkit for getting the most from the opportunities that exist today for marketing accounting firms online. From here, it's going to be totally down to you as to what you do with them. The methods here range from being simple one-offs that can be set up in an hour or two, through to activities which will require regular attention for an indefinite period.

If the time investment required to do everything in this book is more than you are willing or able to make, then don't feel too guilty about it. Maybe some of the chapters with their need to understand some of the basic elements of how webpages are built were too complicated for you to understand. If this was the case, don't worry too much. No one is forcing you to do **everything** in this book. Even if you decide to put just a couple of the strategies described here into action, you will probably still be ahead of the majority of your local competitors, as accounting tends to be one of the more conservative professions which is slow to adopt new marketing methods. This means that currently few practices are taking full advantage of all of the opportunities offered by internet marketing and social media.

Knowing the principles is one thing – putting them into practice is quite another. All of the time you will have spent reading this book will have been wasted if you don't take the first steps required to actively use these tools.

CREATING A MARKETING CALENDAR

Unless you are incredibly self-motivated and organized, the chances of your putting together a successful social media and internet marketing campaign is pretty remote without a timetable with deadlines on it. As a result, I recommend your putting together a marketing diary which will allow you to keep a track of what needs to be done when in order for you to achieve your goals one step at a time.

If you would rather keep track of your plan in a paper diary, that's fine, but I would recommend instead that you put your plan on your computer instead because you are going to need to be in front of your computer in order to put all of the steps into practice in any case.

If you are not already using a computerized diary, then I can recommend Google Calendar for the task, which you can access at:

www.google.com/calendar

One of the advantages of using Google Calendar is that you can set it to send you reminders as to which of your tasks are due when, and you can also access it from your smartphone, allowing you to check on it from anywhere.

Most of the strategies that I have described in this book have two elements to them – the first step is a one-off exercise in order to set them up and then there is a second step, which is to keep the operation going on a daily, weekly or monthly basis.

To start off with, focus on setting up all of the elements of the campaign which you are intending to use. Prioritize them in order of importance and set yourself a realistic period of time to achieve all of the steps.

Your first priority is probably going to be to sort out your website. Chances are that, if you were sufficiently switched on about the promotional possibilities offered by internet marketing and social media that you thought it worth investing some of your hard-earned cash to buy a book about it, you already have a website. However, chances are that, after reading through this book, you will realize that there is probably a lot of room for improvement there. There's probably a need to rewrite your copy according to the rules I gave you for copywriting in chapter 2 and for search engine optimization in chapter 11. If this is the case, it will take you a lot less time than if you had to build an entire site totally from scratch. However, you still need to spend as long as it takes to optimize it, because your website is the bedrock that much of your internet marketing strategy will be built upon.

After that, it's optional as to the order in which you take on the rest of the opportunities. Personally, I would recommend ensuring that your business is listed in Google Places and all of the other major directories as a top priority because it shouldn't take you too long to complete. In addition, it could lead to your getting quite high up in the search engine rankings even without the long and laborious task of finding sites to link to and trade with.

Next I would recommend your starting with the social media networks. LinkedIn, although not the largest or 'sexiest' of the social networks, is going to be the most useful one for building up your address book with the contact details of excellent prospects in the form of many small business owners. Another advantage of LinkedIn is that you don't need to constantly make updates to your stream in order for it to be an effective tool. Once you are all set up on LinkedIn, I would suggest you next set up your Facebook business Page and then go on to Twitter.

Google AdWords can be added into your mix of promotional activities at any time after you have optimized your website. If you want to see some fast results and don't mind paying for them, make it one of your top priorities. Although it might take a while to set up your account and get it running properly, it shouldn't take too much of your time after that to keep it generating new, well-targeted leads other than a bit of tweaking here and there.

Once you have all of your accounts set up and optimized, the hardest part might be over, but it doesn't mean that you can put your feet up and relax. Instead you will have to do a little work every day in order to keep your campaigns running. Divide each of the tasks you will need to perform on a regular basis into daily, weekly and monthly tasks.

For example:

Daily: Respond to everyone who has contacted you via the social networks, select the most interesting pieces of news, both local and professional, to post to your social media profiles, and set the scheduler on your social media dashboard to drip-feed postings onto Twitter throughout the following day.

<u>**Weekly:**</u> Check on all your statistics coming from Google Analytics, your AdWords dashboard, Facebook Insights, etc. in order to check trends and make adjustments to your strategy if necessary.

<u>**Monthly:**</u> Arrange your big promotion for the next month and send out your monthly newsletter.

Set a specific time each day, week or month for taking care of all of these tasks so it starts to become part of your regular routine – a quiet time when you will not be distracted by the needs of your main job. The end of the working day is an excellent time for your daily activities – then you will have the whole day's worth of news to choose your main news items from. The weekly and monthly activities will take a little longer, so you need to allocate a bit more time for them. These are the times when you will need to get a little creative – to keep asking yourself, "What if?" and allow your imagination to run wild with new ideas that you can try in order to improve all of your marketing activities. There is never a 'perfect' solution when it comes to marketing – there is always going to be room for improvement and, with statistics available that will show you the results of most of your activities, it allows you to test new ideas constantly and see what kind of results they bring in.

How much time you spend on testing and implementing new ideas is totally down to you – there are only so many hours in the day after all. Be aware, however, that there is the law of diminishing returns with most forms of internet marketing activities. If you keep on working to the same 'tried and tested' formula all of the time, your Friends, Fans and Followers will start to get bored of what you have to say and your messages will have less and less impact over time.

INTEGRATING YOUR MARKETING INTO ALL YOUR BUSINESS ACTIVITIES

Unless you work alone, you need to ensure that **everyone** in your practice is involved in all of your marketing activities in order to get the most out of them. The results of your activities impact everyone in your company, from the receptionist right up to the CEO. If anyone in your organization starts thinking that marketing is not part of their job, then they need to be put right. The more successful you are in integrating your marketing activities into everything you do as a company, the better the results will be.

You should also try, wherever possible, to do whatever you can to get anyone who is dealing with your company in a personal capacity to join your online marketing activities. One of the main benefits of online campaigns such as social networks is the ability to keep in regular contact with prospects. This is of paramount important to accountants because you are marketing for the long-term. Unlike retailers or restaurants, for example, much of your activities probably won't see an immediate return – not every company is looking to change accountants every day. One day, however, the majority of them will – and you need to position yourself to be at the front of the prospects' minds so that, when that day arrives, they don't even need to bother to start Googling for options – they just need to pick up the phone and give you a call to set up a meeting.

Every person that you have contact with in the course of your business activities who doesn't end up either joining one of your social networks or signing up for your monthly newsletter should be thought of as a lost opportunity. You should do everything that you can do in order to make sure that a person gives you their permission to become part of your network. If you have a receptionist, you should definitely tell them about this fact and make it their responsibility to try and ask each person visiting your office if they would join your network.

Anywhere that your company name or logo is featured, you should also ensure that, at a bare minimum, your website address is also included. This includes any signage that you have and any printed promotional material, including all your business stationary – your letterheads, fax sheets, envelopes, etc. The most important piece of stationery for this purpose is your business card. If you have space on your card without it looking too cluttered, include the addresses of your Facebook business Page, LinkedIn account and Twitter feed as well. If there's not room to put them on the front of the card, consider putting them all on the back of it rather than leaving it blank. It's a shame to have all of that really useful space going to waste.

Even more important than your business card is to ensure that the details of your website and all of your social media networks are included as part of your email signature. Make sure that this signature also appears on any emails sent from your smartphone as well. 'Sent from my iPhone' only helps Apple with their marketing – it would be much better to change the message so that it helps you with yours instead!

Make sure that all of the links to your accounts with the social networks as part of your email signatures are clickable, leading straight to your page so that the recipient can start following your streams with just a couple of clicks. If you make it too much hard work for them to follow you, then they probably won't bother. Don't just list the networks; actively ask them to join you there as well in order to maximize the number of people following you.

If, after reading about all of the free or inexpensive means of promotion that you can get online through the methods contained in this book, you are **still** planning on using more traditional methods of advertising such as local newspapers, then make sure that your website address is included there also. I would really suggest though that you think long and hard before you invest any more of your marketing budget into advertising in 'old media' however. OK, so maybe I am a little biased in my opinions about the benefits of online versus more traditional means of promotion, but you should now have the tools available to try and compare the effectiveness of both methods. The most expensive methods for getting your message in front of prospects that I have covered in this book are Pay-Per-Click advertising on Google AdWords, LinkedIn and Facebook. In each of these cases, however, you will know exactly how much you are spending for each prospect that you reach. Compare this to the cost of acquiring each new prospect via advertising using 'old media' if you can – unfortunately not only is 'old media' generally a lot more expensive than 'new media', it's also usually difficult to work out what type of return you are getting from it.

Personally I think that the only forms of traditional advertising that will come close to seeing the same type of returns that you can expect from your online marketing activities will either be free editorial coverage that you might be able to achieve through a PR campaign, or perhaps some small classified ads in well-targeted sections of the local newspaper. As hundreds of other local businesses are discovering every day, virtually every other form of advertising is a very expensive alternative to promotional activities that are conducted completely online.

If you work for a larger practice which has dedicated sales people, they need to be involved with the creation of your internet marketing and social media campaign right from the inception. For them, your online activities are going to be a godsend if they previously relied upon cold-calling potential clients in order to find new prospects. If you implement all of the strategies in this book, plenty of prospects are instead going to be finding you, or else your sales people are going to be 'lukewarm' calling to prospects with whom your practice has already had some initial contact with before at least. As I mentioned right at the start of this book, you will be practicing Seth Godin's Permission Marketing process of 'turning strangers into friends and friends into customers'.

But all of your hard work is going to be in vain if you don't have procedures put in place ready to handle the inquiries and leads which you should be generating from your campaign. Once a prospect has made contact with you, you need to make sure that their query is handled as quickly and as efficiently as possible. There is a saying that internet time moves seven times faster than it does in the non-virtual world, such is the pace of innovation. With Google searches, it's just as easy for a prospect to find half a dozen new accountants to potentially give their business to as it is to find just one. When looking for a new accountant, a lot of people are likely to contact several companies with questions as it doesn't take much longer to send six emails as it does just one in order to test them all on their levels of service. If one of your competitors is more on the ball than you are and replies to a prospect's questions in half an hour while it takes you a couple of days to get back to the prospect, then the business is probably as good as lost, no matter how good your marketing was. As smartphone penetration increases, customers have come to expect almost instant answers to their questions. If they don't get them, it's on to the next company. You are, after all, in a service business and prospects need reassurance that you are going to provide them with it right from the first contact.

After the first contact, you are going to need to keep track of the prospect's progress through the sales process and this is where CRM systems such as Nimble, which I mentioned in chapter 7, become highly useful tools. You've put so much effort into getting these prospects to get in contact with you – don't fall at the final hurdle!

So that's it – there is no more to this book – there are no chapters on blogs, or podcasts, or YouTube channels, buying banner advertising or any other strategies that you might read about in more general books on internet marketing. This is because all of these methods are time-consuming or expensive and are of little use for a professional business such as yours which is only interested in a small geographic area. The tools that I have given you here should be all that you need to take your online marketing activities to the next level.

Although there can be no guarantees as to the results that you can achieve by putting all of these principles into practice (a lot will depend upon whether your competitors are going to be using them as well), I am pretty confident that, with a reasonable amount of effort, you will soon be attracting more clients than you can cope with. In today's economic climate, that's an excellent problem to have!

Many thanks for making your way through to the end of this book and I wish you the best of luck with all your marketing activities. If there's anything here that you didn't understand – or if you have any feedback, either positive or negative, I would love to hear from you, so please drop me a line.

If you found this book to be useful, then I would like to ask one big favor of you, and that is to help me out a little by posting a review of the book on Amazon or any other online retailer that you are signed up with. Just type my name, 'nick pendrell' into the search box and you should find the book in a couple of clicks.

Thanks in advance for helping me out.

Nick Pendrell

Email: nick@informerbooks.com

Web: www.informerbooks.com

Facebook: www.facebook.com/InformerB

Twitter: @InformerB

JUST ONE MORE THING ...

Give a man a fish and he'll eat for a day

Teach a man to fish and he'll eat for a lifetime

"But I don't have **time** to go fishing every day! I'm a busy accountant!"

If you've read all the way through this book, you should have learned how to find pieces of a virtual fishing rod which are given away free on various different websites and know exactly what to do in order to keep reeling in a succession of big fish new clients.

Having the tools now at your disposal is one thing. Finding the time to use them effectively is another though.   Maybe you're thinking that you just aren't going to find all the time necessary to put all of the elements of your internet marketing and social media campaign together and then find time each day to keep them active. Or perhaps all my talk of HTML and Meta Tags sounded like I was speaking in an entirely different language to you.

If this is the case, then there is an alternative to having to do everything yourself. Informer Books' sister company, **Informer Marketing**, has set up a number of affordable programs just for accountants like yourself which can take some or all of the strain off your hands at prices that even the smallest of practices are still going to find affordable and incredibly good value compared to alternatives such as advertising in local newspapers.

Informer Marketing has developed several different packages, so there's sure to be one that's just right for you, no matter what size of marketing budget you have.

Choose from:

Monthly Bronze

This **completely free** service gives you a weekly newsletter that keeps you up-to-date with what's happening in the world of internet marketing and social media. With changes happening to sites and services on a weekly basis, make sure you sign up to receive this free newsletter to keep your knowledge fresh and to ensure that this book never goes out-of-date.

Monthly Silver

Struggling to think of something useful to post in your social media streams each day? Let us help by sending you a daily newsletter of ready-to-post status updates which you just need to copy and paste into your streams so that it takes less than five minutes a day to keep your business in front of your clients every day of the week.

Monthly Gold

All the same tools as in the Monthly Silver package, plus an hour per month of mentoring, feedback or any other kind of assistance you require. Everyone needs a little help with their marketing campaigns from time to time. Maybe you don't understand the first thing about HTML and need a little help adding some code. Maybe you want a second opinion on a marketing idea you've come up with. Maybe you aren't getting the results you expected and need someone to ask what you might be doing wrong. The Monthly Gold package gives you peace of mind that you're never going to get 'stuck' in your marketing activities. Just email, Skype or call us for an instant solution to any problem you may have.

Monthly Platinum

Leave everything to us to take care of all your internet marketing and social media needs. We'll communicate with you at the start of each month to let you know what we're planning and to find out what your needs are for coming period and then we'll take care of everything for you. It's like having your own in-house marketing department, but at a fraction of the price.

*　　　*　　　*

Informer Marketing can also help you to get your marketing campaign off the ground in the first place. Leave the hassle to us and we'll get your campaign up and running in a matter of days. Choose from any of the following options:

QuickStart Silver

Features all of the following services:

- A professional Facebook business 'mini-site' featuring an incentive for potential clients to 'Like' it.

- A Twitter account all set up for you ready to start posting straight away.

- An online Seesmic social media dashboard account all set up and ready to go

- MailChimp mailing list set up

- Listings on Google Places, Bing Places, Yahoo Places plus another ten major directories

- A fully functioning mobile website from Onmobile

QuickStart Gold

Features everything in the Silver package, plus:

- A complete rewrite of your website copy optimized for sales and search engines.

- A Google AdWords campaign all set up and ready for you to start using.

- A Google Analytics account ready for you to use.

QuickStart Platinum

The complete bespoke solution. Allow us to make a complete audit of all your current internet marketing and social media promotional tools and activities and we'll make improvements and additions as necessary.

Pay for just the elements that you need.

*   *   *

All of the Gold and Platinum packages are restricted to one business per local area to ensure that there is no conflict of interest. So sign up quickly if you want to take advantage of these packages before your competition does and it's too late!

For prices on all of these packages or to sign up, please either email us at **nick@informerbooks.com** or else head to the following page of our site:

www.informerbooks.com/local-business-marketing/

CPSIA information can be obtained at www.ICGtesting.com
Printed in the USA
BVOW041405120112

280409BV00016B/3/P